"PROBES DEEPLY INTO THE PROBLEMS OF
PARENT–CHILD RELATIONS."
—*The New York Times*

"A great deal of sympathy and understanding has gone
into the writing of this book. Those who read it—and
their number should be countless—will remove
themselves from the ranks of amateur parents."
—*National Parent–Teacher*

"Practical...the general practitioner, governess,
schoolteacher, and others who have close contact with
children and parents will find it useful."
—*American Journal of Psychotherapy*

"Based on a wide experience in conducting child-
guidance clinics, it is to be recommended for reading by
all parents facing the difficult situations frequently
associated with behavior disorders. Many case histories
throw light on the specific problems."
—Henry R. Viets, M.D., *Hygeia*

RUDOLF DREIKURS, M.D., was an eminent child
psychiatrist who practiced in Chicago. Along with this book, he
was the author and co-author of many other child-rearing and
family guides, including the classic *CHILDREN: The Challenge*,
as well as *Logical Consequences*, *The Challenge of Marriage*, and
Discipline Without Tears.

THE CHALLENGE
OF PARENTHOOD

NEW AND REVISED EDITION

BY RUDOLF DREIKURS, M.D

A PLUME BOOK

PLUME
Published by the Penguin Group
Penguin Books USA Inc., 375 Hudson Street,
New York, New York 10014, U.S.A.
Penguin Books Ltd, 27 Wrights Lane,
London W8 5TZ, England
Penguin Books Australia Ltd, Ringwood,
Victoria, Australia
Penguin Books Canada Ltd, 10 Alcorn Avenue,
Toronto, Ontario, Canada, M4V 3B2
Penguin Books (N.Z.) Ltd, 182–190 Wairau Road,
Auckland 10, New Zealand

Penguin Books Ltd, Registered Offices:
Harmondsworth, Middlesex, England

Published by Plume, an imprint of New American Library, a division of
Penguin Books USA Inc. Previously published in a Hawthorn Books edition.

First Plume Printing, January, 1992

10 9 8 7 6 5 4 3 2 1

 REGISTERED TRADEMARK—MARCA REGISTRADA

Library of Congress Cataloging-in-Publication Data

Dreikurs, Rudolf, 1897-1972.
      The challenge of parenthood / Rudolf Dreikurs.
          p.   cm.
      Previously published: New and rev. ed. New York : Hawthorn Books,
c1958.
      Includes index.
      ISBN 0-452-26707-2
      1. Child rearing.   2. Parenting.   I. Title.
HQ769.D65   1991
649'.1—dc20
                                                                      91-39647
                                                                      CIP

Printed in the United States of America

PREFACE TO THE
REVISED EDITION

Since this volume was first published in the United States ten years ago, developments in the field of education and child guidance have corroborated the suggestions presented at that time. Some, controversial then, are now becoming more generally accepted. One is less inclined to regard restrictions imposed on the child as repressive and therefore damaging; the tendency to be overpermissive is recognized as more detrimental. Emphasis on demand-feeding diminished in favor of a more orderly procedure.

There is wider acceptance today of the fact that parents need specific instruction in child raising. The focal point for corrective procedures is shifting to changing the interaction between parent and child, replacing the tendency to concentrate on unconscious processes within the child. Consequently, our method of working with mother and child simultaneously is now preferred by many who previously considered it as essential that mother and child should each have a different therapist or counselor.

New problems have also arisen during the last ten years, which require either additional comment or reconsideration and alteration. Childhood psychosis has come to be viewed in a new light during the last decade. Some of our child-guidance techniques have been refined during this period. The family council has become an essential feature for the democratic family. Its technique and procedure, not described before, deserve an important place in a book on the upbringing of children in the contemporary setting.

On the occasion of the tenth anniversary of this volume a brief review of its history may be indicated, since it seems in a peculiar way to reflect the cultural changes of the last few decades. The original manuscript was written in German, during the democratic phase of Austria. When Austrian Fascism came into power, publication of a book on education based on the application of democratic principles, became impossible. No German publisher was willing to take a chance. The first published edition was in Dutch, since Holland maintained its democratic tradition. Shortly before Hitler invaded Austria, a very brief realignment of all democratic forces took place. In this period an Austrian publisher accepted the manuscript for publication. However, Hitler's forces invaded the country before the book was published, and the author, who was fortunate enough to have left his native country, succeeded in getting back the rights to his book just before the publishing house was dissolved.

It is significant that the full publishing rights were obtained by the present publisher, since we have in the United States more practical democracy and equality than anywhere else. Nowhere else in the whole world—except perhaps in the new State of Israel—have women and children gained the status of equals with men, submitting to no one, claiming their full rights and rebelling openly if they are not granted. Therefore nowhere else are techniques of dealing with each other as equals as urgently needed as in the United States. We need new traditions for raising children. Our efforts to provide guideposts for their establishment may encounter opposition on the part of all who fail to realize the full implication of the democratic principle for family life; but knowing the meaning of the democratic evolution, we cannot doubt the eventual outcome.

Chicago, 1958

CONTENTS

III. THE DIFFICULT CHILD

INTRODUCTION

My dear Parents:

We talk a great deal about the problems which children present to their parents. Do you realize that it is you who are our real concern? Parenthood is a challenge to you; but you, as parents, are also a challenge to us. I say this, first, in my function as a psychiatrist. My greatest ordeal are parents who ask me to "cure their children." When I counsel them, I am torn between sympathy for them, because they are miserable and suffer, and indignation when I see what they are doing to their children. This book, which I dedicate to you and your heroic task, may reveal the ambivalence which I share with most practicing psychiatrists. Some psychiatrists go to extremes: one blames with blasting fury the mothers who spoil whole generations so that they become unfit for social living; the other regards most parents, especially mothers, as emotionally sick people who need psychotherapy. It is difficult to strike a balance. I must ask your forgiveness if I, too, do not always find a way of expressing myself without stepping unduly on your toes. You must recognize that it is more dangerous to attempt guidance by writing a book than by having a private consultation with a patient. In a personal interview I can sense when I hurt a patient's feelings, and can correct my mistake immediately. I do not see you while you read this book, so I cannot step in when it disturbs you. I can only assure you, most earnestly, here at the beginning, that I do not want to hurt your feelings. Above all, if you get discouraged by reading this book, then it would have been better if it had never been written. No benefit can be gained by causing discouragement.

Unfortunately, there is no way to guarantee that a reader will extract from a book what the author intends to convey.

I wish to give you information and encouragement, because I know that you need these most in your tremendous job of rearing your children. However, a book is passive and permits you to find in it what you are prepared to see and digest. The optimistic reader will easily find in this book reassurance for his optimism; but the discouraged, pessimistic parent may perhaps—against all my intentions—find only new justification for his defeatism. As I said before, I can only plead with you to watch your emotional reaction while you are reading.

But you—and by "you" I always mean mothers *and* fathers —are a problem not only to the psychiatrist. You are the greatest problem to society as a whole. You are in a most strategic position, more than any other group of citizens, to decide the development of our nation. You are the link between the past and the future. In other times, when progress was slow and human society was static, when there was little change from generation to generation, the task of parents was relatively simple. What they learned from their parents was transmitted to their children. Today we are living in a crucial period of our human society. Social conditions, moral values, and the ways of everyday living change rapidly. In your function as parents you stand with one foot in the past and step with the other into the future. No wonder that you are torn, without realizing what causes you the discomfort. You experience the consequences of this dilemma in your daily contact with your children. But you probably do not know that your daily trials and tribulations are highly significant of our present culture and its upheavals. Parenthood today leads only too often to frustration. More than anything else you wish to make your children happy, to prepare them for a successful and comfortable life; yet you do not know how often you harm your children, stifling them more often than guiding them.

Let me be more specific. The social and cultural changes which occur almost under our eyes are of epochal consequence. They signify the end of a cultural period which started five or six thousand years ago, they herald the dawn of a new era of humanity which we have labeled the "Atomic Age." True enough, the discovery and utilization of atomic energy will hasten the development of new ways of living, of our whole social organization and culture. But the characteristic and most fundamental element of the new era seems to be linked with the concept "Democracy"

From the beginning of our civilization mankind has sought the ideal of democracy as a basis for harmonious social living. But the dream has never come true. Only now can we visualize its possible realization. The basic idea of democracy is the recognition of a fundamental social equality of all human beings. When this stage is reached, a new society will be born.

You may ask, "What does all this have to do with my problem as a parent?" Parents are in trouble because they are caught in the net of confusion characteristic of the transitory cultural period through which we are passing. All human relationships show the same confusion. We wish to live in peace and harmony, but we fail miserably in our efforts. We fumble, shift from one approach to the other, and, instead of solving our conflicts, we create new ones. This is obvious in domestic and international relations alike. The conflict between nations, races, and creeds, between management and labor, between men and women, between the generations and between parents and children, is tainted with the same confusion and contradictions. The problems which you experience with your child have a fantastic similarity to the problems between the United States and Russia, between the white man and the colored, between management and labor, between men and women—wherever one group fears to lose its power to the other. The headaches are the same everywhere, as are the mistakes that we make.

Raising children is an application of social living. Because we are almost illiterates in the art of living together, you as parents are as nonplussed as your fellow workers in other fields of human relationships. The proper way of training children is identical with the proper way of treating fellow human beings. The methods of child training can be equally applied to the conflicts of any human relationship.

You have undoubtedly realized that democracy is the only satisfactory way of life. You dislike dictatorship, you do not want to be pushed around, you believe in the rights of the little fellow. But how about you as a father or a mother? I have seen many truly liberal men who are veritable dictators in the home, laying down the law to their womenfolk and children. The methods which you use in rearing your children are probably the same used hundreds of years ago by your forefathers, based on reward and punishment. Little do you recognize that such methods presuppose an unreasonable, unintelligent, and unreliable inferior being who has to be tamed with bribes and threats. Yet that is the course most parents are pursuing. While these methods may have been successful in previous times when they corresponded to general social relationships, they are bound to fail today. Today we have overthrown the emperors and kings, the dictators and tyrants who treated their subjects as ignorant, helpless dependents who required rule with an iron hand. We know that given the opportunity, people can take care of themselves. Today we seek democracy.

This book attempts to show you how you can establish democracy in your home, how you can prepare your children for life in a democracy, where they can take on responsibilities without being dominated or coerced. Many of you may have tried to grant your children freedom and self-expression. But as you have not learned from your parents the efficient methods of training children in the spirit of freedom, you are inclined to confuse freedom with anarchy, self-expression with indulgence, liberty with license. And you fail because your methods neglect the basic requirements of social living. When you fail with your ideas of freedom and liberty, then you feel compelled to revert to the old methods of authority, severity, and force. Most of our contemporary parents vacillate between indulgence and suppression, with damaging effects on their children. We cannot blame parents for their inadequacy.

Nobody has taught them what to do; they themselves are the victims of our confusion and conflict. They must be recognized as one of our foremost national problems. Unless we, the educators, psychologists, and psychiatrists, fulfill our duty to help them through instruction and counsel, the problem and challenge of today may become the menace of tomorrow.

It is only recently that psychiatry has entered the field of education and child training. Heretofore this field was exclusively in the hands of religious teachers, educators, and philosophers. These were the men who studied and established ethical principles and educational methods. The psychiatrist became aware of the educational problem in his treatment of the emotional maladjustments and personality difficulties of adults. He found damaging childhood experiences and improper training at the roots of the conflicts of later life. He recognized the psychological mechanisms and motivations behind disturbing behavior. He discovered the inner reactions of children and adults to outside influences. Through psychiatric study and investigation we know today how children feel when they are exposed to the "normal" way of child training, and how their experiences lead to misbehavior. The psychiatrist still has to fight against a public prejudice originating in the days when psychiatry was principally concerned with insanity and mental derangement. Yet today the psychiatrist can help you to understand your child. The methods of child training which he suggests are based on the observed psychological reactions of the normal child. We are not concerned with the moral issues involved; we do not refer to ethics and to educational philosophy. We are only interested in how children feel and why they misbehave. And we want you to understand what we know. Perhaps we can also help you to understand your own reactions to and the reasons for your own behavior toward your child.

In this sense, please accept this book as my contribution to help you—to stimulate you to study and learn about parents and about children. Training of children today is an heroic task, almost an art. Without deliberate effort to master the tools of this craft you cannot hope to succeed.

It would be preferable to read a book of this kind, before your child is born. I hope that in the not too distant future similar books will be used in high schools to train adolescents in the understanding and handling of little children. Eventually such a training program will be recognized as obligatory, as an integral part of the general knowledge, not less important for the individual than knowledge of the three R's.

However, this book is written especially for those who are already involved in the tribulations of parenthood. We are bound to make mistakes with children, and our times, especially, do not permit our children to grow up without problems. But regardless of how many or few difficulties you may have with your children, regardless of how insignificant or disastrous they may appear to you, there is always a chance for improvement. It is never too late to reconsider your methods and attitudes toward your child—and it is never superfluous. Your children never will be angels, to be sure, but you can always become a better parent than you have been. To that end this book is dedicated.

Sincerely yours,
RUDOLF DREIKURS, M.D.

I. THE PSYCHOLOGICAL BACKGROUND

Chapter 1

The Situation of the Parents

I_T IS easy to *become* a father, but difficult to *be* one." [1] To provide support and adequate care for your children is an exacting responsibility; but your life is further complicated by petty annoyances, caused by behavior you consider superfluous and puzzling. Children can be the source of highest pleasure, and they should be. The majority of parents actually do enjoy their children, at least at times. Yet, numerous are the occasions when children cause you annoyance, distress, grief, and bewildered anguish. As the same frictions and conflicts exist all over the country and, indeed, all over the civilized world, we may suspect that common, fundamental causes are behind them.

You are often too involved to comprehend the reasons for these difficulties, so you may look for scapegoats. You may place the blame on economic conditions, or the bad disposition of the child. Others may consider the rest of the family responsible—the husband accusing the wife, the wife the husband, and either of them their respective in-laws. Few realize the extent to which *they themselves* are contributing to the difficulties encountered in rearing their children.

To understand the common parent-child relationships requires a thorough investigation of those mistakes which parents are apt to make. Intelligent action is impossible without

[1] Translated quotation from Wilhelm Busch.

complete comprehension of the issues involved. Positive and constructive steps can be taken only after past mistakes and misdirected attitudes have been recognized and abandoned. Knowing what *not* to do is a great help in determining what should be done.

Everyone who deals with the problems of bringing up children must be sympathetic with the difficult position of the parents. The hardships and tribulations of parenthood are truly numerous. It is pathetic to watch parents fumbling about, bewildered by the disparity between their goals and their actual accomplishments. The vast majority have the sincere desire to be good parents. They try their best to bring up their children to be happy and successful. The behavior of the parents influences not only the present parent-child relationship but the whole future life of the child; it is the most important single factor in his development.

Love

There is no doubt that you love your child. He is part of you and closer to you than any other living being. His proper development depends on your love.

Love is regarded as the deepest and most beautiful human emotion. How is it possible, then, that this feeling can cause so much misery and suffering? Only too often people torture themselves when they love; only too often is love received as a cumbersome burden.

Love between parent and child is commonly considered the purest form of love: it is free of the complexities of sex. Mother love is the essence of sympathy and understanding and of selfless devotion. And yet how much grief and anxiety mothers experience because of their love! And how much suffering is the lot of their children!

The personality of the child should draw strength and impetus for its harmonious development from this love. No living creature needs as much love as a newborn child. His first feedings and earliest attentions require all the mother can give.

And yet a child can be stifled by an excess of love, hindered in his development and almost ruined. This may seem contradictory. Can there be an excess of the good and beautiful? We must realize that people call many emotions "love" that are far from being worthy of the name. The struggle of their daily lives, the precariousness of their existence have stimulated in them wrong concepts and attitudes which make them incapable of really loving. For them love has *possession* as its sole object; its characteristic is fear; its intention is receiving; its course is often jealousy. Being egotistic and irresponsible, this love considers only the lover—his wishes and his needs. He thinks that he loves because he suffers.

A true mother subordinates her own desires to the needs of her child. But some parents, driven by a domineering and selfish love, disregard the real needs of their child. They disturb his sleep, exhibit him as their masterwork, and treat him like a doll designed expressly for their amusement. Their "love" moves them to trundle him about at unsuitable hours, to hug and kiss him beyond all reason. They even deny his need to be fed on a schedule since their "love" will not let them bear hearing him cry. For the sake of their "love" they make him their idol. They cater to all his whims, often to the extent of making him despot of the family. In their desire to secure all his love they frequently shut him out from the outside world, preventing normal social contacts with friends and playmates. Such "loving" parents make their child a slave or a toy, and predispose his development into the following channels: he either will become wholly unfit for a normal life, causing endless grief and worry with his hopelessly tangled problems, or he will eventually resent the golden cage and become rebellious and stubborn.

But even pure and selfless love has its hidden pitfalls. It prejudices, and thus hinders, a fair judgment of the child. Love has a right to be blind, but education should never assume this privilege. If you love, you may tend to overlook faults, which consequently develop unchecked. You may tend to overrate your child and hence encourage him to acquire a false conception of his personal importance. Thus your love for your child may often complicate your relationship. Like any other form of love, it easily leads to a certain dependence on its object; and you run the risk of being ready tools in your child's hands, rather than his guide and teacher.

Anxiety

The situation is especially difficult when love for one's child is mingled with anxiety. Discouraged individuals are prone to overestimate the frailty of human nature and the hostility of the surrounding world. When they become parents, they are doubly anxious about their offspring. For, of all living beings, a baby is undoubtedly one of the most helpless.

Excessive concern over the child's welfare is a personality fault. If you doubt your own ability to face life, you may feel certain that your child also is incapable of meeting life's problems. On the other hand, the more self-assured you are, the more confident you will be that your child, too, will find in himself the power and the means of coping with existence.

There are many sources of parental anxiety. One of them often is the selfish love mentioned above. Parents who love their child egotistically are generally timid, discouraged individuals who fear for their own well-being. Every moment holds the threat of danger, and they are unwilling to face any risks. Parents are attached to their children, and the loss of a child would be a dreadful blow to any one of them. But, luckily, not all make this contingency the very core and basis of their educational efforts, seriously threatening the child's development and his very existence.

Your anxiety may often be further intensified by your feeling of responsibility. You may live in constant fear of neglecting some important aspect of your duty, and magnify every little fault of your child until it seems a sure sign of his ultimate ruin. The less practical knowledge of child training you have, the heavier you may feel this burden of responsibility.

As parental love may move you to overestimate the merits of your child, so anxiety for his welfare may lead you to overrate his defects. Both processes may take place concurrently. At one moment the child is the acme of perfection; yet at the same moment he is full of drastic faults that bode ill for his future.

Expectations

If you show these concurrent tendencies to overrate and underrate your child, you are probably an ambitious individual who expects your child to fulfill the desires of your own thwarted life. This hope for vicarious satisfaction deepens the conflict between your pride in the child and your dissatisfaction with him, because your exaggerated standards of achievement are often much higher than the child can meet.

What should you expect of your child? One might think that parents would be content if the child became a useful and happy human being. But unfortunately many parents act as if children were born to fulfill the personal desires of their mothers and fathers—to reap *for them* a belated harvest of contentment, honor, and happiness. Some ambitious parents long to see their children become persons of power and distinction. If the father has suffered the consequences of a poor education, he may want his child to be a scholar. If he has had to work his whole life long, he may be determined that his son shall lead a life of ease and enjoyment. Whoever feels that he has been slighted and maligned may rear his child as his avenger; and one who has been disappointed in the love of the opposite sex may wish to satisfy his ungratified desire through the love of his child. A woman who considers herself frustrated in her relations with men may be inclined to regard her son as the one man who belongs to her, whom she will never lose and who will never prove faithless.

All these desires and expectations make the child a pawn of parental battle, especially when mother and father are at variance. Pulled in several directions at once, he must disappoint both parents in the end. By and large, their expectations as parents are much more likely to meet disappointment than fulfillment. *The child must lead his own life.* His personal aims and ambitions arise from motives quite different from those of the parents.

Demands

Thus, more is often required of the child than should be expected. If he is to become a useful individual, he must adapt himself to some orderly pattern of existence, learn to think and act in compliance with social regulations, adjust himself to his environment, and develop a sense of responsibility. He must acquire the graces that are requisite to social living. To ask this of your child is only right and proper. However, your demands seldom stop here.

Perhaps you expect perfection. You rarely stop to think whether you yourself could serve as model for what you demand of your child. Perhaps you believe that by asking for more, you will receive at least a part of what you desire. This is a fallacy. Such a technique will do nothing but accustom the child to ignore *all* your demands. You may require the strictest truthfulness from your children—but are you yourself so completely free from deceit and falsehood? The child must never be lazy . . . is your own industry so beyond reproach? The child must obey blindly and never talk back . . . but are you such paragons of unquestioning submission? A double set of values is impossible; the child is just as much a human being as his parents.

On the other hand, your interest in your own peace and comfort may make you sometimes be self-indulgent. A great deal of what is asked of the child is not so much to further *his* development as to preserve your personal comfort. In this case, the just claims of the child are often neglected. When you want to rest, the child must keep quiet; that is correct. Yet, he must give up his right to rest whenever you desire to keep him up. Such an attitude neglects the requirements of the child's development.

The Conflict of the Generations

From the erroneous attitudes we have just discussed—egotistic, domineering love; extreme anxiety for the child; doubt of his capacities; unjustified expectations and unreasonable demands—arises the bitter struggle between parents and children which is as characteristic of our age as the conflict of the sexes. Differences in temperament and outlook do not explain the lack of cooperation between parents and children. There must be deeper reasons for the frequent frictions. Often it is a struggle for power that leads to a violent clash of interests.

Man today feels threatened from every quarter. His economic future is increasingly uncertain, as are his social position and his political influence. Hence his personal importance is very often challenged. He is painfully aware of his insignificance in a world full of peril and humiliation, so he constantly searches for defenses and safeguards. It is for this reason he is so egotistic in his love, so uneasy and nervously eager to provide himself with a retreat from potential dangers. This is why he is ever watchful for any possible means of bolstering up his self-esteem. What could be more natural than to look for this sort of assurance from his children? Over them, at least, he can expect to rule. But unfortunately he is mistaken in this assumption. Children may be small, weak, and dependent; but anyone who ventures to match wits with them will soon discover that youngsters are more than able to hold their own in a contest with their elders. They do not consider the consequences, and hence are completely ruthless in their choice of tactics. Moreover, their minds are generally much more agile, more cunning, and more inventive than those of adults. Probing and groping, without ever being consciously aware of his intentions, a child has practically inexhaustible resources from which to draw a great variety of tactics in warfare. The deeper parents allow themselves to be drawn into the fight, the more seriously will their authority be impaired. And as their position becomes less favorable, they only fight the harder to maintain their superiority and personal prestige. They fail to realize that in doing so they are thwarting their own purpose. A whole series of disciplinary measures,[2] whose uselessness has long been demonstrated, is still employed for no better reason than that these methods seem to aid parents in their struggle for superiority over their children. In earlier times such methods might have succeeded to some degree in preserving an external show of parental authority; but under present social conditions, with increased equality in the relationship of man to man, any efforts in this direction are quite futile.

At present, the incentives to false attitudes toward one's children, and hence to conflict with them, are much more obtrusive than in earlier times. The position of mother and father, both inside and outside the family, is more disadvantageous and insecure than ever before. But, what is more significant, the difficulties of this situation are greatly intensified by the *prevalence of very small families.* This increases the uncertainty and anxiety of the parents. Their affections are concentrated on only one or two children, and their personal expectations and demands have often to be met by a single child. Formerly the parents' love and hopes were apportioned among a considerable flock of children. Even then one of the number, often the eldest or the youngest, was likely to be most exposed to parental emotions. But generally, in a large family, the personal conflicts between parents and children do not so strongly affect any single child. The children are more occupied with one another, and the parents must distribute their attentions more widely.

We know, of course, that the conflict of the generations is not restricted to the family. Its effects are equally evident in the business world and in public life. The old fear the young, and the young feel themselves slighted. Strife and suspicion,

[2] See Chapter 4, "Nagging," "Fault-finding," "Physical Punishment."

vanity and spite throw up their walls between the generations. As a consequence, the conservativism of the elder wants to block the vigor of the young, and the younger generation wishes to push the older stumbling block aside, while a combination of young enthusiasm and old caution might serve the whole community much better. Instead, older people are just pushed aside as soon as they lose the qualities of youth. One cannot distinguish whether these dissensions begin in the family and spread from there, or whether they penetrate from without into the family. The processes take place simultaneously and run parallel courses. Mankind in general is seized with discouragement and has substituted for the fundamental spirit of human cooperation a frantic struggle for personal superiority.

This striving for superiority leads to the demand for perfection in children. Without realizing the import of their actions, parents tend to magnify every fault in the child. By systematically disparaging him they may unconsciously try to emphasize their own adequacy and to appear superior, at least to the child. These same tactics are often employed against other fellow human beings. By disparaging and degrading others, many try to inflate their own deflated self-esteem. Many unwittingly take a selfish interest in the shortcomings of others, even of their own children.

The following case history will serve to illustrate this almost unbelievable fact:

A sixteen-year-old girl with various anxiety symptoms was brought for treatment by her mother who complained that her daughter was untidy, that she never put away her own clothes but cluttered up the house with her belongings and also neglected all her other duties. The girl had to be specifically told and then repeatedly urged and reminded to do her chores. In the course of treatment it became evident that the girl—an only child—had been badly spoiled and had never been taught to assume responsibility for herself. In a short time it was possible to make her aware of and willing to undertake her own obligations as a member of her family. But soon the girl, in turn, had a complaint to make. Her mother, she said, had the habit of pressing and admonishing her even before she had any chance to set about a task. Her duties were constantly held over her; on the other hand, the mother would stop her from her tasks on the grounds that she, the patient, would be certain to make a mess of them.

I sent for the mother and explained to her that she would have to allow the girl more freedom of action if she wanted her to be orderly and helpful. I assured her that I could do little or nothing unless she changed her behavior toward her daughter. She promised to follow my advice and to give the girl more opportunity to look after her own affairs. But the patient reported that nothing had changed at home. It was quite as if I had never spoken with her mother. Every remonstrance on the patient's part to the effect that she could very easily get along by herself met with violent opposition from the mother. Finally, I had to send for the mother again to ask her why she persisted in this attitude. She became very excited and refused to accept the blame. She insisted that the daughter was too awkward and unreliable to be left to herself, and claimed that if she were actually thrown on her own resources she would keep no order at all, and make a mess of her life. Only by the use of considerable persuasion was I able to make the mother see the whole point of the treatment—that the girl should experience the full consequences of her slovenliness.

On the following day I received an urgent call from the patient: her mother had suffered a nervous breakdown. This development presented a new aspect of the problem-situation. The patient's family had once lived in a luxurious home, but had been compelled by circumstances to cut expenses and move into more modest quarters. Both the father and the daughter, who attended college, were active outside the home all day, and the mother, with a consequently limited contribution to her family's well-being, began to feel that no one needed her any more. Her husband and child could get on very nicely without her. Any housekeeper could take her place—*if only the daughter were not so helpless*. This, apparently, was her sole remaining claim to usefulness. The clumsier and more slovenly her daughter, the greater her own sense of importance. If her child should ever learn to stand on her utterly useless and superfluous. Of course, she had never been fully conscious of this motive behind her actions. As it was explained to her, she realized that she had been selfishly interested in *maintaining* her daughter's faults, and hence had unwittingly encouraged them.

This illustration is by no means a rare or exceptional one. In this case, it was possible, by treating both mother and daughter, to cure the neurosis of the latter, and, by establishing a new and better relationship between them, to satisfy the needs of the mother in a different way.

The Parents' Sense of Inferiority

There is no doubt that most parents feel keenly their inadequacy in their relations with their children. Many of their mistakes in child training are the result of their sense of failure, whether real or imagined. Anxiety, extravagant claims upon the child, the tendency to belittle him reflect this subjective feeling of inferiority. One expression of deep discouragement is indecision.

In child training, if your attitude is indecisive, without any real plan or purpose, you may be first severe and then indulgent, now despairing and the next moment dotingly confident. This attitude expresses itself in a continuous rotation of methods and techniques. Beatings are followed by exaggerated displays of affection, and scoldings by promises and rewards. Every offer of advice is met with the stereotyped response, "I tried that before—I've tried everything." Because of their indecision, such parents are incapable of following advice. No sooner have they taken one course than they veer to another. They lack the courage to pursue any definite line of action. They use their bewilderment as an excuse to evade their real responsibilities.

A purely defensive type of evasion finds its most striking expression in nervousness. "Nervous" parents find their "nervousness" a most convenient refuge, and an acceptable reason

for neglecting their responsibilities. They never tire of avow-
ing the good intentions which their "nerves" prevent them
from carrying out. They are not vicious people but are really
invalids, who are unable to find the way to give and take and
who pay dearly for their self-indulgence. They need help and
sympathy and should undergo competent treatment before
tackling the problems of their children.

Sometimes the parents' "nervousness" comes to light only
on sporadic occasions. "My nerves are worn out," or "I can't
stand it," is the typical excuse for an action that cannot be justified on more tangible grounds. This explanation is commonly
offered when, for example, parents have struck their child and
then realized their mistake, or when they have said or done
something that was neither expedient nor justifiable. Inability
to "take it" is the standard excuse for a situation in which one
feels helpless. You may feel that the child has got the better of
you and are unwilling to admit defeat. To save face, you resort to any visible means that will preserve the appearance of
authority. The most usual are whipping, scolding, and threatening. If you wish to obscure the true nature of this open
struggle for power or to palliate the methods employed, you
can always resort to your "nerves" or temper. This stratagem
also yields the added privilege of evoking a special consideration of your own desires.

The Parents Are the Victims

We must recognize that your feeling of inferiority in dealing with children may often be completely justified. Children
begin at infancy to play an active part in the establishment of
inter-personal relationships within the family. The child does
not merely react but learns to act in accordance with his own
ideas and purpose. His active stimulation and provocation begins very early—within the first year of the baby's life. Parents often fail to recognize the child's plans as decisive ele-
ments in the family situation.

An infant's actions are not based on a conscious plan. His

mental development does not permit conscious thought and decisions. But his actions may be none the less determined and intentional. A baby who wishes to be picked up because he once experienced the pleasure derived from being held will acquire a great variety of tricks to get the desired result. The older the child becomes, the greater his efficiency in devising stratagems and stunts to which the parents and other adults succumb long before they realize what has happened. The first years of a child's life are filled with a growing awareness of his physical functions and the people and objects around him. He is constantly observing, experimenting, and experiencing. As a consequence, the child knows more about his parents than they know about him. The average child can manage his parents much better than they can influence him. No wonder that so many parents feel inadequate in dealing with their children.

What Do Parents Know about Education?

Another factor which often contributes to the parents' lack of self-confidence is their ignorance of proper methods of education. Even in normally balanced and self-assured individuals this ignorance may easily produce a feeling of frustration; but when coupled with a deep sense of inferiority it completely warps the parent-child relationship.

The fact that parents are poorly prepared for their function as educators is generally recognized. Every trade or craft must be learned before it can be practiced; yet one of the most difficult of all, the task of rearing the young, is entrusted to persons who are utterly untrained to perform it. Systematic study and practical training are indispensable to the educator. Yet where can fathers and mothers find time and opportunity to undergo this preparation?

However much we may deplore this situation, and however vigorously we should try to correct it in the course of time, we must admit that the lack of instruction alone is not the worst obstacle. "A little knowledge is a dangerous thing."

If parents knew nothing at all of education they sometimes might be better off. They would be more likely to follow their common sense and seek advice at the proper times. They would often be more willing to listen to reason. As matters stand, however, everyone thinks he knows a little about education and often this little is wrong. All of us have experienced "being raised," with the attendant problems and contingencies. But what memory do we retain of our reactions to the methods practiced on us in our own childhood? Poets and novelists are able to recall and describe the discouragements and humiliations, the disillusionments and sufferings of childhood which often far outweigh the pleasures of being a child. But few parents remember this. In their attitudes toward their children many take their own parents as models. They may be willing to make some changes in the old scheme. They may adopt more liberal policies in certain respects because of memories of bitter experiences; or they may lean toward stricter discipline if they feel that their own parents were too lax. And in doing the opposite of what their parents did, they may err just as much. But these changes—which often represent a fusion of the paternal and maternal methods employed—do not alter the fact that in rearing their children most people *follow the example of their own* parents.

As a result, the same errors in child training are handed down from generation to generation. Today this accumulated bulk of false principles weighs upon the present generation of parents, who live in a changing world with different ideas about human relationships. Their situation, moreover, has grown worse with the prevalent custom of very small families. Formerly, when large families were the rule, much less depended on the pedagogical skill of parents. Then, the children largely educated themselves through their contacts with each other and with their neighbors, and the parents' lack of training was far less disastrous. However, at no time did the principles of scientific education reach the parents. They were always reluctant to take advice, for they believed, as many still do, that their early experiences as children qualified them to rear children of their own, in their own way, in their philosophy of life and in the same pattern of relationship that existed when they were small.

Any effort to convince a father who was brought up by the rod that children should be reared without violence, generally provokes the protest, "*I* was brought up like that, and *I* turned out well enough. Why shouldn't I bring up my children the same way?" Like all parents who take this attitude, he never stops to think how he *might* have turned out if he had enjoyed a different and better upbringing. It is as true today as in the past that one of the chief results of breeding and raising seems to be the transforming of intelligent children into rather stupid adults. This is the effect of a dogged process of *discouraging* children; and although this fact has been given recognition ever since Rousseau, not much has changed in the practice of home training. The father who "believes" in spankings has no notion of the extent to which the beatings that he received as a child have impaired the happiness of his married life, his relations with his friends, and finally his attitude toward his own child. In some respects he may have developed "well enough," but at the same time he has become distrustful, brutal, and tyrannical.[3] The same is true of all mothers and fathers who justify their parents' principles of education by reference to their own success in life. It is impossible to estimate how many unnecessary handicaps, defects of character, and undeveloped potentialities might have been avoided.

Educating the Educators

The age-old vicious circle of false premises and principles perpetuating themselves must be broken before we can hope to reduce the difficulties of education, lighten the burden of parents, and correct the faults of their children. This is not possible without a rehabilitation of the *parents*. If we are to have better children, the parents must become better educators.

[3] See Chapter 4, "Physical Punishment."

They must learn to understand children, to know what goes on in their minds, and to comprehend the motives for their actions. And secondly, they must learn to distinguish between the correct, that is, the effective methods of training, and the wrong and worthless.

However, it must be recognized that knowledge is not enough. Many teachers who were endowed with the most profound pedagogical insight and achieved the highest success with other people's children have failed miserably with their own. One of the most glaring examples was Rousseau himself, the pioneer of modern pedagogy.

Fathers and mothers have also many emotional obstacles to surmount. Emotional maladjustment is the consequence of wrong attitudes, such as defensiveness toward life, anxiety for the future, the struggle for power. The education of the educators, the key problem of modern pedagogy, must be attacked from two sides. Enlightenment, the transmission of necessary factual knowledge, is one objective; the other is the development of the educators' personalities. Parents are themselves like children—and sometimes "problem" children—who must be "brought up." But it is not an easy matter to influence adults from without; to a great extent they will have to accept the responsibility of educating themselves. They must learn to know and understand themselves. They must first overcome their distrust of themselves in order to adopt a balanced, confident attitude toward their children. Then, and only then, can they desist from a struggle for power and avoid the conflicts that disturb their child's harmonious development.

If you wish to increase your enjoyment of your children and to strengthen your own educational efficiency you must work toward your own improvement. You must be ready to reorient and reform yourself time and again and to learn from your children as well as from your own experiences. You must be willing to accept all the moral obligations which you lay upon your children. When you realize that the observance of order and regularity is fundamental to the child's development, you must submit yourself to the same regularity and to consistency. If you are unseemly, you can expect to contribute little to your child's conformity.

The behavior of the child is his actual *answer* to your behavior. Education is not a mechanical device imposed from above; the child is not merely the insensible object of your will. The rearing of children implies a constant interaction between parent and child. Parents' and children's actions correspond, as the participants in a dialogue respond to each other. The resultant process is called education and is the product of activity on both sides. The child's behavior corresponds to and changes with the behavior of the persons around him. His ability to adapt himself to the persons with whom he is in contact is greater than that of adults. His personality is not yet fixed, and he is more keenly observant, more sensitive, and more flexible. You must learn to recognize in your child's behavior the reflection of your own disposition and character.

The Position of the Mother

In addition to the impact of his personality, every person who takes part in the rearing of a child exerts a particular influence through the special function that he performs in the family. The most important person in a child's life is the mother.[4] It is she who, from the hour of his birth, is most immediately concerned with the child; and even in the earliest infancy he responds to her behavior. For the child, either boy or girl, is most closely attached to his mother—unless she fails in her function. Even outside duties which prevent her from spending much time with her child do not necessarily deprive her of her place of honor in her child's life. All she needs to do is to prove to him that she, his first and most constant companion, is absolutely trustworthy and dependable in all her relations with him. He will forgive anything in his mother but un-

[4] A discussion of the separate functions of the various members of the family cannot take into consideration the personalities of the various individuals. A strong personality within the family may take on more importance for the child than his or her family position would otherwise warrant.

reliability. Understanding, sympathy, and a little tenderness will give her a permanent lease on his affections. All other attributes of motherhood—anxiety, solicitude, indulgence, vigilance, and the like—are unnecessary, and even harmful. The mother must lessen her attentions and not occupy herself too much with the child, particularly as he grows older. The warmth he needs and naturally expects from her can most often be adequately expressed in a minimum of words or actions. None of her actions should lack this warmth. Then the child will be willing to be led by his mother.

Thus, even the business or professional woman can give her child what he needs from a mother, especially as the child grows older. She can always provide an element of permanence and security in "the racing fight of men and things." A governess, however capable and affectionate, cannot replace the mother, owing to the restrictions on time and responsibility that generally are put on her activities. But where a governess fails, a stepmother may often succeed. There is sufficient evidence to prove that stepmothers and foster mothers can be accepted as mothers in the fullest sense of the word.

The Position of the Father

The father's significance for the child is derived from the position allotted to the male in society. The masculine position in society is undergoing a change at present. Therefore, the role of the father as the educator of his children is changing, too. There is a remarkable difference in the position of the man in the various countries. In the United States the masculine authority is gradually diminishing, while in Latin America and in some parts of Europe it is still more or less unchallenged. This may, to a certain extent, explain the reluctance of the average American father to take any responsibility for the upbringing of his children. Very often he says he does not want to interfere with his wife's handling of the children. Discussions and lectures about education and child guidance are almost exclusively frequented by women, and it is rather difficult to get the fathers interested. This masculine behavior, however, seems to be part of a bigger problem, as it coincides with an obvious masculine tendency to yield all interest in psychology, art, and literature to women. The average American man tries to maintain his superiority by restricting his activity to business and politics, and by regarding the support of his family as his main duty to the home.

The father has, however, a definite function in the development of his children, even in families where the mother tries to occupy a typical man's position. He is still the wielder of vested masculine authority in the family, and he is still the main wage-earner and chief provider. His foremost characteristic in the eyes of the child is his quality as a worker, as a member of a trade or profession. This is true even during periods of unemployment which are considered exceptions to the general rule. The father is generally regarded as the practical and efficient member of the family who has and exercises some special ability. If this function is contested, his natural function in the process of education may become seriously impaired.

The influence of the father is often reflected in the child's attitude toward work and practical achievement. It is the father who is best equipped to spur him on to make something of himself; but, conversely, it is also the father who can easily discourage him so that a boy doubts whether he can ever be a "real man," and a girl assumes that her efficiency will never amount to anything. (However, many children may become discouraged by the example of a perfectionistic and very efficient mother.) The routine home training of the children belongs to the mother, and any open interference from the father, any public effort on his part to oppose her methods, is usually ill advised. Especially grave is the error of father or mother who attempts to counterbalance extreme indulgence and laxity of one parent by equally extreme severity and strictness. Such "compensation," far from improving, only aggravates the situation. One parent can only modify the other's policies by frank discussion and agreement. Under no circumstances should the children become aware of differences between the parents.

Even though the father may play no active part in educating his children, the children are still likely to take him as a representative of strength and power, because he is generally taller and stronger than the mother. He represents what is left of the old masculine ideal of the past. To the children, his behavior signifies masculinity. For this reason, his pastimes and pleasures take on importance beyond their actual significance. He is "the man" around the house, the first pal of the boys, the first sweetheart of the girls. Owing to his limited time at home, he can best serve as an ideal and also as the last authority, as a court of higher appeal.

Especially important for the children are the accord or discord between father and mother and the character of their relationship. These not only set the atmosphere of the entire family and lead either to harmony or disunity, but also give the child his first and most vivid impression of the relations of the sexes. Both parents have the function of assisting the child in the development of the harmonious personality, guiding and stimulating his physical, intellectual, and emotional growth through his social adjustment.

The Position of the Grandparents

Grandparents often contribute much to the child's happiness, but they may also seriously interfere with his training. Theirs is the function of pure love; they demand nothing, but give always. Thus, they tend to spoil their grandchildren, and hence their influence should be carefully restricted. Infrequent calls and occasional longer visits with them add warmth and pleasure to the child's life. They can afford to be kind and gentle since, unlike the parents, they are free from responsibility. They take a pure delight in the sheer existence of the child and in his well-being.

However, it is risky for parents and children to live with the grandparents. Under certain circumstances, his grandparents may be obliged to assume the parental responsibilities; in this case they function as aging parents of late-born children. But it is quite a different matter when grandparents meddle in the parents' methods of training—and this is likely to occur if they all live under the same roof. In such a household the conflict between the two older generations heightens the tension between parents and children, and the child soon learns to play one authority against the other, especially if the grandparents take his part against father and mother and treat the parents themselves like children to be reprimanded and corrected at will. In general, a grandmother is more frequently disturbing than a grandfather, because she is more inclined to interfere. Sometimes one can reason with grandparents more easily and successfully than with parents; still, grandparents should take no part in the actual education of the child.

Chapter 2

The Situation of the Child

To UNDERSTAND a child is to know human nature. It is possible to comprehend a person intuitively; but a clear, rational understanding of a personality can be reached only through insight into its development. This insight is obtainable solely through a systematic, psychological study of his childhood. Alfred Adler's technique enables a trained student to reach a scientific understanding of a person, be he adult or child.[1]

It is our main concern here to grasp the significance of the child's total personality, the fundamental structure of which remains fairly constant throughout the various stages of his life. Changes in personality traits express only his answer to changing conditions and do not necessarily involve a profound change in structure. Recognition of the *basic* concepts governing the formation of the child's personality contributes more to the understanding of a particular child than does an awareness of the incidental behavior patterns which he exhibits while passing through various phases of his development. Every external change which a child undergoes at different

[1] For an understanding of the theoretical background of our techniques, the following books will be found helpful: *Understanding Human Nature, What Life Should Mean to You, Guiding the Child,* and *The Education of Children* by Alfred Adler; *Guiding Human Misfits* by Alexandra Adler; *Corrective Treatment of Unadjusted Children* by N. E. Shoobs and G. Goldberg; *Individual Psychology, Your Nervous Child,* and *Our Children in a Changing World* by Erwin Wexberg.

ages (and which will be discussed in Chapter 5) is simply a variation on the theme, understandable only on the basis of his basic personality. In each case, therefore, our attention will be focused on the structure of personality in its unique, individual entity.

The Life Plan

From the day of his birth, the child begins to acquaint himself with the world he lives in; he experiments with his body, learns to use it, and tries to understand the people and objects of his environment. In short, he attempts to make sense out of his world and its problems. Although this takes place before conscious thought is developed, the child displays a high degree of intelligence, albeit not on the verbal level. While still in infancy, he discovers ingenious means of overcoming difficulties. For example, a five-month-old boy with a muscular weakness of the upper eyelids was observed attempting to remedy this impediment by slumping his head to one side and using his little fists. Careful observation shows that all actions, from earliest infancy on, are purposeful, even if the child is not aware of it. We can understand a child's actions only by recognizing the goal which he unconsciously pursues.

The child early utilizes his impressions and experiences to construct a plan for his subsequent conduct. While still an infant he learns to turn the attitudes of his parents to his advantage. For instance, as soon as he realizes how his parents respond to crying, he will cry whenever he wants to be picked up. Even at this age the child is quite receptive to certain impressions, and speedily adapts his behavior to new experiences. This mental capability—we may call it intelligence—is an important compensation for his physical helplessness.

As the child grows older his impressions and experiences become so complex that he could never assimilate them all if he did not integrate them into some system. Here again the purposiveness of his conduct is apparent from the manner in which he develops. He responds naturally to his own physical and psychological constitution. He recognizes his physical powers and limitations through his experience with his own body, by the ease or difficulty with which he can perform certain functions. In this way he encounters his organic constitution, his physical endowment through heredity, all of which are called the "inner environment." His psychological constitution develops from interactions with his surroundings, with his parents and the other people concerned with his education, and with his brothers and sisters. The more intimate his contact with any one of these persons and the more pronounced his dependence upon them, the greater the part this relationship will play in the structure of the child's behavior scheme. But the child is never the passive object of external influences. What appears to be mere reaction on his part proves, by close observation, to be spontaneous, purposive activity in accordance with a definite plan of behavior. In every child, in fact in every human being whatever his age, this plan assumes a distinct, individual form. For this reason each new situation and each disciplinary measure will invariably meet with different responses from different children, depending in each case upon the subjective way in which it is interpreted and assimilated. Repeated impressions of the same kind will actuate the child to develop his plan in a certain direction, that is, to adapt himself specifically to these impressions.

In most cases this behavior scheme is so skilfully contrived that a casual observer would never realize its remarkable consistency or even suspect its existence at a time when the child's age precludes conscious thought. It often has the effect of a mystic revelation when the trained worker unveils this secret plan before the parents' marveling eyes. The most puzzling eccentricities and mannerisms suddenly take on meaning, baffling paradoxes become sensible, and every action can be recognized as a part of the child's secret scheme of conduct.

Peter, three years old, is the pride and joy of all who know him. His natural charm, his vivacity, his clever little speeches and bright remarks make him the constant center of attention. But occasionally he displays a very ugly temper. He is often stubborn, kicks, howls, and screams in order to get what he wants; but the next moment he turns on a most innocent smile that disarms everyone. He has a wonderfully refined technique for concentrating interest on himself; all his actions revolve around this tendency. His precocious flights of fancy and speculations on his future are simply attempts to thrust himself further into the limelight and attract more attention—as, for instance, his expressed desire to play the big bass in an orchestra. (The small boy gaining significance by using the big instrument!)

This boy is an only child and has never been with children his own age and size. Being small, his significance always depended on those larger than he. By experimenting and observing the reactions of others, he soon discovered the tactics which presumably would give him the best opportunity for asserting himself. He then proceeded to improve this scheme, "unconsciously" but nonetheless systematically; and now he is engaged in amplifying this method by every means that offers itself.

This aim—to attract attention and make oneself the center of interest—is pursued by a great many children, and is especially characteristic of the only child or the youngest. However, in each case the plan of action is different. Only the inadequacy of language, the want of precise terms, compels us to use the same words to describe a great variety of somewhat similar tendencies. When we speak, for instance, of the child's calculated desire to be the first in every endeavor, we must bear in mind that this is only a general theme of which each specific case is a subtle variation. The plan to be first can assume shapes and colors of a thousand different kinds.

It is relatively easy to change the child's latent and sometimes obscure plan of behavior up to about the sixth year. When experience teaches him that a course of conduct is impractical, that a method will not get him what he wants, then he promptly sets out on a new course and tries to find other and more effective methods. It is much more difficult to make such a shift after his sixth year, however. By that time the child's developed mental powers permit him to preserve his old schemes by employing a series of tricks and ruses for their maintenance. Of all his impressions and experiences he chooses to rely only on those which coincide with his plan. Thus he develops a so-called "tendencious apperception scheme," that is, the ability to adjust his apperceptions to his own personal bias. This biased or falsified apperception is characteristic of all adults and keeps them from learning from experiences which do not fit their personal outlook on life. People "make" their experiences; not only do they register only what fits into their schemes, but very frequently actually provoke the experiences which they anticipate or desire.

The scheme which a child has tried and tested to his satisfaction in the specific situations of his childhood becomes his permanent plan of conduct, his *life plan*. This basic scheme remains unconscious even when he grows up into adulthood. He seeks reasons and arguments for justifying his conduct without ever realizing that a definite plan controls all his activities. Whenever the logic of life makes it impossible for a person to act according to his plan, he tries to evade the issue; if this fails, he may withdraw from the logic of life altogether.

The mother of eleven-year-old John complained that her boy, who had always been an excellent student, industrious and striving, had suddenly changed. He no longer did his schoolwork and did not care about marks. The only interest he showed was in sports. John's story was simple enough. He was the son of a prominent Austrian industrialist and had grown up in a small village where his father's plants were located. He had considerable status in the community as the "crown prince of the big man," dominating not only his younger sister, but also all the children of the village. He was by far the best student in the school, which was "honored" by his presence, and he was, as a matter of course, the leader in all of the children's games.

When he became ten, his parents decided to take him to Vienna to start the customary secondary education. Here, in the big city, he found himself unable to maintain his former position. His methods did not work any longer. Most of his schoolmates were scholastically much more advanced than he, who had attended only the small and inadequate village school. Furthermore, they made fun of him as a country boy. Unaccustomed as he was to playing a subordinate role, he lost all interest in schoolwork and stopped making any effort in that direction. But discovering that he could still outdo the city children in sports, he transferred all his interest to athletics and football—to the great surprise and regret of his parents, who could not understand the change that had come over their son. In their opinion, John showed a complete lack of ambition and they simply refused to believe the psychiatrist when they were advised that, on the contrary, the boy's too great ambitions had caused the difficulties.

Every human being is guided in his conduct by a definite plan which forms the basis for a *unified personality* that encompasses all the apparent inconsistencies of his nature and actions. The life plan gives each person his individuality, resulting in a distinctive life style, a peculiarly personal "gait through life." It determines the character and disposition of every individual and molds his destiny to a great extent since it constitutes the motivation for all his actions.

Heredity

If one does not understand a child's motivations and fails to discover his hidden plan of conduct, one may be inclined to regard many peculiarities, faults, and extraordinary qualities as the outcome of "natural" predispositions. Man is subject to the same laws of heredity that control all other living beings; but in man's existence the operation of these laws is restricted to certain immutable factors, such as certain physical features *which are beyond the reach of individual training and education.* Thus the stature and build, the color of hair and eyes, and a great many other physical characteristics are unequivocal results of heredity.

However, the same is not true with regard to psychological qualities, traits of character, and abilities. These undergo tremendous development and are quite different in the infant and the grown man. They are mainly the products of training and discipline, of numberless commissions and omissions, of trials and errors and readjustments. There exist connections between a person's development and the original hereditary foundation, but they are not so simple as is often believed. The general tendency is to deduct from the final result the existence of a corresponding predisposition. Thus the predominance of good qualities in an adult is supposed to indicate a good hereditary background, the prevalence of defects a bad one. But this assumption is wrong. The best potentialities will lead to nothing if they are not developed. Every human activity is extremely complicated and cannot be mastered without training; and the individual who lacks this training will never develop special capacities, no matter how favorable his predisposition.

There is, moreover, another complication of the issue. A natural infirmity or inherited defect does not necessarily lead to a permanent deficiency, but, on the contrary, may provide the impulse to extraordinary achievement. In his effort to overcome any difficulties that may occur, the child may concentrate on the very function that caused the greatest difficulty. This intensive self-training in the exercise of any defective part or function—be it an internal organ, a sense organ, or perhaps some lacking skill or ability—may give rise to an exceptional development of this part or function. Many outstanding accomplishments, physical, intellectual, and artistic, have resulted from the overcompensation of a handicap, especially of an inherited organ inferiority.

The child's ultimate development is not simply the result of original disposition. Through the interplay of neglect and cultivation the child arbitrarily molds his powers and qualities in accordance with his plan.

In the development of personality the inherited foundation

is less significant than the acquired superstructure. The child's endowment is not as important as *what he does* with it—a fact that is proved by the following observations. In the vast majority of families the first and second child are fundamentally different' in character, inclinations, and interests. This would be impossible if their development were determined solely by predisposition. There is no law of heredity which can explain why the greatest differences in character, temperament, and interests exist between the first and second child. The marked differences are due to purely psychological factors. The two children, even though they may sometimes get along well together, are usually serious competitors. The elder, who has once been an only child and has had his parents to himself, is afraid of being deprived of his privileged position. He sees his mother's affection and solicitude diverted to the second child, and he comes to feel that the newcomer is usurping love that is rightfully his. What superiority he may possess by virtue of his age is threatened. He sees the younger child gradually encroaching on one after another of his old prerogatives, and he fears being overtaken and left behind.

The second child, on the other hand, must always cope with a rival who has had a head start in everything, who can walk and talk, eat and dress by himself, perhaps even read and write. In the struggle to assert himself against his rival each child will develop merits, corresponding precisely to the other's faults, with the result that two distinct personalities will emerge. If one is vivacious, the other will be quiet; if one is slovenly, the other will be orderly and neat. Untidiness and neatness, magnanimity and pettiness, phlegmatism and sensitivity, gentleness and brutality, sentimentality and matter-of-factness—these are some of the typical contrasts between the first two children.

Often one child will resemble the father and the other the mother. This would seem to confirm the importance of heredity; but here again it can be demonstrated how psychological factors lead to a certain type of development. The striving to be like mother or father is sometimes the sequence of a family contest for authority in which the children take sides with one parent or the other. In some instances one of the parents may be moved by some external resemblance to claim one of the children as particularly "his own." Or in other cases the child himself may come to regard the father—or the mother—as especially powerful and worthy of imitation. Thus a great variety of motives may lead a child to develop the character and habits of father or mother. Therefore, an existing similarity in character between child and parent cannot serve as final evidence of inheritance. It is improbable that we shall ever be able to decide exactly how far the influence of heredity extends in man, since the process of education begins on the first day of the child's life. At this time we can scarcely determine the hereditary factors, good or bad, that operate in him; and later we can never distinguish between the results of heredity and the effects of education. In the main, the "phenotype" covers the "genotype" so completely that the latter is removed entirely from scientific examination.

The belief in heredity and "natural" aptitude still exerts a detrimental influence on the minds of educators. It leads to a fatalistic pessimism. Instead of applying better methods of training, the discouraged parent or teacher uses the argument of poor natural endowment to justify his own inability. "He is just like his father!" The more dismayed and helpless a parent is, the more firmly convinced will he be of the immutable force of heredity. This assumption will hinder him even further from understanding the real forces that work in the child and determine his behavior.

Social Interest

Is man by nature good? The answer to this question reflects the fundamental outlook of the educator and differentiates the various theories of education. Parents or teachers who believe that they must *tame* the natural badness of children will adopt measures quite different from those adopted by parents who feel that it is their prime duty not to *impede* but in every way to encourage the development of sound natural impulses and energies.

But we need not involve ourselves too far in this philosophical controversy for the simple reason that the point of what man *is* by nature seems to be irrelevant. The essential fact is that everyone can *become* good. However, the term "good" —if we attempt to define it—leads to another problem in ethics. Let us, however, accept the conventional meaning and follow popular opinion, which knows no "absolute" values but establishes norms of conduct according to a more utilitarian viewpoint. In everyday usage the concept "good" is relative, as it refers to the rules and precepts laid down by communities. Anyone who follows the rules of his community is regarded as "good." Understanding and observing social rules requires a special quality that we call social interest. For a good many thousands of years men have led a collective life and found it necessary to cooperate with one another and to adapt themselves to the requirements of the groups in which they lived. Each human being brings into the world a sense of social participation, a heritage from this collective past, which is at the same time a necessary basis for his own individual existence. He needs it from the very start in order to hold his own within the first small group into which he is born. The baby makes himself understood through cries and gestures and smiles. He learns rapidly, and from the first day of his life begins to adapt himself to the regulations that he encounters.

But social interest must be further developed, for the amount of social interest that the child acquires will decide the success and happiness of his entire later life. It will determine the extent to which he can cooperate with other human beings—whether he can win and hold friends; whether he will arouse antipathy or meet with approval; whether he can rightly grasp each situation as it arises and act accordingly. The social interest is the expression of human solidarity and is revealed in the feeling of belonging to others, in the interest taken in other people and in the problems of the common welfare. One experiences it as an urge to live with others, to work in partnership with them, to make useful contributions. Accordingly, an individual's social interest can be roughly measured by his ability to cooperate, his willingness to respect the rules of human society even though their observance may involve personal sacrifice. The burdens imposed upon us by fate or our fellow men are an unremitting test of our social interest.

In adults the complexity of life often prevents an accurate appraisal of their social interest. It is easier to evaluate it in children, as their correct or incorrect conduct is more obvious. The child's social interest determines whether or not he behaves correctly, that is, in proper keeping with conditions at school and at home, in the company of other children, or alone by himself. The child continually faces new group problems; he cannot solve them satisfactorily unless his social interest is allowed to develop freely and fully. In this light such qualities as politeness, obedience, industry, honesty, modesty, and self-reliance assume a new and more specific importance.

The educator must, therefore, recognize the factors that advance the growth of social interest and avoid those that impede its development. This point of view will permit a better evaluation of the methods of child training used heretofore.

Social Insecurity

The natural need of the child to conform to the group into which he was born encounters many difficulties. All the errors committed by parents and teachers constitute obstacles; and all the mistaken methods of training—dissimilar though they may be, or even diametrically opposed—produce the same effect. Parents may be too indulgent with the child or too severe; they may pay too much attention to him, or none at all. But whether they are overaffectionate or unnecessarily harsh, whether they humiliate the child or idolize him, the results are almost identical: instead of conformity they foster rebellion and antagonism.

This hostility—which, strangely enough, may be mingled with affection—is directed primarily against the parent or educator. He appears to the child as the representative of the society as a whole since he acts as the agent of its laws. Therefore the rebellion first directed against parents expands continually and uniformly to the different aspects of social life. *The struggle against the educator invariably develops into a struggle against all order and regulation.* What is the consistent cause of this revolt, first against the educator or parent, then against society?

A feeling of solidarity is possible only so long as one is assured of being accepted, of not being slighted or neglected. A newborn baby may experience at first pleasures or discomforts of only a physical nature. But he is not merely a biophysical organism; he is a human being. As such he soon recognizes social relationships as a source of pleasant or unpleasant sensations. As a consequence, he brings his physical needs into harmony with the regulations of the group and subordinates the importance of his bodily functions to the necessity of establishing social contact with his environment. Henceforth it is the quality of these contacts that chiefly controls his well-being. The greatest pain, the deepest suffering of childhood, does not grow out of physical illness and bodily discomfort. Far more oppressive is the sense of being excluded from the group. The feeling of not belonging, indifference, disregard, and neglect are the most painful experiences of every child.

The child suffers without clearly realizing the cause of his unhappiness. Every human being, if barred from his group, feels that he is in some respect or other made *inferior.* This sense of inferiority does not enter the child's consciousness, but is quite as evident in his actions as in those of adults, and its effects must be counteracted by the same method in the child as in the adult—*by raising his self-esteem.* The small child is particularly sensitive to being slighted. His position in the family gives him sufficient grounds for assuming that he is inadequate and inferior. He is much smaller, more awkward, and more dependent than the other persons of his circle, and receives his status only through others, bigger and more important than he. His rights must often give way to those of others, even when he is pampered—and then perhaps even more so. How often do children feel completely ignored! The child's efforts to compensate for this social insecurity usually lead to a striving for power—the characteristic effect of a sense of inferiority. Whoever feels socially lowered seeks to rise. Every human being wishes to be significant.

The revolt of the child stems from his exaggerated feeling of inferiority, which at the same time constitutes the prime obstacle to the development of his social interest. Instead of remaining interested in social participation, the child who feels inferior becomes more interested in his own elevation. His efforts toward social integration are diverted to a drive for superiority. From this tendency develop all the failings and weaknesses of the child, all his bad habits and deficiencies.

Inferiority Feeling and Discouragement

The child's difficulties can be traced to a sense of inferiority and to a peculiar drive to make up for real or imagined social deficiencies and weaknesses. There are two principal compensations for inferiority feeling—surrender or overcompensation. Similarly, all hereditary or organ inferiorities permit one of two possible courses of action: either they lead to the evasion and neglect of the impaired function, or they give impetus to a special development of this very function, resulting in exceptional achievement. For example, some children who are born with poor muscular coordination will be inept and clumsy; but others with the same defects manage, through persistent self-training, to acquire an unusual degree of physical skill. Natural deformities cause some children to become asocial and backward, but in other cases provide the impulse for outstanding accomplishments. Defects of the eyes may lead to inadequate vision, but more frequently the result is a special development of visual qualities, as keen observation, artistic and visual sensitivity. The same contrary possibilities are inherent in all the difficulties that arise. The child has the choice of giving way to them or learning to overcome them. What, then, determines his choice?

The only factor that decides the issue is the *courage* with which the child approaches his problem. As long as he is not discouraged and believes in his own powers he will struggle unceasingly to master the difficulty; and the innate courage of a child, *unspoiled by faulty training,* is remarkably great. For this reason the defects that challenge the child and arouse his energies at the very outset of his life—such as organ inferiorities of the eyes—are much more likely to result in overcompensation than in evasion and failure; for at this early age the child's courage is usually still intact. Physical handicaps which the child experiences at a later period are more likely to lead to lasting defects. Children can accomplish a great deal that is impossible for adults. This striking ability of children is generally attributed to their greater mental vigor and their brisk, new energies; however, it probably is due to the greater courage which they possess in childhood as compared with adult life.

If it is true that children are by nature courageous and unhesitatingly attack any obstacles that confront them—even the difficulties presented by their own bodies and imposed by heredity—why then do they gradually lose this courage? Here the effects of improper training become apparent. A great many educators, professionals and laymen alike, are not aware of the importance of courage and hence disregard this fundamental need of the child. *They continually diminish the child's self-assurance.* All the many (and sometimes heterogeneous) errors of education converge at this point.

The child may be discouraged by having every obstacle carefully removed from his path, so that he is denied the chance to experience his own strength and the development of his capacities. Similar is the result if too many and too great obstacles are put in his way so that his powers prove insufficient, and he consequently loses self-confidence. Without knowing it, parents discourage children in a thousand small ways, and the cumulative result of these discouragements is the growing sense of inferiority in the child. Overprotection and neglect, indulgence and oppression, despite their fundamental difference in kind, result in the same breakdown of the child's self-confidence, self-reliance, and courage. There is no connection between his sense of inadequacy and the child's real ability. At the beginning of life, at the period of greatest helplessness, he is much less troubled by feelings of inferiority, and attacks his problems much more courageously than in the later years, when he is actually much stronger and more capable. The self-evaluation of a person does not depend on his actual abilities or deficiencies, but on his own interpretation of his comparative status in the group, on his subjective judgment of his relative strength and ability, on his biased appraisal of his deeds as success or failure, and on his own supposition of being adequate or inadequate in handling his problems, which are mostly social. Courage is the prerequisite for successful living—discouragement and the sense of inferiority lead to maladjustment and failure.

The Struggle for Superiority

The mere evasion of a difficult task does not satisfy a discouraged individual. The tangible task may be removed, but the sense of inferiority lingers and continues to press for compensation. Nobody is content to be inadequate. Deeply rooted in every human being is a desire to have a place in the community. Hence the need for personal importance that assures the status of an acknowledged member of the group. Human beings are conditioned to feelings of inferiority. The human race experiences its *biological* inferiority in the struggle for life, being badly equipped for the fight against nature. Man also is impressed by the realization of his *cosmic* inferiority, being aware of his cosmic insignificance, visualizing his future and inevitable death.

The child experiences his inferiority still more directly, through his smallness in the world of giant adults. While biological and cosmic inferiority affect the human race as a whole, stimulating mankind to compensations, to the mastery of nature, and to spiritual, religious, and philosophical growth, the *social* inferiority of the child affects him alone, distinguishing him from the rest of the group. Comparing himself with parents and relatives, with older and with younger siblings, he never feels secure in his position. This constant fear of losing his position is accentuated by the atmosphere of competition, which is characteristic of our present society and which penetrates into the family, thereby corrupting the relationship between all members of the family group. As long as the child is courageous, he will try to prove his importance by useful accomplishments, by social contributions. Only when he becomes discouraged, does his social interest become restricted. Then the road to useful achievement may be blocked, so that the child seeks means of increasing his personal superiority on the "useless side of life" (Alfred Adler).

The urge for superiority moves the child to lay down certain guides for his conduct. This is done mainly in an intuitive way, since his rational powers are still limited. He may try to model himself after a person who seems powerful and influential. The ideal of masculinity, so overrated in our social system, may exert a strong attraction. The child uses every opportunity to increase his prestige. This striving for recognition is especially obvious in children who have developed a strong feeling of inferiority. The ideas of superiority reflect the child's concept of "security." As he is not sure of being accepted and of being good enough, as he *cannot rely on his*

own strength, he expects to be secure through outside support.
Being loved, getting attention and admiration, having power
over others, and receiving service—these are his ideas of
security. Some children do not consider themselves socially
acceptable unless they can do something unique, or be the
leader of their group, or succeed in depressing other children
to a lower level. In these cases their contribution to the group,
even though it might be socially useful, does not reflect social
interest, but interest in themselves; they do not act for the sake
of contributing, but for the sake of self-elevation, of gaining
recognition and significance. The vast majority of misdeeds
are a sign of the fictitious superiority for which a discouraged
child is striving, by getting undue attention, dominating with
his violence and temper, or punishing others for his own feeling of rejection and being disliked.

All the faults of children, all their frailties and petty vices
are miscalculated efforts to get ahead of others. They are
directed against both the parent and the social order. By elud-
ing definite demands and tasks required of him, the child gains
a kind of superiority over the parent. In any contest with the
child the parent or teacher is at a marked disadvantage. He can
never gain more than a sham victory, and in the end he must
admit frustration; the child gets his own way, and the educator
has a permanent problem on his hands.

Stubbornness in the child is, therefore, not only an expression of revolt, but at the same time a tool for securing power.
It breaks down all the bounds of order and parental authority.
Between the ages of two and four the child reaches a fuller
understanding of the system and general structure of the family
group, and by ill-advised pressure he may be forced into opposition and become gradually discouraged. For this reason
he frequently develops a stubborn period. This is the time
when conformity should be achieved; but, with our system of
small families and with the shortcomings of our present-day
methods of education, this result is rarely attained without a
struggle.

Conscience

In the first years of his life the child acts unconsciously. His actions are not based on conscious thought on the verbal level. Nevertheless, his actions are intentional and have a purpose. His various purposes are obvious to the experienced observer; but the child may be wholly unaware of them, especially when they are directed against his environment. He may realize that he wants a ball, a glass of water, or to go to the toilet, but he is not aware of wanting attention or showing his power. Such intentions are just as definite and must be recognized if one wishes to understand the child.

At first the child's actions are automatic, empiric, opportunistic, and unrelated to each other. As his radius of action and his understanding grow he comes to understand the larger implications and significance of behavior. He gradually realizes what is *right* to do and what is *wrong;* he acquires an insight into the general rules of the social game. If his relations with the family group were free of any antagonism, he would accommodate himself naturally and without objections to its laws. But as matters ordinarily stand, he finds it more important to fight for his position. His efforts to gain superiority as a compensation for his precarious social position are bound to be eventually at odds with moral precepts. Then, only two ways are open for his subsequent development.

His opposition to his parents and other members of the family may be so strong that he loses sight of common interests and drops every vestige of fellow feeling. The result is open rebellion—the child refuses to acknowledge any order and willfully resists all rules and precepts. In such a case his conscience remains underdeveloped. He does not accept moral standards and social conventions.[2] A similar lack of conscience may be found in children who grew up in a family which in itself is at odds with society and does not recognize general standards of correct behavior.

[2] See Chapter 6, "Psychopathic Personality."

The other possibility to express antagonistic intentions is more frequent and almost the rule. The child remains attached to his parents and accepts law and order in a general way. He develops sufficient conscience, he knows what is right and what is wrong and he tries to conform. His "common sense" expresses his feeling of belonging; he thinks in line with the others. That does not prevent him from wanting to do things his own way, against his "better judgment" and against the standards which he had accepted in general. He acts in such instances according to his "private logic" which can be called his "private sense." He knows what he should do, but decides to the contrary if he thereby can gain something for himself. He pretends to accept the rules, but breaks them whenever they interfere with his efforts to gain position and prestige. He follows them only if his prestige is not endangered.

This conflict between "common sense" and "private sense" is characteristic not only for the child but for adults as well. We admit to ourselves only those intentions which conform with social prescriptions. Actions which serve socially unacceptable intentions seem to arise against our own will, almost as compulsions, without apparent rhyme or reason. Since they are anti-social, we cannot accept responsibility for them if we want to maintain our good intentions. Consequently, excuses are sought to explain such perplexing actions, impulses, or emotions.

The child learns by experience the value of good excuses. Whatever he does wrong will find less criticism and retaliation on the part of the parents if he can find a plausible excuse. Parents are receptive to good excuses because they themselves, in their own conduct, rely on them. Nothing upsets them as much as an open admission of bad intentions on the part of the child. This is a defiance which they cannot tolerate. But as long as the child seeks an excuse he demonstrates at least his good will. It makes a great difference when a child, after breaking an object, says he is sorry it happened because it slipped out of his hand, instead of admitting that he was angry at mother and wanted to hurt her. While there can be no doubt that that was his real intention, the child himself remained unaware of his real goal. If a child is asked why he misbehaves he cannot give a satisfactory answer.[3] In many cases he will say that he does not know. Such an answer often infuriates the disciplining parent; but nevertheless it is correct. The excuses which the child may give are merely rationalizations. He may invent them just to mitigate the scorn of the parents, or he may really believe them. As a rule, the excuses are made up for the benefit of the parents; but as the child grows and his conscience develops further, he seeks excuses for himself, to quiet his own conscience.

A five-year-old girl was in strong rebellion against her domineering and overprotecting mother. The mother could not understand why the child was so unreliable. When she went to visit a girl friend in the neighborhood, she never came home on time, nor could mother find her where she was supposed to be. The child was very bright and frank. We asked her whether she liked to do what mother told her or whether she did only what *she* wanted. Surprisingly, she answered that she did what she wanted. Q. "And when mother tells you what to do?" A. "Then I don't listen." Q. "And when mother asks you to listen?" A. "Then I start to talk, too." Q. "What does mother do then?" A. "Then she tells me to be quiet and to listen." Q. "And what do you do then?" A. "Then I forget what she told me." This child had no difficulty in admitting her intentions to herself. As she grows older, if she does not lose her desire to show her mother who is "boss," she will reach a stage where her intentions become intolerable to her conscience. Then she may learn to conceal her real intentions and use neurotic alibis, which she is already preparing. She may develop a compulsive urge to talk, or a real, not pretended, forgetfulness.

Conscience and conscious will are only part of the total personality. They are developed simultaneously with the

---

[3] See Chapter 3, "Disclosures."

ability to talk and to express thoughts verbally. Conscience, or the awareness of good and evil, is necessary for the child's development. However, its educational significance is often overrated. Education on the verbal level is directed only toward the child's conscience and consciousness. Such education must regard all other aspects of the child's personality (emotions, habits, impulses) as being beyond the reach of will and knowledge. As such motivations are often not understood and resist correction on the verbal level, they are often regarded as an incorrigible mass of inherited predispositions, senseless instincts, or deep mystical emotional urges. However, these expressions of the child's personality are the *true indications of his intentions*, not admitted because not in accord with his conscience. Pointing out to the child that he is wrong might be necessary if he really does not know that he was wrong. In most cases he knows it very well, and an appeal to his conscience is superfluous—no, it is actually harmful. It intensifies the child's inner conflict between his "common sense" and his "private sense" which existed already at the moment when he misbehaved. Preaching and moralizing lead to the development of guilt feelings, which is one of the most misunderstood psychological mechanisms of our times. Very few recognize that guilt feelings are not an expression of remorse but, on the contrary, a preparation for continuous misbehavior. Guilt feelings are only found in people who *pretend* to be sorry for something they have done and intend to do again. Regardless of how much one regrets what one has done, one does not develop a guilt feeling if one is willing to do the right thing now. Guilt feeling must be distinguished from active remorse; it refers always to what happened in the past instead of considering what should be done in the future. The child may realize that he did wrong, but he does not realize which intentions were responsible for his action, and maintains the same intention, leading to a repetition of the same mistake. Therefore, increasing the child's guilt feeling blocks his improvement. Instead of being preached to, he must be made aware of his real intentions.[4]

Revealing to a child his immediate purposes may often abruptly change his methods of obtaining his goal. As soon as he becomes aware of his anti-social intentions, he can no longer reconcile them with his already developed conscience. He has not yet organized this complicated scheme of self-delusions with which we adults manage to pacify our conscience by fooling ourselves with excellent rationalization. It is difficult to make adults realize their real intentions; their well-established rationalizations permit them to maintain their belief in their good intentions, even if their actions obviously point in the opposite direction. When a young child is informed that he wiggled in his chair just to attract attention, he will—in most cases—stop wiggling. (No such result will be obtained by telling him that it is not nice to wiggle.) This device to obtain his goal is no longer useful once he discovers its real meaning. If he still wants to attract attention he will seek another method to get it, again without recognizing its meaning unless made aware of it.

The recognition of the limited value of conscience does not prevent the realization of how important it is to develop the child's conscience. Without adequate conscience, social adjustment and social living is impossible; but conscience alone is not sufficient. It is necessary to recognize, supervise, and—if necessary—stimulate a change in the child's "private goal" and his life style. Otherwise the child develops an outlook on life and chooses methods to obtain his place in society which are not conducive to his happiness and to his ability to live harmoniously with others. If the child misbehaves, he reveals thereby only the erroneous concepts which he has developed about himself. Moral preaching, reproaches, or appeals to his conscience are futile. They do not affect his impulses and emotions. These will change only when his intentions and

[4] See Chapter 3, "Disclosures."

concepts are not longer in opposition to his conscience and conscious thinking, and in accordance with social obligations. Correct social attitudes alone permit an integration of the conscious will and the emotional desires. Any antagonism between conscience and emotional impulse disappears once the "private goal" falls in line with "common sense."

The Family Constellation

The attitude of parents and teachers is the most frequent but not the only source of the child's feeling of inferiority. His position among the brothers and sisters plays a great part in the growth of his character. The relationship between the first and the second child produces uncertainty in both, and the ensuing competition leads to characteristic personality differences. The less courageous of the two—the one who has been pampered, or perhaps is physically the weaker, or who has in some way been neglected—is the more likely to turn defeatist. It is inviting disaster when the parents make a fuss over one of the two because he happens to be a boy, or because he is especially weak or delicate. Often the older is forced into opposition by the parents' failure to understand his heightened sensitivity and hostility after the birth of another child. In other cases, the unusually rapid development or exceptional ability of one child may be regarded by the other as a serious threat to his own status.[5]

Thus the child's position in the family entails a great variety of trials and stimulates the development of certain traits and qualities. The second-born child is generally the more active, both in good and in evil; he acts as if he had to make up for lost time. The first-born, on the other hand, may be troubled his whole life long by the feeling that he may again be deposed.

The second child becomes a middle child when the third is born. First, he may believe that now he will enjoy the same superior position his brother held over him. But soon he dis-

* See Chapter 2, "Heredity."

covers that the new baby has certain privileges which are denied to him. As a consequence, a middle child very often feels completely slighted and abused. He has neither the rights of the elder one nor the privileges of the baby. Unless he succeeds in pushing himself ahead of his two competitors, he will likely, the rest of his life, hold the conviction that people are unfair to him, that he has no place in the group.

For this reason the first and the third child very often form an alliance against their common competitor. Alliance between children is always expressed in similarity of character, temperament, and interests, as competition leads to fundamental differences in the personalities. The fourth child is frequently similar, that is, allied, to the second child. But one must keep in mind that no general rule can be applied, for the establishment of alliances and competitions depends on the fashion in which the children of each family inaugurate their relationships and equilibriums. The situation may be quite different in each family.

The only child has a peculiarly difficult start in life. Like a dwarf among giants, he spends his entire childhood among persons whose capacities are far superior to his. For this reason he may try to develop techniques and qualities that will gain him the interest and approbation of grown-ups without particular achievement on his part. He readily acquires the knack of attracting the interest and solicitude of adults either through personal charm and grace, affectionateness and amiability, or by the typical expedients of the weak: helplessness, shyness, timidity. The only child often balks at group activities unless his mere presence assures him a certain distinction.

The youngest child resembles an only child in many respects; but in others his position corresponds to that of the second-born, and accordingly he develops a considerable urge to put himself forward. His efforts to outdo all the other children may be remarkably successful. Since he has to use a whole bagful of tricks to mask his situation as the smallest of the family, he often becomes quite inventive and adroit.

The considerable differences in age among the children of large families may lead to the spontaneous formation of groups, or cliques, within the family, each group as a whole assuming the position of the first, second, or middle child. A child born many years later than the previous one often develops the same traits as an only child.

If a child, for any reason, stands out from the others, he may find it particularly difficult to develop his social feeling. This might be true, for instance, of an only girl in a family of boys, or of a single boy with a number of sisters. A strikingly ugly or sickly child has much the same problem to contend with. Conspicuous advantages or merits, too, may impede the development of social interest. Parents must realize that feelings of inferiority may arise from too much recognition. An unusually attractive child, for example, can be very easily discouraged where practical activity is concerned, since it is so much simpler for him to win recognition and favor through his external appearance than through actual achievement. His vanity leads him to expect constant admiration and praise, and he is all too ready to retreat from any situation in which this approval is not easily or completely secured.

Each individual's start in life is different. No two children have an identical background for their development. Hence the problems of upbringing are identical in no two cases, even for the children of a single family. Parents may think that they rear all their children in the same way and that the reason for the diverging results must lie in some inherited differences. In this they are wrong. In the first place, mothers and fathers do *not* treat all their children alike. However strong their effort to be completely impartial, one or more of the children will be closer to the parents than the others. But even if the parents succeed in treating one child exactly like another—the oldest and the youngest, the strong and the puny, the boys and the girls—even then there will be disparities in their position, and conflicts. As a consequence, each child will react differently to the parents and to his situation as a whole. Each has his own distinctive childhood and, therefore, builds up a life plan that is definitely his own. The life styles of the youngest children of two different families probably are more similar than those of the youngest and the middle child of the same family; so strong is the influence of the family constellation. The experiences by which a child develops his life plan are infinite in their variety. We cannot hope to recognize them all, but we can understand the conclusions which the child draws from his premises. Comprehension of the child's interpretation of himself is the only basis for proper guidance and assistance in correcting a maladjustment or in improving a noticeable deficiency in the child.

II. THE METHODS OF TRAINING

Chapter 3

The Efficient Methods

You must realize the psychological factors which influence the development of a child's personality; otherwise you lack a basis for your educational efforts. Your success in rearing your child can be measured by the degree of social interest developed and exhibited by him. The development of sufficient social interest should be the main goal of your education, if you are interested in the happiness of your child and his future physical and mental fitness. You cannot accomplish this goal without observing the following general principles: (1) your child must be brought to respect order and accept social rules; (2) warfare and conflicts with your child must be avoided; and (3) your child needs constant encouragement.

These basic principles need further amplification:

1. The proper growth of your child's social interest requires that he recognize his close contact with others in the group. Education is the process of furthering his development as a social being. By learning to respect order and follow the rules of the social game, the child will become willing and able to cooperate with others. The adjustment of the child to social living is the most important method for making him a happy and harmonious human being.

2. Conflicts with your child prevent the growth of the necessary sense of solidarity, and damage the relationship of

parent and child. Moreover, any fight with a child is senseless and futile. Harmony is the only basis for social education. Nothing can be accomplished without reaching agreement. Objections are sometimes raised at this point by parents who themselves were brought up on discord and coercion. Is it possible, they ask, for children reared in completely peaceful surroundings to bear up under the struggle for existence? A calm atmosphere in the nursery is, in their opinion, a faulty preparation for later life.

The most cogent evidence to the contrary is provided by those who were brought up in quiet, peaceable families. As a rule, they are not incompetent in the struggle of life, but manage to keep well above water. Personal conflict is not necessary in the proper preparation for overcoming reasonable difficulties. It represents only hostility, strife, agitation, and is inseparably bound up with hateful feelings and impulses. It is the prelude to strong words and violent actions, and stirs up dissension and vindictiveness. It creates bullies and underdogs whose defensiveness in their domestic relationships does not contribute to the solution of any social problem, but creates new ones.

It is true that the child must learn to fight—but not against you who ought to be his friend. There are enough outlets for his combativeness. The inanimate world gives him many chances to expend his energies, to overcome obstacles, and to experience a sense of victory. Later on, similar opportunities will present themselves in his relations with playmates and schoolmates. He must learn to contend with hostile forces and to pit himself when occasion arises against aggressive, malevolent, and spiteful opponents.[1] However, it is most important that he learn to reach agreement, to settle differences with friends and associates, without fighting. Conflicts, in the sense of

[1] See Chapter 3, "The Atmosphere of the Family."

rivalry and the experience of self-assertion and triumph over others, are not essential for the child's development, notwithstanding the present social emphasis on competition. Competition must not be regarded as an indispensable stimulation. Differences of interest and opinion are inevitable; but they never necessitate unfriendly or hostile attitudes.

Pernicious and futile conflicts can be completely avoided if parents familiarize themselves with the technique of peaceful education. Because of their unfamiliarity with such techniques, they, like other untrained persons, may be unable to solve any difference or clash of interests in a peaceful way, based on mutual respect. Generally, they either fight or give in. Both methods fail to accomplish their purpose: they do not lead to agreement. Fighting means violation of respect for the other one, and giving in is disrespect of one's own dignity. Either alternative invariably leads to new conflicts, where those who lose out rebel and seek another opportunity to reestablish their lost prestige. Most parents are completely helpless when confronted with a situation where the child's interests and theirs do not coincide. Many go so far as to battle and give in at the same time; either struggling with the child and finally surrendering, or first indulging the child and then awakening to the consequences and fighting. The proper educational techniques exclude fighting or yielding. Whatever can be accomplished without conflict or surrender is generally to the good, because it leads to agreement. Compromise may be agreement, but is not necessarily so. Both parties may feel defeated and dissatisfied. Compromise is agreement only when a common ground, acceptable to both, is found. Otherwise, it is mutual imposition.

3. Encouragement is the medium for all constructive influence in education. The child needs it as a plant needs water for growth. Since he begins his life in complete

helplessness and is exposed to a succession of disheartening experiences throughout the period of growth, he needs conscious, deliberate, and systematic encouragement to develop self-confidence, strength, social interest, self-reliance, and any skill and ability to meet life successfully.

It is not feasible to assign any particular educational approach to any one of these three categories, since the three divisions belong together. Adjustment is the objective, peacefulness the technique, and encouragement the substance of child training. Accordingly, most of the processes of education involve all three aspects. This is true of the simplest single measures—the giving of orders, for example—but much more so of that varied composite of disciplinary influences that goes by the single name of "authority." There can be no doubt that children require guidance and that you, the educator, must secure respect and must be in a position to carry your points without undue interference, especially when the child is small and limited in his comprehension. But the means of winning and preserving authority are multiform. Authority may be earned through understanding and good will, or it may be imposed by brute force. It may be built upon your *personal* superiority, or it may be the expression of an order which is binding upon *all* members of the group, of which you yourself are also a part.

Thus the factors entering into child training are extremely diverse and complicated. In the following pages some of the simplest factors will be discussed.

A. Maintaining Order

THE ATMOSPHERE OF THE FAMILY—Every community has its customs and usages. And every family is a community in itself. If wrangling and contention, disorder and slovenliness, suspicion and self-interest are allowed to set the tone of the family life, the child will adopt these practices and attitudes, no matter how favorable his disposition and hereditary background may be. For this reason the results of education depend largely on the atmosphere of the family. If the rules of conduct prevailing in the home do not accord with those stipulated by society in general, the child will be faultily prepared for the problems that he will encounter at school, in his profession or job, in his sex relationship, and in his social contacts.

The parents' example is of greatest importance. How can the child develop orderly habits if his mother and father are careless and unmethodical? Why should he be industrious if no one else in the family applies himself to a systematic routine of work? How can he acquire affable manners if vulgar squabbles and name-calling are daily occurrences in his home? Only under one condition will the child's development pursue a course exactly opposite to the example set: if the child is hostile to his parents. In this case, a bad example may stimulate a child to develop acceptable patterns of behavior. It is not uncommon that an honest, capable man or woman emerges from a degenerate family, this favorable result being more probable when the child found somebody who supported him in his stand against his parents. But one should not rely on the potential benefits of a bad example. The better the atmosphere of the home, the more likely it is that the child's development will be gratifying.

The home atmosphere is determined in part by social and economic factors, in part by the parents' general outlook on life, and in part by their characters, their level of education and refinement, their intellectual and spiritual interests, and the quality of their marital relations. It is impossible to change the whole background of the family; but some of the important factors can be modified through insight and understanding. It is even possible for resourceful parents to use unfavorable circumstances which cannot be avoided, such as disease, and economic or social predicaments, as stimulation of constructive attitudes and motivations.

Parents should prepare the way for their child's satisfactory upbringing even before his birth. If they quarrel, the spirit of discord will permeate the entire home. Kindness, mutual respect, and forbearance are necessary prerequisites for successful cooperation. From his mother and father the child derives his first impressions of mankind at large; consequently, they must keep a close check on their own conduct and improve it to the best of their ability.

You also give your children their first conception of the great world beyond the family, and it is significant what picture you give them of this outside world: how you speak of other people; whether you discuss your neighbors with friendly interest and understanding, or merely gossip about them and treat them condescendingly; whether you try to be fair-minded, or are hypercritical and too ready to believe the worst of everyone. Most prejudices are put in children's minds by their parents.

Children see the universe through their parents' eyes. Therefore your view of the world is of greatest importance. It is of great advantage if you have some definite, well-established outlook on life; any definite belief—whether religious (the particular denomination is immaterial), or secular, based on ethical or scientific principles—acts as a constructive force. The more clear and adequate your view of the world, the more consistently will you observe a moral order, and the easier will it be for your children to accept social conformity.

Your attitude toward the problems of life is revealed in your conversation. What children hear at home is of the greatest importance to their development. You must be careful of what you say in front of your child, *and never underrate his powers of comprehension.* He understands a great deal more than you imagine. He may be unable to grasp some words logically and rationally, but even at a very early age he is able to gather the essential meaning of the conversation between adults. You should present the world to him in such a fashion as to stimulate his mental and spiritual growth. Pessimistic views, expressed by you and people around you, will not induce children to be happy and contented. Constant talk of the depravity of man and of the world cannot stimulate them to become useful members of society.

You should show the child the beauty of the earth and the dignity of art. He can be taught delight in nature and the pleasures of thought and knowledge. He will take an early interest in such topics if you talk of them at the dinner table and while taking a walk with him. The atmosphere of the home itself, apart from any special educational measures, serves to guide the child's spiritual, intellectual, and emotional development. It exerts a lasting influence on his character, his temperament, and his mentality. Much arduous labor will be saved in his later training if his upbringing is calm and constructive from the beginning.

We must realize that the perfect domestic atmosphere is hardly to be found in our era of insecurity, strife, and intense competition. Parents, however, must be warned against the temptation to shift the blame for lack of harmony to conditions in general, to grandparents and in-laws, or to each other. This will only tend to aggravate a situation that is already strained and will give rise to further conflicts. You can change and improve conditions only by watching *your own* conduct and by trying in every way to improve your own contributions. Economic difficulties, character defects or incompatibility of the parents, crowded quarters, undesirable neighbors or relatives, or illness—that is, any disturbance of domestic order and peace—will require increased attention to the methods used in influencing the children. Resentment and discouragement, carrying a grudge, regardless of how justified and understandable it may be, will only add new hardships to an already difficult situation and may impair the child's development more than the original, detrimental situations.

THE OBSERVANCE OF DOMESTIC RIGHTS AND OBLIGATIONS —Social living requires certain rules of conduct. Some of them are all-inclusive and apply uniformly to all members of the group; others serve to fix the respective rights of the individual members. Probably no family has ever actually codified its laws, but their validity is nevertheless firmly established by tacit agreement and custom.

Parents often believe that they have set up binding rules governing such items of conduct as cleanliness, orderliness, veracity, gentleness, and industry. Only if they themselves follow these rules will the child recognize them as obligations that hold good for everyone, and accept them as a matter of course. *The essential premise is that the rules must be subject to no exceptions.* Otherwise they will appear to the child not as necessary forms of a general social order, but as a scheme of unfair impositions.

Naturally, each member of the family has different functions which imply different rights and different duties. Children, and adults too, are sensitive to inequality, and are suspicious of anyone who seems to enjoy more privileges than the rest. They often vindicate their resentment against their own role by referring to their sense of justice; actually they are motivated only by a sense of rivalry and by their rebellion against the existing order as a whole. Such rebellion reveals that the child has not recognized and accepted the fact that father and mother, the elder and the younger children, have, logically and unavoidably, different functions and, hence, different *responsibilities* with their concomitant "rights" and privileges. There is no social group in which all the members have identical functions and privileges at all times. The most important point is the fact that difference in function does not mean social inequality. (This must be recognized by the rest of the family in order to be impressed on the child.) Each member of the family can and must receive full recognition *in his particular function* and must be conceded full importance as a significant and appreciated member of the group. It is his social right: to be appreciated, recognized, and respected for what *he* is and does, regardless of what the others are and do.

One is too easily tempted to disregard, within one's own

family, this necessary right of every member to be respected in his functions. The wage-earner and supporter, generally the father, has certain natural prerogatives. His work schedule necessarily affects the family's daily routine. But this does not imply that the functions of the other members are inferior or worthless. The wife and mother should not be relegated to a secondary position. Her many duties give her certain privileges. She has deciding influence in matters of training and discipline, and jurisdiction over the daily life of the child. Her function, however, does not give her the right to look down upon the husband as though she were a queen or ruler. Any infringement on another's social status leads to an impairment of his functioning. *The less recognition and respect are granted to the function of any member of the family, the less adequately will he perform this function.* This is an axiomatic truth which can be confirmed by numerous experiences in any social group, especially in family life. It has far-reaching implications for the rearing of children.

What are the rights of the child? You ought to consider this matter very seriously. Since a child owes his life and subsistence to his parents, you might feel that he has responsibilities only to you and no rights of his own. Or you may be inclined to reason that you have all the responsibilities and owe everything to the child, since it was through your will, not his, that the child came into the world. Such attitudes are detrimental to the child's final adjustment. He is a full member of the family, with *definite rights and definite obligations*, from the first day of his post-natal life, even during the period of his complete physical helplessness. If he is deprived of his natural privileges or if he gets too many, he then often tries to assume a great many others to which he has no just claim.

The baby's right to rest, to sleep, and to have regular feeding periods[2] has already been mentioned. As the sphere of the child's activity expands, his rights multiply. He is entitled to enjoy an increasing degree of freedom and independence, to

[2] For details, see Chapter 5, "Nursing."

develop his own initiative, to experience *his* strength, and to have suitable opportunities for play with companions of his own age. Even when very small, he needs opportunities to make useful contributions, to help around the house and be of service to others. It is his privilege to make certain decisions regarding his own person, and to be allowed considerable leeway in the choice and the manner of acquiring necessary practical abilities.

In addition, the child needs a certain amount of *recognition*. When you belittle his activities, you curb his growth. You must realize that the play of children is as serious and important as the work of adults. It is essential to growth and broadens the scope of their experience in much the same way that conscious study broadens the mind of the college student. Through play the child acquires the skills and capacities needed in later life. He learns the use of his body and the form and meaning of the objects about him. He gains dexterity, both physical and mental, and develops the ability to live and work with other people. It is a mistake to think that children's play is entertainment, like the play of adults. *Everything that the child does is a serious preparation for life.*

Likewise you must show your recognition of your child's first attempts at independent action—his early efforts to wash and dress himself and to keep his clothes and toys in order. Especially important is the principle that the activity of any one child of the family, irrespective of age or sex, is neither more nor less significant than the activity of any other.

The responsibilities of each child are in direct relation to his rights and privileges. Both his rights and his duties are inherent in his natural functions. Sleep and rest, for instance, are not only his duties, but his rights. The younger child has not only the "duty" but the "right" to go to bed earlier than older siblings. The child must fit himself into the family pattern. He cannot be allowed to disturb the order of the household, and he must learn to respect the rights of others just as they respect his own. Reciprocity is the basis of cooperation, and requires a dynamic equilibrium of the rights and interests of all the individuals composing the family.

CONSISTENCY—The child must be clearly aware of what is expected of him before he can adjust himself properly. The more generally applicable laws exist, the more quickly will he grasp their meaning. Children learn only by the recurrence of similar experiences, and hence can comprehend definite rules and injunctions only if these apply uniformly, at *all* times and under *all* circumstances. Every inconsistency on your part clouds the child's understanding of the principles that should govern his conduct.

You will, for example, have great difficulty in training the child to wash his hands before meals unless you establish this habit at the earliest possible time, and then hold firmly to it, with no exceptions allowed. An order must be carried out in all cases to which it applies. Once children realize that a rule is permanently binding and invariable, they will accept and follow it automatically. Hence you must be particularly careful when the child first encounters a new responsibility. His first impressions of a new situation will strongly influence the course of his subsequent conduct. You cannot afford to be indulgent at the beginning, in the mistaken belief that the child will learn to meet the necessary requirements as time goes on. This is an invitation to regard the task as unimportant. A child acquires habits of order and cleanliness only through the consistency of established rules. If he is not *always* obliged to straighten up his books and papers after studying, he will feel that he does not need to comply with sporadic commands to this effect. If occasionally, when time runs short, he is allowed to go to school only half washed, he will have every reason to think that thorough bathing is unimportant. One day you insist that the child respond immediately to your slightest suggestion; and the next day you do not care if he ignores your repeated calls, and are perhaps even amused when through ruses and cleverness he leaves his task undone. If this is your way of giving orders, how can you expect the child to mind you?

You frown upon lying; you impress the child with the disgrace of falsehood—and the following morning you may send him to the door to tell a bill collector that you are not at home. What must be his general conclusions about the ethics of lying? Or perhaps the child shows off for the benefit of guests. Everyone laughs at his pert remarks, and you feel highly flattered. A few days later, while you are having a serious conversation with a friend, the child tries the same antics. But this time, oddly enough, you become angry and send him to his room. How can he understand that the same actions can please you on one occasion and annoy you on another? If you cannot learn to be consistent in your demands, the child can scarcely be expected to follow your orders.

DECISIVENESS—Before you ask anything of a child, you must know exactly what is necessary. If you are not certain of what should be done, you can consult with the child. "What do you think about visiting grandmother tomorrow? Or do you have too much schoolwork to do?" In such a case a definite demand should be avoided since it might be necessary to retract it. This is especially important in dealing with older children. In all instances you must decide carefully whether the situation requires, or permits, a definite order.

But when a decision has been reached you must firmly insist on the execution of the instructions. The very tone of your voice will tell the child whether or not he can expect determination. His powers of observation are extremely sharp; and the expression of your face, the inflections of your voice, betray your thoughts and purposes to a far greater extent than you perhaps imagine.

Firmness, however, is not to be measured in terms of loudness. Many mothers and fathers think that they have to shout in order to produce a proper response. But quite the opposite is true. A great expenditure of lung-power generally indicates some inner uncertainty which the child will at once recognize and turn to his advantage. An order, it is true, must be resolute, but it will be much more effective if delivered in a low tone. It is the *inflection* of the voice that brings out the firmness of our intention.

Commands or direct orders should be used very sparingly if they are to maintain their effect. They should be reserved for real emergencies when danger is afoot and the child must respond immediately. On most occasions it is best to avoid direct commands, for it is impossible to supervise their execution with the proper care unless there are very few of them. And if the child ever comes to feel that he does not need to comply immediately with your orders, your word will carry scarcely any weight at all in the future.

Most commands can be replaced with friendly *suggestions:* "Wouldn't it be nice if . . ." "I would enjoy having you do . . ."

NATURAL CONSEQUENCES—Letting the child experience the natural consequences of his misbehavior is the most important method of preserving order. Any direct intervention—in the form of commands, exhortations, or scoldings—works only from without. The child feels more or less forced into a certain mold of conduct. Correct behavior, however, arises from within, when the child voluntarily and spontaneously adjusts himself to a situation and develops the proper impulses of his own accord. If inwardly he is not prepared to observe order, all educational efforts will be of small and temporary value. But he cannot arrive at this inner acceptance of order *until he realizes that it is more satisfying to respect the rules of conduct than it is to violate them.* This process involves no personal submission or humiliation. It is the only means by which the child can willingly learn to accept unpleasant as well as pleasant responsibilities, to modify his own desires when necessity arises.

Opportunities to let him feel the unpleasant results of transgressions will arise in the natural course of events, unless a false pity leads you to spare him such experiences. Often you may be misled by pride or by a perverted sense of shame for your child. He fails to get up at the set hour, dallies away time in dressing, and finally is late for school. Yet you are often perfectly willing to write an excuse for him and save him from experiencing the effects of having wasted time. Or, in order to keep him from being late, you help him in what should be his own duty.

Natural consequences of violations, which automatically impress the rules of proper conduct on the child's mind, are encountered frequently enough without special effort on your part to create them. If you are careful not to destroy any of these valuable opportunities by a miscalculated zeal to keep your child from discomfort, you can let him learn by experience. If he fails to watch his step, he will fall. (A doorsill between two rooms provides a natural occasion for such an experience.) If he puts his left shoe on his right foot, he will feel the pinch. If he is slow, he will miss some fun or activity. Natural consequences can have their proper effect only if the adults of the family do not interfere. Such restraint will subsequently save both you and the child a multitude of annoyances.

In some cases, however, it is necessary to contrive certain experiences. You can devise harmless means of showing the child that a stove is hot, that a needle pricks, or that a chair may fall over backward. Such facts are highly important; a casual method of calling them to the child's attention is far more impressive than intimidating him with wise, dire warnings. Likewise, you must see to it that certain consequences are invariably forthcoming. If the child is unpunctual at mealtimes, he should find that meals have already been served for all but him. If he fails to gather up his playthings, he ought not to be surprised if he is unable to find them the next day. If he is too slow in getting ready for walks and excursions, he should discover that you have gone off without him.

But the child must never consider these unpleasant effects of nonconformity as punishments[8] or hostile moves on your part. On such occasions you must maintain a perfectly passive but benevolent attitude. You may express regret that the child has to go through these painful experiences, but in no event should you relieve him of them. He will not consider such an attitude as mean or hostile, if beneath it he can recognize the consistent order that regulates your conduct as well as his, if the consequences are not imposed arbitrarily by the power of an adult, and if their *logic* is obvious.

This effectuation of natural consequences is one of the most powerful methods in the training of the child. It teaches respect for order and develops conformity. Yet it is one of the most difficult techniques to acquire, as parents have not been trained to think and act in this way. Many find it difficult to understand the fine distinction between "consequences" and punishment. From a superficial point of view it may sound like hairsplitting. One method is just as uncomfortable for the child as the other; why, then, make the distinction and stress the importance of a difference? From a psychological point of view the difference is tremendous. And children are more responsive to psychological factors than to rational formulations. They may rebel equally against punishment and against "consequences" and may try just as hard to evade either of them. But this is only a temporary reaction, and soon the common sense of the child will make him realize that you were probably right. Consequences are acceptable to the child; punishment at best is only tolerable.

You must train yourself carefully to utilize this method of education. Its application requires thought, deliberation, and

---

[8] Rousseau and Herbert Spencer, among others, describe these natural consequences as "natural punishments." This term is unjustified when the consequences are the inevitable outcome of blunders. The effect in such cases is quite analogous to the unpleasant consequences that adults must accept as the sequence of improper conduct. If a man refuses to work and accordingly fails to earn a livelihood, or if he is surly and people shun his company, these results are not punishments and are never regarded as such. They are simply logical consequences; and children should be taught to consider the natural effects of their behavior in this same light.

imagination. When you act impulsively in a conflict situation you merely continue the fight and try to impress with your power, but you are unable to use the impersonal consequences of a disturbed order.

A few signposts may help to distinguish the fine but all-important line separating natural consequences from punishment. One has already been discussed—namely, that consequences must have an inner logic understandable to the child. Telling him he cannot go to the movies if he does not eat his dinner has no logic; but if he does not come home from the movie on time, it is reasonable that he be told he may not go next week.

There is another difference which is extremely important and yet is often difficult to grasp. Consequences are a natural *result* of misbehavior—but they are not retaliations. If you say, "You have misbehaved, now you must . . ." that is punishment. Consequences are, rather an invitation: "As long as you misbehave, it will be impossible for you to . . ." It emphasizes less what *did* happen, than what will follow—in the future. Instead of closing the issue it opens the door for future adjustment. A good example of this structural difference may be provided by this simple situation: The child is loud and unruly. It is punishment when you say, "I can't stand this commotion any longer, now go to your room and stay there!" Quite different is the approach when you say, "I am sorry that you cannot stay here with us if you disturb us. Perhaps you had better go to your room until you feel you can behave properly." In either case you must insist on his leaving the room, but in the first case the isolation is final and ends an episode, while in the second case the child may return as soon as he feels he is ready. It is up to him to change the situation.

Leaving the child a choice is always extremely important, especially in tense situations when he refuses to comply. Adults who act logically instead of psychologically will find it difficult to understand the significance, because for them it makes little difference which dire consequences one has to endure; but for the child it is very important if you tell him, "Do you want to leave the room by yourself, or shall I carry you out?" In our adult opinion the unpleasant duty of leaving the room remains in either case equally unpleasant. Not so for the child. If he can decide for himself, he feels important and is less reluctant. Even if he does not answer, you can always say, "If you do not want to go by yourself, then I will have to carry you." In the majority of instances, when the child is not yet too stubborn and hostile such an approach will save the situation. If the child is older, you can no longer carry him out. In this case the choice is between his or your leaving the room. And if he follows you, you leave the house. If he follows you then, the situation may yet be saved if you disregard him, whatever he does. But this is an extreme case; with most children the spell is broken at a much earlier stage. As a rule the child responds to the first choice if he feels that you are in earnest, especially if he knows from previous experience that you mean what you say.

Another factor, distinguishing consequences from punishment, is the tone of your voice. If you speak in a harsh, angry voice then you *punish.* If you maintain a friendly attitude, you emphasize that it is the *order* which has to be observed, not your personal desire or your power. In the first case you take a stand against the child and consequently he feels rejected. In the second case you object only to the child's behavior and his personal value is not threatened. The distinction in the voice expresses the difference in relationship. In punishment your anger disrupts the relationship, while in consequences you maintain your sympathy and friendliness.

While you can be sympathetic in applying logical consequences, you must be wary that your exaggerated and misdirected sympathy does not weaken you just at the moment when the child may learn by experience. A misplaced sympathy may make you succumb to his clever efforts to talk himself out of his predicament. Promises, solicited or voluntary, are the pitfalls of your weakness. In this critical moment he should never have "another chance." (He should *always* have this other chance another time, as the past should never be held over him once the consequence has taken place.) This is not the time for talking, but for action.

I shall close this most important section with one brief illustration.

A boy of eleven was brought to me by his parents. The contest for power which was their basic conflict was reflected in the one major symptom which caused endless friction within the family —the boy never came home on time for supper. Whatever punishments or rewards the parents attempted made no impression; he was always late. I suggested the simple solution of refusing him supper if he were late. But the parents, in this case the father, could not see the logic of such "punishment." After all, "a boy needs nourishment." It took me more than half an hour to convince the father of the necessity of trying this method, at least for one week. When he returned the following week he told me it did not work. I was greatly surprised and asked for details. The father assured me that the son received no supper when he came home late the first day, the second day, and the third day. I have found that as a rule children are not this persistent if they really miss their supper. Querying further as to what had actually happened, I asked whether the boy were actually given no food on these occasions. The father said, "After all, we could not let him go to bed hungry!"

There we were! It broke the father's heart to see his son go to bed hungry—but the same soft heart did not prevent him from spanking and punishing the boy severely for his defiance.

B. Avoiding Conflict

OBSERVATION AND REFLECTION—Situations which are of prime importance in guiding the child's development can never be fully utilized without careful thought. It is impossible to rear a child without reflection and deliberation. If you act automatically and impulsively, and permit yourself to be carried away by momentary whims and notions, you will always be at a loss when dealing with children. For children are deliberate and persistent in devising new and effective means of achieving their purposes—of soliciting your concern and evading unpleasant duties. Here again we see *how sharply the child observes.* He is quick to discover the slightest weakness of parents, teachers, and adults, and to take advantage of it. He is adept at playing off one adult against another. He knows exactly how to vary his tactics to suit mother or father and have his way with both. In one case, stubborn defiance may turn the trick; in another, wheedling and begging; and in still another, tearful self-pity. He adapts himself to each situation and to each individual.

In this respect you have much to learn from your offspring. In order to determine the methods of training best suited to any given set of circumstances, you must observe the child carefully and then decide on the best procedure to follow in the particular case. You will change a bad habit most successfully by recognizing and giving free play to the unpleasant consequences that logically result from it. But this cannot be done without thought and reflection, since the sequence of cause and effect must be made obvious to the child. You should consider beforehand what his reaction will be. He may not calmly accept unpleasant experiences, but struggle against them, wheedle and cry, and perhaps respond with some new mischief. An important principle to observe is this: *You can work on only one aspect of the child's behavior at one time.* If you try to do more, you will be unable to accomplish anything. For example, you can make the child feel the consequences of picking his nose by refusing to touch his hand afterward. No matter what his response, you must remain completely unmoved, or you destroy the effect of the measure. It would be impossible to correct a bad habit and at the same time attempt to check the various reactions of defiance which should be regarded as the child's answer to the pressure.

All methods of child training are effective if they are employed *sparingly*, but persistently. The motive and the means of intervention should be provided by reason and not by impulsive emotions. In the process of education it is vitally necessary that we eliminate, as much as possible, emotions which play havoc with, and yet so often completely dominate, the activity of the educator. Worry, irritability, and anger—however understandable they may be—are the expressions of a sense of weakness and futility. They arise only when we are at our wits' end or when we feel that we have yielded too much ground and must somehow take a firm stand. But any action resulting from this sense of weakness is bound to be wrong. It is humanly understandable that malice or hostility in your children may move you to indignation and anger. A person who gives vent to these emotions may be forgiven as a human being, but not as an educator. If one sees a boy tormenting an animal, one may be sufficiently outraged to slap him. But in this case one must realize that the slap was not the act of an educator, but merely that of an infuriated human being. The act may be justifiable, but it is more than doubtful whether it would break the boy of his habits of cruelty.

Education is impossible unless the educator is confident of his ability and efficiency. "Losing control of yourself" indicates your loss of self-confidence. Hence, if you ever become excited by the child, or if for any other reason you are in danger of losing self-control, it is advisable to drop everything for the moment and to leave the room. Then you can regain your poise and be calm again; not until then will you be capable of reflecting and deciding what really should be done.

Do not say that you have no time to think—that you are overburdened with work and worry. Of course, thought will take time, but not nearly as much as is required for continual admonishments, reprimands, and punishments which are wholly ineffectual and harmful. A little time for reflection will spare you a great deal of agitation and turmoil, and actually save time in the long run.[4] It may seem simpler and quicker at the moment to strike out at random when the child is naughty. However, restraint and thoughtful consideration will permit you to act more rationally and economically.

This advice naturally does not apply to real emergencies. At such times you are not required to exercise an educational function but to avert an acute danger by immediate action. Again we must remember that the opportunity for instruction and discipline will come later, when the critical moment has passed. In these moments of danger, nothing can have an educational value. Reprimands serve more as a release of your tension than as a means of future prevention. But situations which involve real danger are far less frequent than you, in your anxiety for the child, may be led to believe.

RESTRAINT—One of the most fundamental bases for influencing children—and one very seldom fulfilled—is the exercising of the greatest possible restraint. A policy of observation, with a minimum of intervention in the child's activities, is advantageous not only in moments of stress, as described above, but under *any* circumstances. If you follow this procedure, your influence, when you do exert it, will be more beneficial, and you will not run the risk of interfering with the vitally important growth of self-reliance in your children. *The best method of education is that which makes itself superfluous as soon as possible and has as its purpose the transformation of the child from an irresponsible object of discipline into an independent fellow-being with a matured sense of personal responsibility.*

The child can assume duties of his own at a very early age, and carry them out on his own initiative. This, of course, is not to suggest that children should ever be neglected. They need love and tenderness, encouragement and stimulation.

---

[4] Parents who are so disturbed that their emotions interfere with their adequate functioning will need psychotherapy for their own reeducation and reorientation in life.

You should never be aloof, but in your capacity as educator, you should intervene no more than is actually necessary. On occasion you will have to take positive action, but these occasions should be rare. Whenever possible you must let the children learn by experience. This can be done only if you learn restraint. It is not your duty to do everything for the child. Such tendencies spring only from undue fear or from a desire to prove your own importance and power.

FLEXIBILITY—If you observe and reflect before you act, you will not adopt any rigid method. You will be inclined to test and verify the immediate effects of your approach. Unreflecting parents tend to follow a set routine, which may have been absorbed from their own parents, or which may have been used on some particular occasion and continued only through sheer force of habit or inertia. Such parents respond with the same routine of coaxing, ranting, and scolding, or even of threats of physical violence, to any misbehavior. Usually the child knows in advance how you will react to any given move. He learns to take your attitude for granted and adapts himself to it—with the result that all your admonition and effort make no impression whatever.

The suggestion to change your methods frequently does not contradict our earlier suggestion to be consistent. Social requirements and standards must be firmly established and must remain constant and definite. But your efforts to make your child realize and comply with them must vary.

There is another reason why rigid methods fail so often. They neglect the specific requirements and needs of each individual child. And even the same child cannot always be treated in the same way. By varying and adapting your methods, by watching the effects and results, and by experimenting with new approaches you can find the adequate means of influencing the child.

This is as necessary for the details as for the larger aspects of education. You must adjust yourself to the different stages of the child's development. Even the amount of attention that he requires is not a stable quantity. In the first months his rest should be disturbed as little as possible. Later on, he will require more attention. But after a few years you must withdraw again, for by then he should be spending more time with children of his own age. During some periods of his life the child will be very amenable to instruction; at other times he will flatly refuse to listen to advice. On some occasions he will voluntarily come for guidance, and under other circumstances he will insist on making his own decisions. A rigid attitude on your part does not allow for the varying needs of each child. The really effective methods of training are adjustable to each specific situation and to the changes that accompany the child's growth.

AROUSING INTEREST—Children will respond more readily to your influence if you are able to arouse their interest. This in itself should be sufficient incentive for you to vary your approaches. Parents frequently complain that their words go in one ear and out the other. Yet the deadly monotony of identical commands, reprovals, and explanations is sure to lead to apathetic reception.

For this reason much depends on the *tone of voice* in which you address the child. The livelier and more natural your expression, the more promptly will the child take notice. Irascibility will never put him into a receptive frame of mind. Many parents, in conversing with their child, adopt a dull, lifeless, or even harsh tone of voice that provokes either unresponsiveness or a response that clearly implies his desire to be let alone. Similarly, the common attempts at baby talk do nothing but bore him; he considers them ridiculous, and rightly so.

Everyone who deals with children encounters numerous situations where it seems to be impossible to effect rapport with the child. The child is so obstinate that no amount of talk or advice seems to influence him. These are the situations in which you are inclined to lose your self-control, because you cannot bear your feeling of helplessness. There is one course of action that can be pursued in any situation, even when you are completely at a loss as to what to do. This technique can save many situations which otherwise seem to be completely out of hand. It consists of figuring out what the child expects you to do next, and then doing *just the opposite!* In any situation, even when the child apparently ignores you completely, he is still counting on your reaction. He might expect threats, outbursts, or physical punishment, or in many cases just scolding or preaching. He is prepared for it and determined to be unimpressed.

You can detect what the child expects, by observing what you feel inclined to do. Your own reactions generally correspond completely with the child's expectation and are exactly what he wants and even provokes. By doing the opposite, you catch the child off guard and throw him off balance. Thus, you not only arouse his interest but, furthermore, force him to reconsider his attitude. At least you have gained a breathing spell which permits new approaches to the child and to the situation. Praising when a child expects scolding, acknowledging his superiority when he expects to be subjugated, indifference when he expects outbursts or at least annoyance, giving him a free hand when he expects to be stopped, are tactics which release the tension and make the child receptive to further action. It is very often possible to use this mutual relaxation for friendly talks to which the child is then willing to listen.

How easy it is to arouse a child's interest and to direct him into a particular reaction is shown by the following anecdote. A man had been much annoyed by the youngsters of the village, who dogged his steps and made fun of his red hair. Finally he gathered them all together and promised to give each of them a penny every day if they would jeer with the proper gusto. The boys were taken aback, but accepted the proposal with enthusiasm, and on the following day they each received the earned penny as agreed. But on the fifth day the man stopped payment. The boys were indignant. "If the redhead

won't pay," they exclaimed, "we won't yell for nothing."
And they went their ways.

WINNING THE CHILD'S CONFIDENCE—Your influence over
your child will be the stronger as you become successful in
gaining his confidence. But love and tenderness alone by no
means achieve this purpose. The child may be greatly attached
to you, yet may still remain hostile and obdurate. You have
not won him over until he no longer is in opposition to you,
and voluntarily accepts your guidance, freely conforming to
your desires. His obedience will depend not only on his belief
in your fairness and consistency, but also on his faith in your
good will and in your practical reliability. Any indication of a
struggle for power on your side makes such cooperation impossible.

It is especially important to know how to win a child over
in disturbing situations. You can arouse his attention by the
surprise tactics discussed above. But more is required to win
his confidence. The best means to this end are friendliness and
genuine benevolence. Children are exceedingly perceptive.
They can distinguish easily between empty gush and true
good will, and are quick to discover who is honestly their
friend and who is not. (This statement is invariably true, even
when appearances do not always bear it out. You may always
have considered yourself the child's friend, when in reality
your attitude toward him has often been unconsciously mali-
cious and hostile.)

Friendliness of tone, therefore, must constantly be maintained. This is more necessary than ever in critical moments.
If you fail to maintain a friendly bearing on these occasions,
you can scarcely hope to advance the child's development.
Whatever you may do, you only increase his antagonism. For
this reason it is essential to avoid personal reprimands or punishments and to allow the child to learn from the purely logical, impersonal consequences of misbehavior. By following
this policy, you can escape the necessity of showing yourself
in an unfriendly light. Harsh words inevitably repel the child.

Mere indulgence will not gain the confidence of children, either. Laxity does not impress them as good will, but as a sign of weakness. You can win the child over most easily by displaying a real interest in him and his affairs—by playing with him, taking him for walks, conversing with him, or telling him stories. But all your activity will be ineffective unless you participate as wholeheartedly and intently as the child himself. Such diversions are beyond the reach of conflict. They are far more effective than flattery or petting, which seldom are free of an unpleasant tinge of possessiveness and condescension. Anyone who shows an active, friendly interest in a child can be assured of his ready attention and willing response when occasion arises.

RELIEVING THE SITUATION—There are innumerable situations that incite a child to hostility and defiance. Hence you should know how to overcome resistance without conflict. The surest method, especially with young children, consists of diverting attention from the point of controversy. If the child is stubborn or if he sulks and refuses to obey, it will be sufficient to find some quick way of arousing his interest. But if he is extremely defiant and refractory, this simple expedient may not serve. Particularly with older children you may be unable to break down opposition quickly and easily. However, by this time immediate action on your part will not be imperative. The older child is more rational. In event of actual danger, he is better fitted to take care of himself; and in other situations you can wait until an opportunity arises for him to experience the consequences of improper conduct.

When little Mary persists in wading toward the deep water, when she takes hold of a pointed object, leans out of an open window, or climbs up on a chair, you will certainly call her to come at once. If she fails to respond, you may try to divert her attention. You may pique her curiosity by saying, "Just look what I have," or whistling loudly, or clapping the hands suddenly—anything to arouse interest. In most instances such means will suffice to avert the danger without agitation. But, of course, if the child is habitually obstinate, these methods are likely to be inadequate. In moments of peril you cannot afford to temporize, but even in emergencies you can usually manage to preserve a friendly attitude. Simply pick up the child, if he is small, or take him by the hand and lead him away.

Unfortunately, one of the most successful means of relieving a situation is too rarely employed. This is *humor*. Many people tend to neglect their sense of humor; they somehow feel it their duty to be solemn and gloomy, and regard an occasional laugh as a lapse of dignity. Yet the quality of humor should never be wanting in dealing with children. If you possess it, your lot will be much easier. You can relieve the strain not only in others, but in yourself as well. If you make someone laugh, he cannot possibly hold a grudge against you. But you must not confuse humor with buffoonery. Wit usually lies in the manner of speech, and often not so much in meaning as in inflection. Also, humor should never be harsh and cutting, or else it will lose its conciliatory effect and only heighten antagonism. The aim is to make the child laugh *with* you. The joke should never be on him.

Examples are not easy to present, since so much depends on the attendant circumstances, the tone of voice, and the turn of phrase. Often, an appreciation of the amusing side of a situation and your own merriment will be enough. Or if no immediate occasion presents itself, you can tell a funny story or anecdote. Small children will often be moved to laughter by the simplest artifice—a bit of string with something dangling at the end, a humorous gesture, or a droll grimace.

However sulky, obstinate, or rebellious children may be, *you* can always remain calm and friendly. This is a principle that all parents *must* observe. A warm word, an expression of sympathy and understanding, will often work wonders, changing the child's repressed defiance and rage into sobs and tears. For in many cases insolence, rudeness, disobedience, and obstinacy are only attempts to conceal a feeling of hurt, of neglect and loneliness. Frequently a sign of willingness to help the child will relieve the hostile tension immediately. But he must first have faith in the honesty of the desire to aid him, and unfortunately he often lacks such confidence in his own parents. See facing page, *80a*, for discussion of "Withdrawing."

C. Encouraging

COMMENDATION—A child's difficulties, as we have seen in the preceding chapter, are always based on some form of *discouragement*. Perhaps the parents themselves or the other persons of his environment have disheartened him, or perhaps repeatedly unsuccessful efforts to master some task or acquire some ability have caused him to lose faith in his own powers. But whatever the reason for his difficulty, and in whatever guise it appears, it is the parent's duty to bolster his self-confidence. Encouragement is for the child's development what water is for the plant; neither can grow without it. It must be shown that he is not as weak and incompetent as he believes. He needs praise, despite or even because of his lack of perfection. But praise should be impersonal and objective. "You've done a good job . . ." "That's right . . ." "I'm glad you can do it. . . ." The child should be commended for what he *has done*, and not for *what he is*, be it good, nice, handsome, pretty, or cute.

If a child is unable to dress himself completely, you can point out how nicely he has pulled on one stocking. Then he may go ahead and try to put on his shoes. You should commend the *effort*, whether successful or unsuccessful. Or perhaps he is a poor writer . . . searching through his papers you can find a page or a line or perhaps only a few separate letters that can be sincerely praised. No matter what the child's failing, you can bring about an improvement through encouragement. The development of character and moral qualities needs the same treatment. Here, too, the child needs recognition if he does not take the right course of his own accord.

If a child is to develop as he should, he must be courageous.

WITHDRAWING. Many children misbehave for the benefit of the parents, either to keep them busy or to defeat them. Withdrawing, the actual physical removal of the parent from the scene, often has dramatic results. A great deal of effort in our child-guidance work is directed to helping mothers extricate themselves from the undue pressure and demands of their children. The behavior of the child is bound to change when the mother refuses to be an unwitting victim. So-called dependent children are usually demanding children. They use some real or assumed weakness or deficiency to put the mother into their service. If mother refuses to play this role, the child often overcomes his inability or weakness and begins to function. A disobedient child is usually a tyrannical child. He is well prepared to resist any pressure brought upon him and very capable of forcing the parents to do what he wants rather than giving in to their wishes. For this reason every attempt to force him into submission is futile; but he can learn the futility of force if the parents are careful not to yield to him.

A temper tantrum is well designed to stifle the best parental efforts. Leaving the child alone is one of the most effective means for correcting such inclinations. The best tantrum is worthless if there is no audience, nobody to be frightened or impressed. Fighting between the children is usually for the mother's benefit. If she stops interfering, being the judge and separating the children, they learn to get along with each other and to solve their own conflicts.

By removing herself in any conflict situation, preferably by withdrawing into the bathroom and locking herself in until the turmoil has subsided, mother can contribute a great deal to the harmony of the family. Such tactical retreat is particularly advisable when mother feels at the end of her wits, no longer able to control herself or to "stand it." Before she, too, loses her temper and becomes involved, she can always bring a door between herself and her child. Emerging from her voluntary retreat she then can again be the friendly, warm person she wants and ought to be.

You must avoid anything that might reduce his self-confidence. You should use the following phrases[5] as much as possible:

If other people can do it, you can, too.
Nothing ventured, nothing gained.
Everyone makes mistakes.
No one was born perfect.
We learn by our errors.
Practice makes perfect.
You make things seem harder than they really are.
A single stroke won't fell an oak.
Rome wasn't built in a day.
All beginnings are difficult.
Don't give up.
Don't let yourself be discouraged.
Well begun is half done.
You're bound to make a few slips.
Try it a few times anyway, and then you'll do better.
You can do it if you want to badly enough.
Difficulties were meant to be overcome.
The harder the task, the more you may gain from it.

Allusions to the child's age sometimes produce a good effect, but they should be used with caution. Otherwise he may feel that he is unable to do something he should have mastered. Comments should be phrased carefully. "There's no longer any need—for me to help you dress," etc. You must always keep a close check on your words and must see how the child accepts them—whether their effect is encouraging or just the opposite.

GUIDANCE AND INSTRUCTION—Introducing a child to a new task or responsibility requires special care to avoid discouragement. It is best for him to learn by his own effort; then each new accomplishment is a tangible step forward. If he is guided too painstakingly, he may easily get the impression that the

[5] From Dr. Alice Friedmaun's *Erziehungsmerkblätter.*

task is too difficult for him and that you doubt his ability to accomplish it. It is advisable to give him only a start, and then let him try for himself until the desired result is produced.

One must note *when* to talk with the child. Talking is worth while only if the child is in a receptive mood for listening. It never pays to say anything immediately after he has done something wrong, because the child will be either rebellious or downcast. The best time for discussion is a quiet, meditative moment when you are alone with the child, chatting or strolling. Just before bedtime, too, is a good time for a half hour of intimate conversation. You can use these occasions to good advantage. Remember, though, that instruction and guidance are wholly ineffectual without friendliness and good will.

In these discussions you must avoid demonstrating your own superiority over the child. Whenever and whatever you teach him, you must make clear that the rules of conduct which he must learn apply consistently to everyone. He should regard you as a fellow-being and as an equal, who desires to help him solve his problems. Any suggestion will be much better received when you say, "Come on, let's do it *together.*" But this spirit of cooperation ought never to induce you to relieve the child of his responsibilities. It should serve only to take the sharp edge off a great many unpleasant necessities. Hence this technique will prove useful whenever the child finds a task disagreeable.

You may often wonder why your child listens more willingly to outsiders than to you, his parents. The reason is that other persons talk with him on a completely equal footing. Parents are inclined to stress their superiority over the child. The more they do so, the less readily will he accept their advice. Genuine superiority, however, does not need expression through prestige and power. You may treat the child as an equal, in spite of your advantage in knowledge, experience, and power of judgment; and the child will be the more willing to recognize your superiority the less it is brought to his attention and the less you demand such recognition.

If you are determined to seem superior at any price you may be embarrassed when you find yourself unable to answer one of the child's questions. Otherwise you can frankly admit that you do not know everything. (You must strictly avoid giving him a consciously false answer; this is the surest way to lose his respect.) It does no harm to admit personal failings and weaknesses. The child would discover them anyway, with keener penetration than you may expect. He will consider any effort to gloss over your own frailties at precisely its face value —as an additional frailty.

MUTUAL CONFIDENCE—By freely admitting your own imperfections you can create a closer relationship with the child. Such frankness will inspire him to greater confidence. He will think none the less of you if you confess that at his age you were neither better nor worse than he. If you are honest, he will credit you with a fuller understanding of his own situation than if you try to make him believe that you were a little angel as a child. Complete comradeship is the best means of winning the child's trust.

But it is not enough to let the child regard you as a human being. You must consider him in the same light. Many mothers and fathers disregard even the most obvious social rights of their children. They have no compunctions against breaking promises or betraying confidences. They show no respect for the child's privilege of maintaining a certain reticence even with his parents and of revealing or keeping his secrets as he chooses. They pry into the older child's correspondence and mortify him by making light of his sentiments and opinions. And yet they are amazed and offended when their children refuse to confide in them. You yourself would not trust a person who treated you in this way. A child is a human being with sensibilities no different from an adult's. As a parent, you cannot *demand* confidence, or take it forcibly; it must be earned. If a child does not regard his parents as friends, they have no one to blame but themselves; and they should not be surprised to find that their influence over him is purely superficial, and that he turns for guidance to other persons who treat him as a human being.

Perhaps you believe it is to the child's best interest that you know everything he thinks and does. But the more you insist on this frankness, the less likely you are to achieve it. When your incessant queries take on the color of inquisitiveness, the child's inner life will be more than ever a closed book to you; and if you continue to press him, you may ultimately force him into lies and hypocrisy. The surrender of one's private feelings and thoughts is an act of the most intimate confidence. If you treat your children with the proper tact and discretion, they will surely be willing to confide implicitly. As the result of the wrong attitudes and approaches used so frequently, very few parents have any notion of what goes on in their child's mind.

Bear in mind that all trust must be mutual. The child needs demonstrations of your confidence. The most valuable indication of your trust is your recognition of the child's worth and importance as a human being. You have many opportunities to display this confidence. Even before the child reaches school age he can be entrusted—not commanded!—to do many useful duties about the house and may make himself helpful in various ways to the other members of the family. You should let him run errands, carry messages to your friends, and attend to some of the marketing. As he grows older, the signs of your confidence will multiply. You can talk things over with him and perhaps ask his opinion and advice on some matters. In this way you make a comrade of your child, and both of you will benefit from your mutual confidence.

Your faith in your child's reasonableness and dependability can manifest itself every day. This is the purpose of the candor that we recommended earlier. You need not hesitate to reveal some of your worries and problems to him; on the other hand, you must never impose your confidence as a burden. Taking him into your confidence does not mean having confidence in him. His development will be seriously impaired if he becomes the permanent repository of your grievances. He will lose his natural simplicity and spontaneity through contact with adult experiences, family squabbles, and marital difficulties which he cannot understand or assimilate. This is a misuse of the child by mothers and fathers who are unable to manage their own lives and have neglected to cultivate friends to whom they can unbosom themselves. It is not a demonstration of confidence in the child, but a sign of bewilderment and loneliness in the frustrated parent, who avails himself of the first opportunity to voice his troubles, without considering the harm he may do.

"MAY" INSTEAD OF "MUST"—In times gone by it was commonly accepted that reward and punishment were standard methods of child training and that no parent could manage without them. Today we realize fully the fallacy of these devices. Both are injurious *as they are merely the arbitrary expressions of parental authority*. The child may eventually submit to oppression, but at the same time his antagonism will be aroused. He must learn to subordinate himself, it is true—but not to the despotic power of any individual. The only conformity that we can legitimately expect is conformity to the social scheme which binds everyone alike. The general laws of natural and social order are sufficiently strong and definite to impress a child of the pleasant and unpleasant consequences of his behavior. That is true only if you as parent don't interfere by protecting the child. That does not mean that you should be completely passive and indifferent and accept an "I don't care" attitude, especially when there is danger involved. You can and should stand by in assisting the child in his efforts to recognize the requirements of any given situation and in adapting himself to it.

In this process, you cannot dispense with the magic formula "you may," but the word "must" should be stricken from your vocabulary. It deprives the child of the sense of being a free agent, of acting voluntarily and framing his own destiny.

"May" is the voice of natural order; "must" is the arbitrary dictate of individual authority. This is not quibbling and hair-splitting. Two little pictures I once saw may make clear the essential distinction. They both show a house on the edge of a forest, with a broad path leading up to the door. In the first is a group of children, dejected and mournful, with bundles of faggots on their backs. In the second, the same children are carrying twice as much wood, but this time skipping along happily. What brought about the miracle? Under the first picture is read, "You *must* go into the forest and fetch wood"; under the second, "You *may* go. . . ."

You can try this system on your own children. If you want your little girl to set the table, notice her reaction when you say, "You must set the table," as compared with "You may set the table if you wish." The difference in the effect will be obvious.

It is best to refrain from negative commands. You should *emphasize the correct procedure instead of forbidding the incorrect*. A little friendly encouragement will produce the most willing response, especially when you can point out a discrepancy between the child's achievement and his real abil-ity—"I am sure you can do better!" An appeal to his self-respect and desire for recognition will often prove effective in guiding him to the desired end.

ENDEAVOR—"If you'll just try, I'm sure you can do it"— this means of reconciling the child to the aims of education can be employed whenever it is necessary to correct his be-havior, to break him of bad habits, or to introduce him to a new task. It is another magic formula. It is an appeal to the child's initiative; it makes him feel grown up, and hence stim-ulates him to concentrate his efforts in a definite direction. Every fault or defect, in fact anything that can be subject to educational influence, is thus transformed into a tangible and solvable problem. By standing aside, and yet maintaining a friendly, benevolent attitude and a willingness to cooperate whenever necessary, you can avoid any conflict. Even though the desired result may not be produced immediately, there is no need for more drastic measures. As matters stand, you have every opportunity to encourage the child and thus strengthen your position as his well-wishing friend. The nature of the difficulty is unimportant. Perhaps it concerns the development of simple skills, or perhaps the overcoming of flaws in character and unpleasant habits that may lead to serious trouble. But no matter how long or tedious the process, you will always be able to sustain your friendly bearing by acknowledging and emphasizing every sign of progress, however slight. This attitude on your part serves unfailingly to clear the conflict-laden and conflict-generating atmosphere. The enemies become allies who *work together* toward an attainable goal.

DISCLOSURES—Thus far we have examined mainly the external techniques of training, but the more far-reaching psychological methods ought not be ignored. Every parent needs some practical knowledge of psychology before he can understand the child and deal with him properly. Accordingly, we discuss in detail the psychological problems in Chapters 2 and 5. The question now is to what extent should you tell the child what you know about him?

The child does not know why he behaves and acts in a certain way. It is generally futile to ask a child, "Why did you do that?" Parents are often infuriated when the child answers, "I do not know." But in most cases that is really true. The child follows his impulses without clear realization of his motives. If he answers truthfully in explaining his behavior these explanations are mostly rationalizations and excuses, not the real reasons. Instead of asking the child the "why" of his actions, you should be able to tell him the reason. Information about his goals and the purpose of his conduct can help the child a great deal. He must understand himself first, in order to change his attitudes. Anybody dealing with children should acquire knowledge and experience in understanding children's problems and in interpreting their behavior.

Precaution must be taken to make psychological discussions

effective and to avoid the possibility of doing great harm. The first consideration should be the timing and occasion for these discussions. They should never take place immediately after some misbehavior, when both child and adult are excited. The second fundamental requirement is that these talks should always be unemotional and factual. If they imply the slightest criticism and reproach, they provoke only opposition and find deaf ears. One must always keep in mind that psychology can be a tool of greatest assistance, but also a weapon of tremendously destructive power. Psychology applied in order to punish and humiliate can damage more than any physical abuse. In order to discuss psychological interpretations, one must be calm and friendly and use the time of personal closeness when exchange of opinion is acceptable to both parties. No matter how correct a psychological interpretation may be, its effects are worse than futile if it is given belligerently or at the wrong time.

Psychological interpretation should not be confused with attempts to analyze, to pry into the unconscious, to dig into deep sources of motivation. We do not advocate psychological analysis on the part of anyone who is not thoroughly trained and qualified to conduct psychotherapy. But we must distinguish between *psychotherapy*, which is a tool of psychiatrists and trained psychotherapists, and *interpretation*, which everyone who is dealing with children should be able to make. The main distinction between the two is the kind of psychological mechanisms and problems which are examined and analyzed; only psychotherapy can reveal the *past* development, the formation of deep-seated concepts, of the life style of the person, child, or adult. Interpretation, on the other hand, is concerned solely with *present attitudes and immediate purposes*.

Every parent and educator should have some psychological knowledge and some understanding of the probable nature of a child's personality. In difficult cases, this knowledge may be obtained through the services of a psychiatrist or a trained child psychologist. But analytical knowledge should never be used for conversations between you and your child; it can serve only as a guide for your general management of the child. You must take cognizance of the child's actions and attempt to influence them. Discussing the questionable action with a child is one of the most successful ways of changing it. An effective discussion, however, should never investigate *why* a child acted in a certain way, but only explain *for what immediate purpose* he did that. The distinction between "why" and "for what purpose" may seem, superficially, to be insignificant. However, it indicates the complete difference between emphasis on the past and on present goals. There may be a thousand reasons which led to a present attitude of a child; but there is only *one* purpose possible for his actions. The search for the "why" is, for the untrained person, mere guesswork; the recognition of the purpose indicates understanding.

The child responds in a different manner to an explanation of *causes* than to an explanation of *the goals* of his actions. Explanations such as jealousy, lack of self-confidence, feeling of being neglected, dominated, or rejected, feelings of guilt or self-pity, regardless of how accurate they may be in explaining the child's behavior, are accepted by the child at best with friendly indifference. It tells the child only what he is. His reaction is quite different when told what he *wants:* to get attention, to show his superiority, to be the big boss, to demonstrate his power, to get even or to punish others. Such interpretations of his true intentions, when correct, evoke immediately a very definite and characteristic reaction on the part of the child. This reaction is immediate and automatic, a "recognition reflex," and indicates the correctness of the interpretation. It consists of a roguish smile and a peculiar twinkle of the eyes, characteristic of the cat who swallowed the canary. The child need not say one word, or he might even say, "No"; but his facial expression gives him away. This discernment of his psychological attitude generally leads to an immediate change in the particular behavior, especially in a young child. Even very young children, as soon as they comprehend the meaning of words, that is, at two years of age, are capable of conscious understanding of their intentions and are inclined to change their attitudes when they are made aware of them.[6] That does not imply a complete change of the life style, but it may lead eventually to a change of basic concepts in relationship to other people.

Even psychological interpretations must be used with care. If repeated or overdone, they no longer are revelations. They should never have a humiliating or belittling effect and should never be translated by the child as fault-finding and criticism. It is generally advisable not to make a definite statement, "You do that because you want to. . . ." Much better are remarks of vague conjecture, "I wonder whether you don't want to . . . ? Could it be?" Such discussions never can do any harm. If you are on the wrong track, you just do not get any reaction. Then you can make another conjecture and the child's reaction will indicate which one was correct.

A five-year-old boy repeatedly threatened to hit and bite other children, especially a little girl cousin. Our first impression was that he felt neglected and wanted to hurt them, to get even. Our voiced interpretation encountered a blank face. We went on probing. Maybe he wanted to show how strong he was. Again no reaction. "Could it be that your mother gets very upset about such threats, and you want her to make a fuss over you, to talk to you about it and tell you that you shouldn't do it?" His face beamed. He was in his glory. The same behavior in another child would have meant something different. For him, it was only a tool to keep mother concerned with him.

A nine-year-old boy had his hair hanging over his right eye. I met him with his mother. In his presence I asked her why she thought he wore his hair over his eye. She did not know; neither did he. My surmise was that he probably wanted his mother to keep reminding him to push his hair back. She could not understand; how did I know that she constantly had to remind him?

*See Chapter 2, "Conscience."

Very simple—if he could not gain her attention in that way, he would not like to have his hair always getting into his eyes. He beamed. That was all that was said. The next day she called me up, quite excited. The boy had asked for money for the barber to have his hair cut.

Two boys, nine and ten years old, annoyed their mother by using bedtime for fighting in their beds. Mother could not stop it and did not know what to do. I had a talk with the boys. I asked them why they went on fighting after going to bed. I did not expect the correct answer to this question, but wanted to hear what they had to say. They both explained that it is so much fun to fight in bed when it does not hurt to be thrown down on the pillows. That was their rationalization.

I asked them whether they would mind if I told them the real reason. Of course, they wouldn't mind. Then I ventured, "Maybe you do it just so that mother will come several times to remind you to be quiet." The younger one said indifferently, "It could be." The older one said nothing, but beamed. One should know that the older one was the favorite of the mother and depended upon her, while the younger one felt somewhat excluded and relied upon himself for his position in the world. Generally, the younger was the one who started the fights, but in this particular situation the older brother obviously had instigated the fights for the sake of getting his mother's attention, bringing her back to the bedroom every so often. Nothing more was said or done about it; but after our short discussion the evening fights stopped and never were resumed. That does not mean that the older boy suddenly became independent of his mother. But this particular method was no longer useful once he recognized his purpose.

Disclosing personal attitudes and goals is also a very effective means of influencing whole groups of children. Group discussions can help greatly in changing attitudes of individuals and of groups and should be used very frequently in classrooms and group-work agencies. Again, the objective is the revelation of attitudes and goals and the significance of the purposiveness of all human actions.

THE CHILD AMONG CHILDREN—Very early the child begins to need companions of his own age. They are essential to his development, for only with other children can he feel himself an equal among equals and learn to adjust himself properly to the social scheme. In the exclusive company of adults he is under- or overprivileged; in either case his position is anomalous, and he is likely to develop into an uncongenial, eccentric type of individual. Continuous association with a single brother or sister is not enough, since this companionship only too often turns into the relationship of superior to inferior and gives rise to feelings of power or weakness. Nor is it enough for the child to play occasionally with chance companions in the street or park. The best opportunity for free and natural adjustment to the social order is provided through an organized group of children under competent supervision. Hence, under the prevailing system of small families, it is advisable to enroll your children from their third year on in a good nursery school or kindergarten; and after their sixth year it is also expedient to send them to a summer camp.

Since we are not exploring the general problems of such recreation groups in this presentation, we shall discuss only the questions that are of immediate concern to parents. Before you select a kindergarten or a summer camp, you should make the necessary inquiries to find out to whose care you entrust your child. Once the decision is made, you have no further right to meddle in the inner affairs of the group. By communicating your dissatisfactions and apprehensions to the child you may easily disturb his adjustment and hence impede his development. Any kindergarten, nursery, or camp naturally has its faults, and could very likely be improved. But you must remember that never in his life will your child belong to a completely perfect group, and that for this reason he should learn early to put up with existing imperfections. Above all, you should never use your anxiety as a pretext for securing special privileges for your child, since this would deliberately frustrate the purpose you are attempting to achieve.

In general, you should interfere as little as possible when the child is with other children. He must find out by himself how to get along with them and how to accommodate his interests to theirs. Missteps will be recognized by their consequences, and the teacher or the camp counselor will know the right way of showing the child how to do better the next time. In cases when his play is unsupervised, you should watch him but reserve your comments until you are alone with him. But whenever you discuss his behavior with him, you must be careful not to inoculate him with your own egotism or misanthropy, your distrust of others, your thirst for prestige, or your timidity, whichever the case may be. None of these qualities will improve his character. He must be taught to regard his playmates not as enemies, but as comrades in whose company he can enjoy himself completely.

What, then, should be your attitude toward fighting? This is a much-debated question. No one is likely to deny that quarrels should be prevented as far as possible, and that serious ill feeling should never be permitted to arise among children. But there are bound to be scuffles. Children will always feel the urge to match their powers, and the child must be prepared to defend himself if attacked. Forbid him to fight, and he will come whimpering whenever another child strikes him. As long as he is small, you can threaten and drive away his adversaries; but what should be done when he is older and you cannot always be on hand to protect him? It seems to lie in the nature of things that the child must be able to look out for himself, and so he must learn to fight like the rest. Naturally he should be kept away from rough and undesirable companions, and you should discourage any rowdy tendencies on his part. A peaceable disposition, however, does not express itself in a dread of fights, but in the ability to find other, more pacific means of settling differences.

Fear of catching disease should not prevent you from sending the child to kindergarten. He is not safer from contagion at home than in school. On the street, in the streetcar, and on visits he is exposed to quite the same dangers as in the classroom. You should not overrate these hazards. We take certain chances in everything we do. Nothing ventured, nothing gained.

It is probably difficult for many parents to send their child off alone to a summer camp. But this valuable practice is becoming more usual year by year. In this case, as in so many others, necessity encourages the growth of a good institution. Today parents often cannot afford a long vacation for themselves, but are glad of an opportunity to provide a few weeks of recreation for their children. The number of summer camps is constantly increasing, since more and more parents are reconciling themselves to a temporary separation from their children. Such a change is beneficial to both sides. It relieves the tension that commonly exists between parent and child. By autumn both will feel a strengthened sense of solidarity and a renewed willingness to meet each other halfway; both can begin afresh, with new courage and reduced hostility. If in the meantime the child has improved, and if you have found time for a little thought and study, a summer vacation may represent a turning point in the family relationships.

D. The Family Council

The growing rights that society bestows on children, and their awareness of their status as equals, make it essential that they be accepted as equal partners in the affairs of the family. Equality in this sense does not mean identical function. Father and mother, sisters and brothers, the younger and the older, can and must perform different functions. But these differences should no longer imply any lowering of status; otherwise they lead inevitably to resentment and unwillingness to discharge those functions that imply lesser social prestige.

The greater freedom that the contemporary democratic atmosphere provides for each member of the family also entails for each a greater share of the responsibility for the welfare of the whole. As long as the parents, and particularly the mother, take on *all* responsibility, and the children enjoy all the freedom to do as they please, an unbalanced equilibrium is inevitable; the children are deprived of useful functioning and tend to be demanding and tyrannical. The experience of freedom, which means self-determination, requires a sense of responsibility; otherwise it leads to chaos.

The family council gives every member of the family a chance to express himself freely in all matters pertaining to the family and the home. He can object to and criticize whatever he does not like; but these objections should lead to *his* suggestions for a solution. The right to criticize implies sharing in the contributions that all have to make toward a happy family life. In this sense, the family council constitutes education for democracy. Such educational experiences are as important for the parents as for the children.

Tradition does not provide us with guiding lines for living with each other as equals. We have to establish them by trial and error. And every family is a pioneer in the adventure of living with each other as equals. If we fail as children to learn how to live democratically in our family, we will have little chance to learn it later, when our arbitrary scale of superiority and inferiority is well established and we try to be superior while actually afraid of being inferior. The family council, more than anything else provides each member with a sense of equal status both in regard to rights and in regard to obligations; in this sense it facilitates the application of democratic principles to family life.

Difficulty in establishing and maintaining a democratic relationship of equals is often responsible for the discontinuation of the family council. Parents may start off with good intentions and a high degree of enthusiasm; but before long, either they or the children violate the basic premises of a democratic procedure, and the council loses its meaning and function. Maintaining a family council requires considerable persistence, a willingness to see one's own mistakes, the ability to change one's attitude and to respect that of others. It needs courage to explore and to chart new courses, without fear and distrust, and the conviction that the others also want to live in harmony and peace but may not know how to achieve this goal.

Without confidence in, and respect for, the other members of the family there is hardly a way to discuss mutual difficulties and conflicts, and no chance for finding any solution.

A few basic principles are suggested to facilitate both the conduct of family council meetings and their maintenance.

a) A certain date should be set for the council to meet each week. It is not advisable to call a meeting whenever one member wishes; nothing is so urgent that it must be settled right now. "Right now" usually means a conflict situation, a clash of interests. That is not the time to talk, since words in a conflict situation are not means of communication but weapons. It is possible to establish in a regular council meeting procedures for emergency situations.

b) All members of the family are invited to participate; but participation is not obligatory. If one member of the family, be it father or child, does not wish to attend, his absence can be utilized to reach decisions that he may not like. Such procedure is usually sufficient to induce the unco-operative member to attend the next session during which he will have a chance to alter the previous decision.

c) All members participate on equal footing; each one has one vote. The age requirement for participation depends on each child's ability to understand what is discussed. Even very young children can contribute and express some of their ideas. On the other hand, any member of the family who disrupts the session can be asked to leave if this is the consensus of the others.

d) The chairmanship rotates, either weekly or monthly, so that every member of the family experiences this privilege and responsibility. It is often assumed that children are not able to function adequately as chairman. This is true, but just as often we find the parent unable to chair a meeting in a democratic manner.

e) The maintenance of the parliamentary order provides each member with the opportunity to express himself freely and with the obligation to listen to the others. If the sessions are used by the parents to "explain," preach, scold, or impose their will in other ways on their children, then the council is not democratic and fails in its purpose. Each parent, like any other member of the family, can merely submit his point of view to the group. The first objective of the sessions should be the willingness of all to listen sincerely to what each has to say. Before any satisfactory solutions can be found, the new routine of listening to each other and understanding what the other means has to be firmly established.

f) Most "urgent" decisions are not as urgent as the parents or a child may be inclined to believe. All members of the family need to acquire the patience to function even under circumstances that are not to their liking. Most parents find it difficult to stand by quietly when something goes wrong or when the child misbehaves. Actually, what they can do and usually are doing may not correct the situation at all, but anything seems preferable to a "wait and see" attitude. In the absence of a decision by the council everyone has the right to do what *he* considers best, but no decision that affects others has validity, unless it is approved by the council. One of the first decisions may be in regard to possible life danger, when—upon an agreed signal—any discussion is omitted and immediate compliance guaranteed. In most other conflict situations it is sufficient for the parent to withdraw and leave the children to their own resources, without an audience.

g) The nature of the decisions requires careful consideration. They should serve the benefit of all, and not any one particular interest. The family council should not be a "gripe session," but a source of working out solutions to problems. Whatever problem arises, the question to answer is: "What can we do about this?" It is important that the emphasis is always on what *we* can do, rather than on what any one member should do. The council cannot function as an instrument of power, imposing its verdict on any one of its members. If some influence should be exerted on any one, then procedure should be a clarification of what all the others will do, if . . . This also includes a plan for action if and when various members of the family do not carry out what they decided at the meeting. In other words, decisions or plans for action are needed either in regard to pleasant or to objectionable eventualities or possibilities. Agreement by all is preferable; but if it is impossible, then the majority has to decide. One must keep in mind that in most cases children are very reasonable when their problems are discussed in an objective way, dissociated from any immediate conflict.

h) Parents are usually afraid of wrong decisions, made against their "better judgment." Such wrong decisions, usually proposed by the children, can be used to great advantage. Instead of trying to prevent such a decision, parents should let the children see what will happen. Not too much harm can ensue. At the next meeting the children will be more careful and agree on a better solution.

i) Once a decision has been made, any alteration has to wait for the next session. In the interim, no one has the right to decide on a different course of action or to impose his decision on others. On the other hand, if a decision for certain actions or functions is neglected by the children, the parents are not bound by it either. For instance, when the mother accepted the responsibility to shop and to cook while the children took on the task of washing the dishes, it is not up to the mother to insist that they do their part; but naturally, she cannot cook either if the kitchen has not been cleared.

j) The family council is the only authority. No individual can lay down the law, make decisions for the others. On the other hand, no one person has to shoulder the full responsibility for the well-functioning of the household. For most parents, particularly for mothers this is a difficult lesson to learn. Mothers are impressed with their sense of obligation and responsibility, and they feel negligent if they do not take care of the needs of all. As a consequence, the children have no chance to take on responsibilities themselves. If mother is willing to accept the family council as supreme authority, she does not have to feel guilty if things do not always go as they should. It is more important that the children accept their responsibility than to have things going smoothly all of the time.

k) Instituting the family council requires the realization that a fundamentally new and untried course of action has begun. It requires time and effort to get all members of the family used to such procedures. Parents and children alike are not prepared for it. They do not trust each other, and consequently do not have much faith in any project that requires co-operation. Children are afraid that this is merely another trick to make them behave and do things that they do not want to do, and parents fear demands and decisions by their children that are out of place. For this reason, the council sessions are often a burden to all. Sometimes it may be difficult to start them, in other cases the first enthusiasm may shortly disappear. Making the council effective may impose hardships on the parents for the time being. But if the difficult period can be tolerated without discontinuance of council sessions, its effects should be highly beneficial for all concerned.

Chapter 4

*The Most Common Mistakes
in Child Training*

No parent can avoid making mistakes in the training of children. You may question the wisdom of being told that so much of what you have done in the process of raising your child has not been exactly right, perhaps has even been harmful. Several reasons may mitigate your concern about your own shortcomings.

First of all, nobody is perfect. And if you demand perfection from yourself, you are bound to become more discouraged and, consequently, to be less adequate than you could be otherwise. We have to accept our children—and all our fellow human beings—despite and with their inevitable imperfections if we want to get along with them and to improve faults. The same is true for ourselves. We can only improve if we first accept our own shortcomings, make peace with ourselves, and then ask ourselves where we are going from here.

Secondly, the present difficulties of parenthood, which we discussed in the first chapter, make it almost impossible for any contemporary parents to find an adequate solution for their educational task. Indicating where they erred is not an indictment, should not be taken as criticism, but merely as helpful information. The best way to act correctly is to avoid acting incorrectly. If you are looking for the proper answer to a difficult educational problem you will find it helpful first to stop and think of what you should *not* do. Then, what you do will be all right. It is very much easier to point out and define a mistake, because errors are always specific. The correct answer to a problem can be found in many different ways, consequently an explicit, constructive suggestion may be restrictive, as it may prevent you from seeking other, perhaps preferable, solutions. It is possible to follow advice literally about what *not* to do, but you cannot be literal about positive suggestions, because correct attitudes depend to a large extent on imponderables, on imagination, sensitivity, emotional attitudes, facial expressions, the tone of voice, and so on. If you learn that it is not good to spank children, you can easily grasp the advice and follow it literally, if you so decide. But any specific suggestion for the proper handling of children can be followed literally and still in a way which is detrimental and offers no solution.

For this reason it seems advisable that you acquaint yourself thoroughly with all the details of wrong techniques. You will find it profitable to learn well what you should avoid doing. But be careful not to be discouraged, because then you make your worst mistakes. Whatever you do on the basis of discouragement and defeatism, guilt feelings and frustration, is bound to be wrong, regardless of how hard you may try to act correctly. There is no sense in "crying over spilled milk," especially when you can be sure that much milk is bound to be spilled in the normal process of rearing children. We have been subjected to abuses by parents throughout the ages and if human nature were not so strong as it is, what would have become of all of us? It is true that we could have been better and that we should try to help our children to become better and happier human beings. But one factor in helping them is to recognize their ability to withstand so many of the bad influences which we exert on them, unwillingly and unconsciously.

In this chapter we will discuss the most common mistakes in child training. All errors arise from the same three sources: (1) the child is not required to observe order; (2) the parent allows himself to be drawn into conflict with the child; (3) the child is discouraged.

Some parents try to avoid conflict with the child by giving in and thus neglecting to educate him to social conformity. Others are bent on *forcing* their children to observe order under all circumstances, and thus let themselves become involved in a bitter struggle. Both procedures lead to disappointment and failure. If we enter into conflict with a child we cannot move him to a proper observance of order; and if we are lax and do not insist on orderliness we will inevitably be forced into conflict with him. There are only the two alternatives— order *without* conflict, or conflict *and* disorder.

One basic principle for maintaining proper human relationships is a mutual respect for each other's dignity. All mistakes in education are the consequences of a violation of this fundamental rule of cooperation. Parents who fail to respect the child will humiliate or enslave, frustrate or overprotect him. On the other hand, they disregard their own dignity and do not earn respect for themselves if they permit the child to boss them, if they indulge the child and make themselves his servants. The great variety of educational mistakes can be reduced in each case either to a neglect of the child's dignity or to a disregard on the part of the parents for their own dignity. Their own vacillation between forcing and giving in is the result of this disregard.

Spoiling the Child

The most serious impediment to the child's development is the parental attitude and technique that we call spoiling. We are faced here with a peculiar and elusive problem. The word spoiling is used at every turn, and yet no one is quite sure of its meaning. It is beyond doubt that the majority of our contemporaries were spoiled as children; even those who most loudly protest against this accusation are longing for a little pampering now, and thus betray themselves. Only a spoiled child yearns for continued pampering.

It is not easy to give an accurate definition of what we mean by spoiling. The term embraces a great variety of actions and attitudes. The very word is expressive of a false method of adapting the child to life. Instead of training him to meet the responsibilities of living, we "spoil" him for these duties—render him unfit to perform them.

At the root of this process is, in most cases, the well-intentioned desire to spare the child certain unpleasant experiences —a desire that is common in anxious parents who are greatly concerned over or strongly attached to their children. Hence the only child or the youngest child is most exposed to this danger, as are children who are particularly delicate or sickly, or who for some reason arouse sympathy and pity—who have perhaps lost one of their parents at an early age or are in some other respect handicapped. A strikingly handsome child is likely to be pampered, and similarly the child whose upbringing is subject to any considerable influence from his grandparents. Anything that heightens the solicitude of the parents also increases the danger of spoiling—the death of the preceding child, a long period of involuntary childlessness, a difficult pregnancy.

The attempt to shield the child from unpleasant experiences generally involves a breach of order and regularity, so essential for harmonious living. This protectiveness may begin almost immediately after birth of the child, getting him off to a wrong start. Even the newborn baby may be stimulated either to conformity or defiance of order and regularity. Definite feeding schedules are not only in line with the rhythm of physiological functions, but also an essential experience for the child to recognize early the benefits of regularity and order. The infant may offer some resistance to such regulation: he may cry whenever he is hungry. (Much of his early crying is misunderstood by anxious parents as indicating hunger or pain, while it often means only that the child wants some attention.) If the parents are intelligent and calm, they will not be tempted to break the well-considered regularity of feeding, unless the child is ill and requires some deliberate changes in schedule. In this way the child will soon realize that he cannot hasten mealtimes by crying, and in a few days he may be accustomed to the stipulated feeding period. Overprotective parents, however, are eager to spare their "helpless child" these first annoyances. They cannot bring themselves to let him "go hungry" especially since the feeding process may be difficult at the beginning and he loses weight regularly during the first days of his life. "Later on, when he's stronger, he'll get used to order." [1] But the older the baby gets, the harder it is to make up for past indulgence, and the more strongly he objects to any change in the irregularity to which he is now accustomed. Moreover, if

[1] Today parents are supported in taking such a detrimental attitude by the current tendency among pediatricians to advise feeding the baby whenever he is hungry. This trend is probably based on certain psychiatric concepts which consider "emotional frustration" as the prime source of human maladjustment. There can be no doubt that some children will develop the desire for regularity by themselves. Many will grow up satisfactorily regardless of feeding schedule or lack of one. It is also true that a too rigid schedule has its dangers if it provokes anxiety in the mother, who watches the clock with apprehension and becomes a slave of a "schedule" instead of just relaxing and accepting regularity herself. But advising parents to indulge children deliberately from the beginning is bound to have far-reaching detrimental effects. It is out of place to compare such deliberate irregularity with reference to the conditions of primitive people or of past centuries when scientific facts about the regular needs of the child were not known. Then, the demand of the child for food was the only guide for the mother. At such times the danger of excessive spoiling of children was not as great. If we still lived in a primitive culture, where order and regularity were rigid and necessary for the maintenance of social living, or if we still had the large families, where children grew up amongst themselves because parents were too busy to interfere with their adjustment, there would be no great danger caused by this most recent relapse into irregularity of feeding. As matters stand today, such indulgence at the start of life coincides with the general tendency of our overanxious parents to spoil their children excessively. There is no doubt that the "demand schedule" may have some beneficial effects by removing a cause for struggle between the child and the parents. But the same effect could be obtained if the parents would avoid concern about the amount of food intake and refrain from pressure and anxiety. The disturbed relationship and ensuing hostility do not begin with the baby who is "frustrated" but with the parents who become anxious and confused. The baby of calm and friendly parents will not fight any reasonable schedule. Happiness is not based on the satisfaction of vague "emotional needs" but on the acceptance of order without rebellion. (For further details see chapter 5, "Nursing.")

the child's health suffers from this irregularity, the mother's solicitude increases proportionally. She may half-heartedly try to enforce some sort of order, but the child will only redouble his outcries, since by now he is sure of success. In the end the mother must give up the struggle—especially as the child's vocal powers are constantly developing.

Every act of spoiling follows the same pattern. The child succeeds in evading a necessary duty, and to quiet him the requirements of order are increasingly violated. One infringement leads to another. When he cries because he wants food between meals, his mother picks him up and rocks him. He likes this; so when he should be lying quietly he starts the practice of crying until someone rocks him again, and, because someone is not present to rock him, he does not get the undisturbed rest and sleep necessary for his growth and development.

Spoiling and pampering may assume a thousand different forms. The child grows up in a hothouse atmosphere in which the natural order that otherwise regulates human conduct is not in force. He is beyond the jurisdiction of the laws that bind all the other members of the family. He is carefully wrapped in a protective layer of tenderness and affection and insulated against the necessity of justifying his existence by accomplishments of his own. Sympathy and indulgence shield him from all the unpleasant consequences of his actions. Continual help of overprotective parents relieves him of any exertion. He does not have to put up with inconveniences. The exaggerated anxiety of his parents keeps him well out of the way of anything that might involve danger and require courage. As a baby he was trundled about and rocked to sleep, and when he is older he will be exempted from many essential tasks. He will not have to dress and wash himself or do his homework alone. He will be catered to in every respect; his desires will be granted without regard to justification, and he will find it possible to get his own way, even in cases where the order of the family will be seriously upset.

All this is a handicap to the basic social adjustment of the child, and he will suffer from it later on when he faces the necessity of subordinating his desires to those of others. For, contrary to their parents' expectation, most spoiled children are not especially happy. Quite the opposite! Life is such that no one can have all his wishes fulfilled, or can be spared the task of making the best of a bad job. But while others accept rebuffs as a matter of course, spoiled children may come to regard them as an unfair presumption on the part of their environment or of destiny itself. The discontent, impatience, and joylessness that characterize so many spoiled children show to what little extent spoiling has succeeded in making life easier for them. Inwardly they never feel that they are quite a match for life, and their lack of self-reliance often causes them to break down under the slightest responsibility or hardship.

Hence any kind of spoiling leads with logical certainty to conflict with the child. The older he grows, the more responsibilities he will have to face, and the more difficult it will be to continue pampering him. But if the parent stops giving in, the child may take this reversal of policy as a sign of unkindness and indifference. He will find it difficult to understand why he must suddenly do without the accustomed amount of indulgence and help, and he will balk at being thrown on his own resources and denied satisfaction of his whims. The parents, accordingly, may have little cause for satisfaction with their child's conduct; they will be vexed, and may add fuel to the flames of dissension by punishing the child for the consequence of their training. The result is the turbulent interplay of severity and laxity, affection and desperation, which may dominate the whole process of pseudo-training.

These may be extreme cases of spoiling. But even spoiling to a lesser degree is detrimental, although it can hardly be avoided entirely. Especially is the only and the youngest child bound to be spoiled a little. You cannot be careful enough in checking the slight infringement of orders, the impositions, and the subtle tricks which your youngster plays on you to induce you to spoil him. Unfortunately, the occasions generally seem so insignificant that you will either fail to realize how these little indulgences disturb your relationship with the child or you may not feel it worth while to make some special effort to stop such tricks as demanding undue attention or putting others into his service, avoiding responsibilities or disturbing the order of the household. Furthermore, we all love to spoil children, to shower them with affection, to protect and mother them, to do little favors, to give them a hand in doing what they could very well do for themselves. It is their emotional indulgence which makes parents insensitive to the needs of orderly human relationship, their anxiety which induces them to be overprotective, and the desire for personal superiority which stimulates them to take undue responsibility. These parents can have our understanding and sympathy, but they have to pay a big price for their small mistakes and will have to work hard to correct the relationship when the unhappy consequences become obvious.

Lovelessness

Parents who really dislike their children are an exception today. However, where the exception is the case, the lot of the children is often wretched and frequently becomes a matter for official inquiry. Unwanted children often grow up without love.[2] Sometimes the merest trifle is enough to draw down their parents' hatred—perhaps a physical resemblance to a disliked relative, or the accident of sex, a girl being born instead of the long-expected boy.

The sense of lovelessness may completely prevent the child from adjusting himself to society. It deprives him of his rights, and arouses extreme hostility and defiance. Without love, no child is prepared to adapt himself to his environment and accept its code of conduct. Superficially he may conform, but

[2] In previous times, stepchildren often shared the fate of unwanted children. At the present time the general attitude of love and sympathy for children permits a friendly and warm relationship with all children, be they stepchildren, adopted, or foster children.

inwardly he is still a bystander. His social sense is atrophied.

The trend toward planned parenthood through birth control reduces the number of unwanted and disliked children. But despite the fact that most parents like their children, the number of children who feel rejected and unloved is tremendous. We can understand the reasons for this paradox. Spoiled children may feel disliked if the parents fail to continue their indulgence. A little boy of seven said openly, "You don't like me, because you don't do what I want." Similarly, not having one's way, not being fussed about or admired, not receiving gifts or attention, is sufficient reason for many spoiled children to believe that they are no longer liked or loved. In the ensuing conflict with spoiled children, parents often reach a stage where they no longer can "stand" undue demands and respond constantly with scolding, nagging, and punishing. Even if these war scenes are interrupted by lovemaking, the child is more impressed with the exhibited hostility and no longer trusts the demonstrated affection. As the fight becomes more violent, especially if younger children push ahead and attain more attention, the child gets attention only if he misbehaves. If he is quiet and nice, mother takes a well-deserved rest. Consequently, such children experience only expressions of discontent, criticism, and reproach, and become utterly convinced that they are not loved. It must be kept in mind that the effect is the same whether the child is actually hated or only *believes* he is. A real or fancied lack of love during childhood, with its consequent feeling of having been mistreated as a child, has been demonstrated in the lives of many criminals.

Excess Affection

A child needs love and warmth for his development, but an excess of affection may do harm. An overcharged atmosphere in the home is a faulty preparation for the normal conditions of life. Many an individual spends his life in quest of the love and tenderness he once received from his mother, and hence he cannot fail to be bitterly disillusioned by his fellowmen. The exorbitant affection that binds a child too closely to his parents makes him ill suited for his later role in love and marriage; it is likely to impair his capacity for love in other forms.

Immoderate affection on the part of the parents may even cause premature sexual development in the child. For this reason it is harmful to kiss children too much (especially on the mouth) or to let them share the parents' bed, if only in the mornings or on Sundays. Unfortunately, however, children are sometimes allowed to sleep with their parents until their tenth year or later—and not because of crowded living conditions.

It is true that a great display of affection promotes a close attachment between parent and child. But if confidence and intimacy are achieved exclusively by this means, their value is always dubious. The child will probably become quite dependent, but neither this dependence nor physical contact precludes conflict with the parents. On the contrary, the pampering that necessarily results from inordinate affection will, in the natural course of events, serve only to evoke and intensify a conflict which, in this case, assumes certain distinctive forms. Open rebellion may not occur; rather, the child may show every indication of good will. But his inner opposition expresses itself in apparent helplessness and inaptitude. A nervous disorder is the commonest manifestation.

It is undoubtedly pleasant to feel the deep attachment of a child and to cherish the physical signs of his affection; but this overemphasis may delude him about his position in life. He may be led to the conclusion that his aim in life should be to win love and affection *through his mere existence*, rather than to acquire recognition through tangible achievements. You should bear these facts in mind when you center on your child all your desire for affection, which perhaps has remained unsatisfied in the other phases of your life.

Dicky is very devoted to his mother; he loves her dearly. He is always at swords' points with the other persons of his environment, but for his mother's sake he tries hard to "control himself" and improve his conduct. Learning, however, is very difficult for him, and his efforts seem to be of little use. He rarely has the inclination to work, becomes flustered in class and is very nervous. Here we see the results of excessive affection on the part of his mother, who in some respects became severe as her boy became increasingly difficult. Until his seventh year, Dick often shared his mother's bed. Afterward he was allowed this privilege only when he was especially troubled by bad dreams; but even later, and for many years, he sometimes spent the night with his mother. He is a most affectionate son, caressing and kissing his mother whenever the opportunity arises. His attachment to her is so great that he can hardly be prevailed upon to leave her.

He began to attend kindergarten at four, but always objected violently to going; and these objections were redoubled when he was enrolled in a summer camp. He continually feels that he is surrounded by enemies, and never tries to make friends. His sole thought is to get home as soon as possible. He began to masturbate when he was only four; erections occurred very early. He is extremely vain and concerned only with impressing others, but has no confidence in his abilities, although he is really above the average, both mentally and physically. He tries to win recognition only by making a nuisance of himself, with clowning and ill conduct (fidgeting, giggling, loquaciousness, etc.).

Withdrawal of Affection

You certainly do not want to expose yourself to the charge of being hardhearted. And yet—strangely enough—you may sometimes try to give this impression. When your child gets into mischief you are "cross." Often this is only a bluff, but sometimes it is sincere. You may believe (like most parents) that this is the best means of disciplining the child—of jerking him into line, so to speak, and overcoming his resistance. There is today a widespread school of psychology that goes so far as to commend and laud this so-called withholding of affection as the sole effective method of child training.

It must be conceded that certain objectives can be attained

by this means. The child is attached to you and to the persons who care for him; and the sense of being rejected, of forfeiting your love and solicitude, is certainly painful enough to cause him to suppress his unruly tendencies. However, it is fallacious to assume that these tendencies actually vanish as a result. The child does not want to lose your love, and will take care to tone down the impulses that meet with your disapproval. But these tendencies will only be repressed, not eliminated. You must use other methods to accomplish that.

What is worse, the child's courage will be seriously impaired by incidents of your estrangement, which makes him sharply conscious of his dependence and littleness. Very frequently your attempt to deprive him of your love will be met with a counter-attempt to force you to display affection. This purpose may perhaps be achieved through spells of fright at bedtime: you have to sit by his bed for hours at a stretch and even hold his hand, or else he will whimper and cry and never go to sleep.

But the most dangerous consequence of "being cross" is the child's resultant doubt of your absolute reliability. How can he acquire faith in human nature and develop his social sense if time after time his best friends suddenly rebuke him? You have at your disposal more suitable means of correcting his faults and making him feel the consequences of bad conduct. For such purposes there is never any need of beclouding your friendly relations with the child. On the contrary, you cannot alter your relationship without implanting in the child's mind the seeds of dissension and conflict. The spirit of comradeship between parent and child will not bear tampering with. A child will sooner forgive a sharp word blurted out in an unguarded moment than forget a cold, deliberate withdrawal of affection—"I don't like you any more." As long as the child fails to recognize this phrase as a hoax and a humbug, it marks the beginning of a struggle, if only a struggle for affection. More extreme forms of "crossness," such as actual unkindness, aloofness, harshness, or continued refusal to talk, are full-blown defensive measures that cannot fail to force the child into a hostile attitude. In reality, you love your children under all circumstances and the child should know this. However, many children do not know it. It was already said that many of our children feel rejected by their parents and think that nobody likes them. They get attention only when they are disturbing and little attention when well behaved. Therefore, they experience mostly scolding and punishment, and come to the wrong conclusions. The fuss which is made over a younger child may also lead them to the mistaken assumption of not being liked.

You may ask, then, whether you should ever show disapproval. You cannot avoid it, and sometimes it is even necessary to show it. Absolute objectivity and matter-of-factness are not only impossible and unnatural, but even insulting. But you must be careful to emphasize *what* you censure: the *child* or his *action*. You can express dislike of a certain behavior if you indicate clearly that you do not dislike the child. The failure to distinguish between the action and the person who acts puts a grave burden on all our contemporaries who have not learned or realized the difference. Consequently, we tend to confuse the value of a person, including our own self, with the value of his acts; and we are inclined to doubt our own value in society if a single one of our actions does not measure up to the standards which we set for ourselves. Parents and teachers who classify children according to more or less incidental failures or achievements, poison their minds, often for the rest of their lives. *There are no bad children,* only discouraged and unhappy ones who have not found the proper method for integrating themselves into human society.

Anxiety

Strong, antagonistic emotions are often caused by fear and anxiety. If you are anxious you may see nothing but the dangers from which you wish to shield the child. You may tremble at the thought that "something might happen to him," and fail to consider that he must learn to take care of himself—that he must acquire the ability to recognize dangers and cope with them on his own initiative. "A burnt child dreads the fire." Timid parents rob their children of valuable experiences. These children remain improvident and are all the more liable to come to harm. They play with matches, turn on the gas, and climb onto shelves. Meanwhile, the parents' anxiety increases and once they slacken their surveillance the dreaded mishap finally occurs.

Five-year-old Tommy takes advantage of his mother's anxiety by running away from her on the street and making her chase him. When she came to me for advice, I explained that a five-year-old boy ought to realize that if he runs away he may get lost, and I told her that she would have to give him first-hand experience of this fact. She could choose the proper circumstances, perhaps in the park or in some quiet street with no traffic. The mother was horrified. What a thing to suggest! What did I, a mere man, know about a mother's feelings?

Scarcely two weeks had elapsed since this conversation when she came to me again in a state of high excitement. "Doctor, just imagine what Tommy's done now! Yesterday I went into his room—and he wasn't there. Then I heard him calling, 'Mummy, Mummy.' My heart practically stood still. For just imagine, Doctor: we live on the third floor, and the windows open onto the steep roof of a balcony. And there was Tommy, sitting on the roof and shouting away! He couldn't be persuaded to come in, and when I tried to climb out after him he moved farther out on the roof. We had to tempt him with promises and candy before we could get hold of him." It was possible to convince her that in this instance Tommy was simply up to his old tricks—he was unable to judge risks, and hence he used them to scare his mother. She finally realized that her anxiety only put him in the way of new dangers.

Children who grow up with any degree of self-reliance are by no means as incautious as their parents believe. In this respect as in so many others, the child's intelligence is greatly underrated. Despite the fact that so many children play unsupervised on city streets and along country highways, statistics prove that more adults than children are struck or run over by automobiles. Anyone who watches the pedestrians at a busy intersection can readily see how much more careless and frivolous the grown-ups are than their offspring, at least in a moment of actual danger. Intelligently reared children show a similar caution in the face of other hazards. Only in the first two years of his life, while the child is still gradually acquainting himself with the nature and function of separate objects, is he liable to expose himself to danger at home. But instead of frightening him with imminent dangers and safety talks—and at the same time arousing his antagonism—it is much more advisable simply to point out the various dangers and arrange some harmless but unpleasant experiences. He will soon learn rightly to evaluate the risks to which he is exposed.

There are children, it is true, who at eight or even older cannot be trusted to cross a street by themselves. But in these cases the blame always rests with the overanxious parents who have failed to let their children look out for themselves and learn proper protection. They must learn to take care of themselves. And the earlier they learn this, the easier will be the minds of their parents.

Frightening the Child

Anxiety induces a great many parents to give their children an exaggerated idea of the perils of life. They think they are training them to be cautious when they dwell upon the frequency of accidents on the streets, the depravity of mankind in general and of kidnapers in particular, the prevalence of disease germs and the necessity of always keeping oneself warm, and so forth. If the child adopts such squeamish, timid notions from his parents, he does not become better prepared for life; he only becomes anxious himself. And it is strange but true that excessive caution leads to the same results as thoughtlessness. Anticipating dangers not only causes hesitancy, but actually drives people headlong into the very dangers they wish to avoid. The evasion of risks requires calm presence of mind and a clear appraisal of the situation. *Hence, overrating danger is equivalent to increasing it.*

Thus the people who are overanxious, and awkward in their motions, are the very ones who are most likely to stumble into the path of an automobile or fall when leaving a streetcar. Courage is better than anxiety as a preventive against danger, and parents who intimidate their children are deliberately putting them in harm's way. The same is true of attempts to shield the child from illness. If he is always bundled up and kept out of every draft, he is simply predestined to catch colds.

It was pitiful to watch grandmother supervise eight-year-old Jerry at his play. "Don't run so fast, you will burst your lungs!" "Don't pull so hard, you will rupture yourself!" "Don't jump down the stairs, you will break your legs!" A child who paid attention to all such admonitions would have to spend his life wrapped in cotton wool in a glass case; but, much to the annoyance of his would-be custodians, a healthy stubbornness usually makes him ignore their nagging.

Another reason, too, may lead you sometimes to frighten your child—an attempt to enforce good behavior—and with no better results. You may tell him about the "bogyman" who comes to get bad children; or you show him the policeman on the corner who "takes away naughty boys and girls." You may consider this a means of making the child more compliant. The expedient may work sometimes, for the moment; but subsequent development will prove your error. The child may become timid, and later on use his fears as a weapon against you, in a thousand possible ways.[8] Never will you profit from intimidation. He who sows fear reaps worry.

Excessive Supervision

Apprehensive parents do not trust themselves or their child or the future; they think only of defense and prevention. This

[8] See Chapter 4, "Withdrawal of Affection."

concern leads to overactivity, to an excess of moves and methods, every single one of which may be adequate but becomes ineffectual and destructive through exaggerated application. From the anxiety of parents grows their tendency to oversupervise the child. They never let him act independently. Every detail of his behavior is prescribed. Parents who are unsure of themselves are equally dubious of their child's ability; the less capable one feels of managing one's own affairs, the more one may try to manage others, meddling and giving advice constantly. Such parents fret incessantly over their children: "You'd better sit in this chair"; "Put the book here"; "Take this pen"; "Wear this hat"; "Don't eat so fast"; "Sit up straight." The inexhaustible stock of parental commands cannot be half inventoried! When the child is near, his parents dictate his every movement. They cannot wait to see whether he can shift for himself. His every activity is supervised, he is exposed to an unceasing series of comments and prohibitions; every action provokes praise or blame, but especially criticism. No day passes without numberless exhortations and precepts.

A friend of mine was a very *busy* mother. On one occasion we began to talk about her overanxiety and constant management of her child. She was not aware of her attitude. I asked her how often she directed the child during one day, with criticism, comment, or command. "Oh, not so often," she said. I asked her to give an approximate estimate. She could not answer. Then I ventured again: perhaps one hundred or two hundred times a day? "Oh no," she answered indignantly. Perhaps ten times a day would be the maximum. So I made the following proposition: I would come over to her house for an hour and observe her. How often did she think she would address her child during this one hour of my presence? "Oh, perhaps two or three times." I made the estimate that it would be thirty times during my visit. She laughed. "It certainly will not be that much." So I came. I was just sitting and watching what went on, counting loudly each time she told the child what to do or not to do. Despite the fact that she was conscious of my presence and reminded by my loud counting, the thirty times were exceeded in less than half an hour. She was simply unable to stop herself.

In order to grasp fully the absurdity of such "supervision" we must bear in mind that educational influences have lasting value only when they make deep impressions on the child. One single but forceful experience, while it does not alter the disposition and character of a child, can provide a stimulus to new attitudes and approaches. Herein lies the value of educational acts; they give the child an *occasion* for thought and reflection. He must take a definite stand and draw conclusions. The development of his personality can be profoundly influenced by a few *striking* experiences, tending in the same direction.

Hence, incessant efforts to influence the child make little impression. They cease to compel consideration and provoke opposition. The child becomes blunted to their effect and no longer pays any attention, since by their multiplicity they often contradict one another. He will either abandon all efforts at independent action, or become sullen, unresponsive, and impudent. Only by *rarely* exerting educational influences can you be impressive and effective.

Excessive Talking

The harmful "busybody" proclivity in child training finds its expression in words. Instead of acting or even thinking, most parents just talk. Whatever the child does, they have something to say. If they do not know what to do—they talk. Talk does not help, of course, as their words do not present any constructive plan.

Naturally, words are necessary. The child needs explanations and instruction, just as he needs amusement; and it is possible to make deep and lasting impressions through words. But too often words are without meaning or direction. You must be on guard against such speech. Every word that has no effect is superfluous and even injurious. It is not an expression of personal contact, but rather of a disturbance in human relationships. Words can be a means of communication—or they can be a tool of warfare. You must decide whenever you talk with the child whether you wish to talk for the release of your own tension, annoyance, or anger, or whether you wish to impress the child. In the latter case you should never talk unless you ascertain that the child is ready to listen. And you must watch your own emotions. Only when you are completely calm are you in a position to talk constructively. Otherwise, your words have the effect of violence; they are offensive and stir up antagonism. If you wish to use words constructively, you must constantly watch their effect and must stop talking if you see that the child is not susceptible at the moment. If you or the child get excited during the conversation then you should know it is time to stop talking.

In the latter event, words must be supplanted by actions. It is better to stop and think than to add another comment or remark that would probably meet with no greater response than the first. Above all, you should *never repeat what you have once said*, and you should never tell the child something he already knows. (Showing him his mistakes falls in the category of useless words, because most of the time the child knows that he has made a mistake.) If your comment was useless the first time, it will be harmful the second—even if it serves its purpose. Repetition exasperates, and irritation acts as the prelude to unpleasant bickering. You should *talk little, think much, and act accordingly*—that is, let the natural consequences take effect. Sometimes when the child has done wrong, complete silence will make a deeper impression on him than the strongest words, as silence can be a very forcible expression of disapproval.

The absurdity and potential harm of words and of certain common manners of speech can be judged from the following assortment.[4]

[4] From Dr. Alice Friedmann's *Erziehungsmerkblätter*.

When the child sets to work:

Don't begin something you can't finish.
I'm curious to see how far you'll get.
You're a fine one to be trying that!
Shoemaker, stick to your last!
Even if you do get finished, what will you have done?
You just want to show off!
Better do your lessons—there's some sense to that.
It isn't as easy as you believe.
You think everything's going to be a snap.
You're biting off more than you can chew.
I don't think you've got it in you.
You won't have the stick-to-it-iveness.
You're interested in such silly things!
If it could be done, someone else would have done it long
ago.

When the child is successful:

That will never get you far.
You're still a long way from being a good student.
You think you're flying high, but there'll be a letdown.
That was just beginner's luck.
More luck than brains!
Even a blind man may stumble onto something.

When he is unsuccessful:

Just look at the money that's wasted!
You see, I was right!
I told you so!
At your age I was making all my own clothes.
I was much cleverer than you.
Your fingers are all thumbs!
Everything you try goes wrong.
Just looking at you is enough to make a person ill!

These and similar phrases discourage the child and impair his actual abilities, yet they are thoughtlessly used in daily life. One must be careful about what one says to a child. Words are intended to be stimulating and helpful, not annoying and inhibitory.

Neglect

Many of the mistakes that we have discussed thus far consist of a superfluity of educational measures. It is a sound principle to interfere as little as possible and allow the child to accumulate his own experiences. But to extend this principle beyond its reasonable limits may imply serious harm. You must be concerned with your children and must occupy yourself with them. Children need not only physical care, but also human sympathy, understanding, and stimulation. If they lack these attentions, they will be injured by neglect and retarded in their development. Their ability to work together with others, to fit themselves into the social whole, may be atrophied.

The limitation that you should impose on yourself is mainly in regard to the application of training methods. A limited number will suffice to preserve order, if they are employed at the right moment. But in your purely human relations with the child, in your cooperation with him, you should impose no limits on your activity and interest. As he grows older the child increasingly needs experiences of fellow feeling and joint activity. From your interest in him he draws the stimulation for his continued development, provided that this interest does not assume oppressive or offensive forms. If you take too little interest in his physical development, his appearance, and his moral and intellectual growth, you harm him as much through your neglect as you do by displaying this interest in such a manner and by such means as to arouse the child's antagonism, thus pushing him in the opposite direction.

Urging

Often the child may require some prodding. If he does, you must encourage him, and in all friendliness call to his attention the need for his cooperation. But if the child offers resistance, any attempt to persuade him is generally useless. It is especially harmful when compliance on his part requires an inner preparation. Urging may be proper when the child should dress himself more warmly before he goes out to play. Such purely external duties may often require a little friendly pressure. But never try to persuade a child to eat, fall asleep, or silence an expression of emotion (crying, sulking, etc.), or to perform any function that proceeds only from an inner motive. Through external inducements you may move him to take a bite of food in his mouth and chew it, but swallowing and digesting it require actual willingness. The same is true of sleeping. You may put the child to bed against his will, but any further meddling disturbs the process of falling asleep. Likewise, the child's emotions cannot be influenced by pressure. He will not stop crying or pouting until he is inwardly prepared to do so. Pressure only increases the inner resistance. Hence words are useless in these instances and are even harmful, since they produce the opposite of the desired effects.

Of course it is possible to influence the child in such situations. All depends on whether you win him over to the proper attitude—making him inwardly ready to behave as he should. He must feel *within himself* the incentive to do what appears necessary. This inner conversion can be effected with relative ease by natural consequences, even when he is at first in strong inner opposition.

Little Eve's objections to taking a nap immediately after dinner vanished at once when she learned that she would not be allowed to stay up in the evening for the chamber music unless she had slept for an adequate time after her meal. Once she refused to eat her cereal; but when she found that nothing else was forthcoming, she said, "You know, Daddy, the cereal doesn't taste so bad any more." Her inner resistance had disappeared. This result could never have been attained through persuasion; on the contrary, pressure would only have prevented the child's sleeping and eating.

Thus even defiant children will readily compose themselves if they are not cajoled and fretted over, but left to themselves. Even crying will cease at once when the child's interest is diverted to other matters. Urging, however, will never have this effect.

Extracting Promises

Utterly futile and even harmful in its further consequences is the attempt to inveigle the child into making promises of better conduct. For example: "Promise me never to say that word again"; " . . . that you'll behave better the next time"; " . . . that you won't fib to me any more!" Generally the child gives his word rather absentmindedly, with no idea but to appease you or avert punishment. Even if he honestly intends to keep his promise, very little is gained. The child has not changed his personality; therefore, his behavior remains the same. And if, from what seems to be thoughtlessness, he repeats his previous offense, then you add to the list of his old faults a new one by branding him with the stigma of faithlessness and unreliability. In order to evade these charges, the child will most likely prefer to be regarded as thoughtless and forgetful. Thus extracting a promise has, in the first place, failed to correct the original fault; secondly, it has added a new failing (unreliability) to the old offense; and thirdly, it has encouraged the child's tendency to entrench himself behind a "weakness."

In order to prevent a repetition of his mistake, you must convince the child of its unpleasant consequences. If a misdemeanor results only in the extraction of a promise, then the child will gladly accept this consequence and, when the next occasion arises, will promise again with perfect equanimity whatever is asked of him. Thus, eliciting promises becomes a ritual through which the child escapes the actual consequences of his actions. Feeling sorry for the child, you may want to spare him the uncomfortable results of his improper conduct; and, to justify your deviation from the logical course of events, you require the child to promise that he will improve himself. Accordingly, you should not be surprised if, in the future, he tries to evade unpleasant situations by blithely promising anything and everything that is suggested.

Then, too, the child will try to use his promises as a means of acquiring advantages. If he wants a demonstration of affection, or to go to the movies or to obtain a treat of some kind, he is willing to make any promise. Or perhaps when something pleasant is in store for him, you may say beforehand, "But I won't do it unless . . ." This gives rise to the same situation as before. Doing something to please the child should be done with no strings attached. If you do wish to make the treat contingent on the child's performing some task or another, then the task must have a logical relation to your contribution and must unquestionably come first, else it may all too easily be confined to the empty words of a promise, and thereby produce the aggravated situation mentioned at the beginning.

Permitting yourself to be bribed by promises which are a substitute for actions will succeed only in developing traits of undependability and grandiloquence in your children. You cannot be too careful in regard to promises. It may be very gratifying when, of his own accord, a child gives a friendly promise. But you must take care that he does not use this as a means of buying himself out of some unpleasantness or of gaining some sort of undue advantage. In any case, nobody should ever extort a promise from a child. It generally invites trouble.

"Pull Yourself Together"

Another effort to induce compliance from the child is attempted as frequently as extracting a promise and is equally detrimental. You may urge the child on sundry occasions to "pull yourself together." You generally don't imply "for you surely will pull through." What you mean is he ought to use his will power; he should not be so *weak*. That is what the child understands. But his conclusions are often different from those which you want him to draw. Instead of realizing his strength, he only feels weaker. He may try to act differently, but only on rare occasions does he succeed. All his *efforts* leave his *intentions* unchanged; he merely goes through the motions of controlling himself. The result is an increased feeling of helplessness. He becomes even more convinced of his lack of will power, without improving his conduct.

This appeal to the child's will power proceeds from a false psychological premise. The *conscious* will is not always in harmony with the actual, more deepseated intentions that produce the child's behavior. Even when he makes a mistake, he has a purpose. Naturally, his intentions in this moment are not friendly, as they express his conflict with a given situation; but while others may recognize the antagonistic tendency, the child himself may remain unaware of it. Telling the child to "take hold of himself" forces him into an attitude that may have far-reaching, but unfortunate implications for his later life. The psychological mechanism that consequently develops constitutes an important basis for the development of the so-called neuroses.

What really does happen when a child "pulls himself together"? His real attitude is in no way altered; his defiance, his protest, his striving for recognition, or his desire to evade responsibilities continue, and certainly remain untouched by such appeal. But instead of recognizing his antagonism and clearing the conflict-laden atmosphere, you demand from him a performance that is frankly impossible under the circumstances. He may "try" not to be lazy or untidy, aggressive or dull. Since there has been no modification of his *inner scheme of purposes*, the effort will not improve his "faults," but will tend to aggravate his sense of weakness and deficient will power. The child points apologetically to his fruitless endeavors; he finds a thousand excuses, becomes forgetful, attends to nothing, and enters into a conflict with himself which really is only a sham conflict and leads nowhere. Intervening in this struggle with criticism and fault-finding, and reproaching the child with his lack of will power, only expedites his hazardous development. Such seemingly weak-willed individuals give in to all their malignant impulses, with the appearance of being unable to "control" themselves. Through their "weakness" and "lack of energy" they force their parents and other persons of their environment to make all necessary decisions for them, and burden relatives and friends with the complete responsibility for their own actions. And yet no one can remonstrate with them, since they obviously "try hard" to fulfill their obligations.

If you do not want to set your child on this road to neurosis, you must avoid the exhortation, "Pull yourself together." When you notice a weakness, it is far better to search for its origin and help the child to alter the *premises* of his behavior. You should not give him the opportunity to believe in his assumed "weakness." When a child is uncontrolled, thoughtless, or lacking in initiative, these flaws are never based on a want of strength or energy. You must recognize his purposes and help the child to solve his difficulties.

Retaliation

Many educational procedures are based on the assumption that every action of the child should receive its reward or punishment. Most parents can hardly conceive of the possibility of training their child without the application of reward or punishment. These methods have been employed throughout the ages and are deeply imbedded in social conditions which characterized human relationships of the past. As long as man was the servant of man, services could be obtained only through force or bribery. The group in power imposed its rule by devious methods of subjugation. Retaliation was a useful tool to this end as long as the powerful one had the stronger methods in his hand.

In our culture the concept of human relationships has undergone a fundamental change. Man has become man's equal, not only in political and social relationships in general, but also in the relationship between parents and children. In the process of mutual retaliation the parent no longer enjoys the favorable position of the powerful superiority. He may try to maintain his superior position, but, without being aware of it, he is influenced by the changed social concepts. In his desire to respect the child as an equal human being, he often makes him his master. Furthermore, the accepted standards of human behavior deprive parents of their right to treat the child as they please. As a consequence, the child's power of retaliation exceeds their own. The methods of retaliation are no longer effective, regardless of the consistency with which they are still employed.

The fallacy behind this theory of reward and punishment is obvious. Both methods are based on the assumption of your power and superiority. If you expose your child to them, you teach him to behave favorably only under your pressure, but not of his own accord. You can, no doubt, achieve conformity through pleasant and unpleasant pressure; but the resulting good behavior is only skin-deep. Any cooperation achieved by pressure is not based on social interest and a genuine desire to conform; underneath remains the rebellion which inevitably leads to anti-social attitudes, disrupting cooperation and breaking law and order. This inner rebellion barely covered by social veneer is characteristic of almost all our contemporaries and explains their social deficiencies. Many are willing to conform only when they can gain advantages or avoid hardships. Their conformity is not genuine, their cooperation not based on their recognition and acceptance of a social order. They regard society as a tyrant to which they have to submit, but not as their own domain which they create and to which they belong as equals. The value of cooperation, of a peaceful order, cannot be taught by reward and punishment. This approach conceals the real issue, by presenting order as an imposition and social adjustment as a submission. For the child, the natural consequences of a disturbed order are the only inducement for real social adjustment. They alone stimulate recognition and acceptance of order independent of the actions of others, regardless of favorable or unfavorable circumstances.

Parents accustomed to retaliation may misuse logical consequences. They may threaten the child: "If you do this, that will happen." Thus they inject again their own power into the social order. They watch like a policeman over the child and are utterly surprised if the child reciprocates, punishing the parents for what he thinks they have done to him. The result is a constant tug-of-war, each party getting even for what the other did before—*ad infinitum.*

The atmosphere of warfare characterizes many procedures employed today by parents who already feel beaten and overpowered by their child. They are not aware of their own motivations in continuing methods which they recognize as being futile and ineffectual. All parents are prone to employ either reward or punishment in child training. We must learn to watch out for them, we must understand their significance and must train ourselves to replace them with more effective approaches.

Insistence on Blind Obedience

You may feel impelled to use force if you regard the child's objection to requests as a grievous curtailment of your prestige (and hence as a defeat on the domestic battlefield of power politics). But is such an attitude justified?

A good many situations, to be sure, require the immediate response of your child. This is true when the child is in impending danger, or when he must be held to the observance of the necessary order. Such emergencies, however, do not occur often; and if demands for immediate response are restricted to these few cases firmness alone will suffice. But to demand submission in every case is a serious mistake. A child has his own thoughts and opinions, and should be allowed to develop them if he is to be successful later on in life. If you cramp the free movement of the child's personality, you check the growth of his will and his power of judgment.

This is by no means to say that, from sheer delight at the first signs of a will of his own, you should give in to him at every turn. It requires thorough and earnest consideration to determine when a child should subordinate his will in the interest of the general order, and when he may make his own decisions without detriment to others.

But even when the child must relinquish one of his desires, it is not always necessary that he acquiesce at once. If parents consider every act of resistance as a threat to their personal prestige, then of course they will find it hard to wait. But their failure to do so will mark the onset of the conflict that should and could be avoided. They react with irritation, anger, and the application of force. If their desire for prestige permitted them a little more patience, they probably would soon come to the conclusion that a little thought goes further than a great deal of violence. They would be able to use natural consequences that steer the child to the voluntary surrender of undesirable wishes and intentions. Or perhaps they could devise some other suitable means of influencing him in the right direction.

Ten-year-old Harry has a friend whom his parents dislike. They have forbidden him to associate with this boy; but their command, like many other similar injunctions, did little good. Then one day Harry lied when his mother asked him with whom he had gone for a walk; and when the lie was discovered, great excitement prevailed. Such a thing simply could not go unpunished! With a little reflection instead of uproar, shouting, and blows, the parents might have begun to ask themselves whether their boy did not have a right to congenial companionship and the choice of his own friends. If this particular friendship was not to their liking, the only right thing for them to do was to find ways and means of weaning their son away from it.

They might have shown him the faults of this companion, and

calmly talked with him of the disadvantages of such associations. But even so, it is questionable whether they would have been justified in taking any drastic steps. It would probably have been best for them to bring their son into contact with other children; they could have invited other boys to their home and given Harry the opportunity to make friends with one of them. The lie that Harry told was the result of his desire to evade painful arguments and altercations. The falsehood in itself should have been reason enough for the parents to scrutinize their previous attitude and question the validity of their approach to the problem. But instead they regarded it as a breach of their command, a culpable flaunting of their authority. Do you believe that after the grand melée the position of the parents is at all improved or that Harry will more scrupulously respect their desires?

We must realize that in dealing with a child it is impossible to accomplish everything *immediately*. This knowledge is especially important at the times when the child is in a certain state of revolt as the result of previous frictions or an increase in his problems or responsibilities: when, for instance, a younger brother or sister is born, when the child begins to attend school, or when he is ill. At other times, too, he may tend toward rebelliousness—frequently between the ages of three and four, and in the period of puberty. In such critical situations the parents' struggle for prestige is especially devastating in its effect. The less self-assured the parents, the stronger the manifestations of this struggle, and the greater their fear of leaving anything undone. They dread the most disastrous consequences if they do not *at once* achieve whatever seems to them important.

Nagging

Pressing impatience readily passes over into nagging. Scarcely any other parental attitude so vexes and antagonizes the child. Harping and caviling from morning to night! And, what is more, the very incessancy of the practice, combined with a poverty of inventive imagination, leads to a monotonous reiteration of the same phrases. Everything is subject to criticism; something is wrong everywhere; nothing is good enough. The pettiest slips on the child's part are represented as heinous offenses.

The pedagogical benefits of nagging are nil. On the contrary, nagging merely strengthens the resistance of the child, promotes disobedience, and hastens failure. If parents would observe the immediate effect that their nagging produces, they might be startled into changing their tactics. But they never stop to think, for their attitude is based upon their own needs rather than the child's; they act from an inner necessity. Even though they advance a thousand reasons for their dissatisfaction, at bottom they themselves do not know the root of their discontent, namely their own disappointment in life and their feeling of frustration. Supervision and nagging are among those measures which aim at belittling and depreciating the child, often enough as a reassurance of one's own superiority. We shall discuss their implications in connection with a related procedure that is also explained on rational grounds, fault-finding.

Fault-finding

Can you imagine rearing a child without finding fault? Probably not. Since time immemorial this has been one of the essential tools of the educator. (But it is certain that outside of our culture group there were, and still are, societies which did not utilize this technique of child training.) We find fault in order to show the child that he has not acted properly. But why such means to this end? We have seen[5] that one can stimulate the child's ability to discriminate between right and wrong by emphasizing the *right*. Usually the child knows before he is corrected that he has made a mistake. With a little experimentation you can see how tractable he is when he is

[5] See Chapter 3, "Commendation."

encouraged and given friendly instruction; by comparing these results with the effects of fault-finding, you will realize how little is achieved by the latter means.

At this point, however, we must make two reservations. In the first place we understand fault-finding to mean (as the term itself implies) only disparaging comments and actions. Saying to a child, "You didn't do that correctly, you ought to do it this way," is not finding fault, but *giving instruction.* Fault-finding involves a characteristic, reproachful tone, and only this form of parental intervention comes properly under our heading.

Secondly, there are, without doubt, children who react favorably to upbraiding. Certain children respond well when they are harshly criticized—but these children respond to no other technique. Friendly persuasion and encouragement seem wholly ineffectual. In other words, the very procedure that has the best results with most children is futile with them. Why is this? In such cases, we are dealing with obstinate and re-fractory youngsters—children who are hardened to conflict and who bend only to force. We shall discuss the psyche of these children in more detail in connection with the problem of physical punishment, since there the peculiar attitude that characterizes them is more clearly discernible.

It is probably true that fault-finding will occasionally show good results in other instances, too, particularly in the case of very ambitious children. But even then it is equally possible that it may have a detrimental effect. When used discreetly and sparingly it may act as a spur to ambition; but, on the other hand, frequent and vehement fault-finding so discour-ages ambitious children that they sometimes instantly aban-don their efforts. Here again we see how an identical attitude on the part of the parents produces different results in differ-ent children.

With the exceptions mentioned above, fault-finding in gen-eral has a fairly uniform effect. It discourages most children and impedes their conduct and their achievement. Hence it is almost preferable if they become inured to their parents' criticism and no longer pay attention to it. But in any event an unhappy vicious circle is created: the parents find fault—the child does not improve—the fault-finding increases—the child gets worse and becomes obstinate—and so on, in the well-known orbit that so often characterizes the relation between discontented parents and their children. How many domestic tragedies have their origin in this faulty relationship?

Especially dangerous is the bad practice of continually reproaching a child with his shortcomings. You should consider the effect, if you feel inclined to remind the child of his awkwardness. Your attitude is understandable, if you are provoked and grieved because you would like him to be perfect. And so you may say to him: "You must have two left feet"; "No one else is as clumsy as you"; "Wherever you step the grass never grows again"; "You're like a bull in a china shop"; "You just touch something and it's broken." Your words do have at least one sure result—they give vent to your own feeling of irritation. But will these statements affect the child? Will they stimulate him to greater dexterity? The opposite effect is more likely, since it is certain that his clumsiness is in large part due to discouragement. He thinks that he is awkward, and then behaves accordingly. You do not tell him anything new, but only confirm his own low opinion of himself.

An analogous effect is produced by repeatedly berating the child with his stupidity, laziness, untidiness, or other faults. If he does not already believe that he has these failings, your remarks will certainly convince him. And then, of course, the defect will take firm root, for such comments completely rob him of the courage to try to improve himself. He thinks, "What's the use of making an effort if I just can't help being stupid (or awkward or lazy)?" He then takes his weakness for granted; and, what is more, he has the satisfaction of seeing others fret over it.

Your discouraging attitude may, therefore, be the direct

cause of the child's contracting a bad habit. This phenomenon can be clearly observed in the case of so-called untruthfulness in children. If you misunderstand the lively imagination of your child and his tendency to confuse fantasy and reality, and accuse him of lying, he may actually think that he is by nature untruthful, and then perhaps he will really begin to lie.

Talk of the devil and he is bound to appear. You may be pushed by your harassment into telling the child your poor opinion of him. In your irritation, you tend to exaggerate his faults, and often your statements may sound stronger than you mean them to be. Is it worth while for the sake of relieving one irritation, to create a dozen new sources of vexation?

Disparagement

The nagging, fault-finding, switch-wielding technique—in short, the disparaging, conflict-generating method of child training—produces in practical application precisely the opposite effect of the one intended.

The attitude of most parents toward bad habits in their child—nail-biting, nose-picking, untidiness, and the like—is displayed in a miscellany of admonishments, reproaches, promises, and threats; yet these are exactly the very forces that might be brought to bear if one wished to *inculcate* such habits in the child. Suppose that someone were to ask the best means of *teaching* a child to pick his nose. Merely setting him an example would prove inadequate, and persuasion would not always work. But there is one method that would unfailingly give the desired result: wait until the child puts his finger to his nose, then slap him; in a little while his finger will be back again, and now you need only shout at him and forbid him to touch his nose. Repeat this ritual; augment the vehement, impatient tone of your voice by threats and slaps; and in a short while the child will acquire the habit of nose-picking. Now, is this not the very method that parents actually employ? The only difference is that they think it serves to *remove* the fault. They are wholly unaware that their method inevitably leads to the opposite result. *Their* parents subjected them to this treatment, and they uncritically employ the same method on their own children.

When a child's defiance is aroused, he offers resistance. Everyone reacts in the same way. One might suppose that, in the course of time, parents and teachers would have observed this fact and given up these ineffective and harmful methods of training. But we note with amazement that this is far from being the case.

The explanation probably lies in the lack of insight we have had into the varying effects of different educational measures on the child. The immediate, superficial results were the only consequences obvious to us. Parents were in the same situation as physicians of one hundred years ago, who, despite their good intentions, did serious harm to their patients because they did not know the effects of therapeutic measures used. For hundreds of years injuries received in accidents or on the battlefield were dressed with lint made of old linen rags. No one suspected that this treatment caused serious, and often fatal, infections. The Viennese doctor Ignaz Semmelweiss was the first to discover the necessity of aseptic treatment, which effectively prevented the artificial infection of wounds.

Just as physicians were previously unaware that wounds should be treated antiseptically, so today the great majority of parents are ignorant of the fact that a child's psychic wounds—which give rise to naughtiness and disobedience, failure in set tasks, and faults of the most diverse kind—must be handled with discretion, lest they be aggravated. Today the modern "depth" psychology makes possible a rational understanding of the inner life of children and of human beings in general, and for the first time it is possible for us to observe and follow the actions and reactions produced by the various methods of child training. Modern pedagogy tries to open the eyes of parents and teachers to the true nature of the child and his shortcomings in order to put a stop to the application of misdirected and injurious methods of training.

Innovators in pedagogy have a much harder row to hoe than those in medicine. It is true that Semmelweiss was given bitter evidence of the obstinacy of his contemporaries, and received contempt, penury, and an early death as rewards for his contribution to humanity; but in time the clear results of his findings could not fail to win recognition. Psychological discoveries, however, cannot be demonstrated with such clarity and cogency; and yet the effects of certain methods of training are obtrusive enough to be recognized by any objective observer. The chief difficulty is that we are not—and perhaps cannot be—objective in our attitude toward our children. Most doctors refuse to treat members of their own families, but no one can escape the necessity of training his own children.

In Chapter 1, attention was repeatedly called to the difficulties that stand in the way of an objective attitude toward one's own children, and mention was also made of the selfish personal interest on the part of many parents in certain methods of training that are of no benefit to the child. What good is even the clearest understanding if one barricades oneself against it, out of an inner necessity? Of what use is the most flawless proof to one who is unwilling to see it? If you scrutinize yourself, you will see how often you feel compelled to slight your child. A great many fathers and mothers are afraid to acknowledge wholeheartedly their child's accomplishments. This is why they are so reluctant to praise, and if, in a burst of generosity, they do go so far as to express approval, they are sure to append some disparaging afterthought. "You were really nice today. Why can't you be so good all the time?" Good conduct is taken for granted; only the slips and sidesteps are called to notice. Parents refuse to recognize the selfish interest that lies at the bottom of this attitude, and they try to palliate it by claiming that otherwise the child might become conceited.

This selfish interest is plainly brought out whenever the child gets into mischief. Anyone who feels self-assured and confident in his relations with his child will calmly and quietly guide him through the difficulty. But not so the parent who feels unequal to the situation. Perhaps he does not know how to meet the problem properly, or has no time for the child at the moment. Usually he is filled with a dread of unpleasant consequences for the child's subsequent development. This is the moment when the deprecating attitude sets in, generally with a violent attack of criticism. The whole list of disparaging methods comes into play in such situation—from ranting to whipping, with a thousand variations in between: scoldings, reprimands, derision, and the like. This impulsive, emotional type of disparagement is part of the regular stock-in-trade of many parents; it manifests itself in all forms of excessive supervision, nagging, and persistent sharpness and irritability.

The same tendency is present, although less obviously, in the case of parents who systematically apply the technique of disparagement as a deliberate formula in child training. There are mothers and fathers who believe that only with severity, with planned humiliations, or with premeditated thrashings is it possible to rear children. They fail to realize that this policy evinces their desire to get the best of the child—to preserve their own superiority by the use of the most extreme coercive measures. Thus the belittling of the child serves the end of upholding parental authority.

Such treatment inevitably leads to revolt. The authority of parents is designed to teach the child to observe order, but the arbitrary abuse in the exercise of authority incites him to resist it. However much he may seem to submit, inwardly he continues the conflict. *Authority that requires force for its maintenance thereby betrays its intrinsic frailty.*

Draconic Severity

Larry is an only child. His mother died when he was three. His stepmother is a good, capable woman, but neither she nor the father understands the reserve and silent antagonism of the boy. Hence they try to "tame" him; his every lapse from grace is harshly punished. His stepmother has some fault to find with everything he does. In the evenings she gives her husband a detailed account of Larry's conduct; and if he has misbehaved, his father refuses to speak to him for days on end. Larry rarely hears a pleasant, friendly word—for he is sulky and does not "deserve" kindness.

Larry is ostensibly an obedient boy. But nevertheless he affords his parents little satisfaction, for he is not a real participant in the family life. Not only is he uncommunicative; his obstinacy comes to the surface time after time. Now and then a defiant word escapes him; sometimes he fails to come home at the proper time, or he refuses to do a task assigned him; and when he does obey, his reluctance is obvious.

By means of these methods it may be possible to "tame" the child superficially, but such unmitigated severity hampers the development of social interest, the growth of the feeling of belonging. In every case it aggravates a sense of helplessness that already exists in the child, and makes him painfully aware of his weakness and dependence. He does not regard his parents as his friends, and he is no friend of theirs. Inwardly he rebels against them, and misses no opportunity of demonstrating his indifference or ill will. The policy of severity, if systematically pursued, may not allow any open sign of opposition; but the concealed acts of hostility are recognized as such on both sides.

Mortification

Many parents believe that they can wear down the child's resistance by mortifying him, and thus break him of certain faults and bad habits. They may require their child to stand in the corner or kneel on the floor, and even these devices do not satisfy the creative imagination that sometimes is stimulated by a sadistic urge.

Whenever eight-year-old Ellen is "bad," she has to kneel down before her father, recite her offense loudly and clearly, repeat this self-accusation several times, and finally request that she be punished. This—as one can readily imagine—is not an easy rule to enforce; and the act of penance is always preceded by a lengthy prologue of shouts, threats, and blows.

The effect of such mortifications is easy to predict. At best, the child habituates himself to these abasements. He does automatically whatever is expected of him. But the mental processes within a child treated in this fashion are far different from what they seem. Tacit sneers and imprecations accompany his meek words and humble actions. Hence he is reared into sanctimoniousness and hypocrisy. The value of his externally good conduct is highly dubious.

The psychic constitution of such children is seriously affected. Not infrequently they develop neuroses; and experiences of this kind often induce disturbances of the emotional life in the direction of masochism. The child finds it possible to transmute the supposed punishment into a source of enjoyment. The parents may believe that they are causing the child discomfort, but instead they give him sensuous pleasure. Thus the child triumphs at the very moment when, to all appearances, he is most abjectly humbled.

Physical Punishment

Corporal punishment as a systematically applied method of child training is falling more and more into disuse. We are gratified to note this fact. But there are still many who raise their voices in its defense, claiming that through whipping children are forced to the recognition of parental authority and superiority. Especially in the first years of his life—so they say—the child is impervious to reasoning, and hence spanking is the only means of persuading him to conform. Even later, it is claimed, whipping must be employed to avert immediate dangers; there are certain situations in which other methods are considered futile. These arguments refer to *systematic* whipping; parents who deal out blows only under emotional stress, when their "nerves" get the better of them, are sometimes aware of the general undesirability of physical punishment.

Accordingly, we must first consider whether situations actually exist which one cannot handle without slapping. How about the baby? Naturally he cannot be influenced by words, since he is not yet able to understand their meaning. But is this any reason for spanking him? Words, after all, are not indispensable in training; on the contrary, they are often superfluous. Hence their inefficacy in dealing with the baby is of no importance. The more effective method of training—namely, the practice of letting children *experience the logic* of requirements and prescriptions—is quite as applicable in early infancy as it is later on. When the child wants to take hold of something that might do him harm, the object can simply be removed and put out of his reach—whether he cries or not. On other occasions, matters can be so arranged that, without actual danger, the baby may experience the painful potentialities of certain objects. Suppose that the child insists on standing up in his carriage and leaning so far forward that he threatens to tumble out. Scolding is effective for a short while at best. This perhaps is a moment when you may consider a smart slap as essential. But would it not be a much more effective procedure if, with all due precautions, you gently tipped his carriage? The sense of danger that this arouses would cause him to sit down of his own accord. If one such experience is not enough, the child can be exposed to several of a similar nature; and the baby may soon lose his desire to provoke unnecessarily these unpleasant sensations of falling.

Much the same is also true of the older child. Once, in a discussion of the undesirability of corporal punishment, a mother brought up the following case as a counter-argument:

The elder of her two young sons had repeatedly turned on the gas in the kitchen. The danger involved in this practice was explained to him to no avail. A newspaper article was read to him, in which he learned how a terrible explosion had resulted from just such a cause; but still he remained unimpressed. Then finally, when he repeated the trick, his mother gave him a thorough spanking. He never did it again; and several years later he told her that whenever he passed the gas stove he was reminded of the punishment and *suppressed his desire to open the valve.* (Note the continuing desire!)

Is it true that in this case spanking was the sole effective remedy? Certainly not! With only little training one can conceive of a whole series of natural consequences of the boy's careless behavior. For instance, the mother might have announced to both children that only the one who knew the gas should not be turned on would be permitted to go into the kitchen to play as often as he pleased; the other one would have to stay out until he was capable of passing the stove without touching it. Such a measure, if carried out consistently, would probably have quelled the disturbance without further ado. There are many similar methods of teaching the child not to tinker with the gas stove.

From earliest infancy, the child must respect and observe order and must accommodate his desires to this imperative. *But physical punishment is never requisite to this end,* even when the child regards it as deserved. If parents only knew what their child feels and thinks when they strike him, they would recoil in horror and never lay hand on him again. (This is true of the normal, healthy child.) In the moment of chastisement, children who are frequently beaten develop frightening thoughts of hate and fury; even a wish for the death of their tormentor is not at all rare. Can you really believe that any impulse toward good conduct will emerge from such experiences? On the contrary, there is every reason to expect that the child will deteriorate further; and even the most savage blows can have no beneficial effect on his attitude. His inner resistance is not broken, but fortified by whipping.

Distinction must be made between children who are spanked only on rare occasions and those who are frequently or regularly spanked. Children who have never been struck before are so dumbfounded by this experience that it may make a very strong impression on them; thus they may make every effort to avoid a repetition. But they, as a rule, are children who have developed so satisfactorily that physical punishment should seem utterly out of place, especially since even isolated experiences of violence are never wholly without profound psychic shock, often with lasting detrimental effects. The child learns to fear and yield to brute force, and a little of his dignity, courage, and self-reliance is destroyed with each stroke.

However, there are children who obey only when they are whipped. It seems sometimes that they deliberately invite punishment. They exasperate their parents with waywardness and impertinence, and appear to provoke anger almost systematically. Persuasion, warnings, and threats are completely ineffectual; and finally the distraught parents give vent to their irritation through blows. Afterward, the child is like a changed person—affectionate, compliant, and well behaved. Such instances can be observed often; and these obvious results are considered to be proof of the adequacy of corporal punishment. But are the results actually as good as they look? Why does the child respond so favorably to bad treatment?

Some theorists advance a rather bold interpretation when they speak of a so-called "desire for punishment," a sense of guilt that supposedly craves chastisement. It seems to me that matters are really much simpler. In these cases we ordinarily deal with children who feel ignored and rejected. Very often a child begins to be extraordinarily troublesome after the birth of a younger brother or sister. Through mischief or naughtiness he tries to divert to himself the attention of his parents. As long as you are not sufficiently vexed, he feels that he is slighted; and he is not content until you are so disturbed that you disregard all other interests. And if, after an outburst of temper, you repent of your conduct and try to make amends by fondling and kissing the child, is it any wonder that he begins to provoke blows in order to attract attention and perhaps even be favored with shows of affection? He simply acts like the farmer's wife who ran tearfully to the priest with the complaint that her husband no longer loved her since he had not beaten her for two whole weeks. Beatings indicate an intensive concentration on their recipient, and it is this fact that drives many children into their peculiar attitude. Sometimes they even enjoy the power to excite their parents to the high emotional pitch required.

This, however, is not the purpose parents have in mind when they whip their child. They think they are training him; but, without suspecting it, they are deliberately making themselves the tool of his desires. His good behavior after the whipping is the price the child is willing to pay for the fulfillment of his wishes; his provocative naughtiness is part and parcel of his unconscious plan either to get attention or to punish and excite the parent.

Some children may respond differently to beatings. Side by side with the child's rebellion against the parent, a seemingly opposite response may occasionally be observed. Brutality usually excites fear and abhorrence, but sometimes it gives rise to a pronounced attachment or even devotion. To a certain extent we are dealing here with the same disturbances of the emotional life that were mentioned in the preceding section. The child nullifies parental violence by making it a source of sensuous pleasure. Such children, too, will often try to provoke blows.

Frequently, stern parents are especially loved and revered in later years. The adult no longer remembers the disagreeable sensations that he felt as a child whenever he was whipped. He will often assert that he is actually grateful for the blows that he once received. Here we recognize the respect that a child shows to everyone who exercises *power*. Thus the rod-wielding father may readily become a symbol of power; and when he no longer is felt to be a menace—*but only then!*

—his children may love him. They may even imitate him; for the children of such parents are the ones who, when they mature, regard whipping as justifiable and even commend it highly. From them we often hear the statement, "I was whipped when I was a child, and I turned out well enough; so it ought to do my children good, too." Yet it is as true in their case as in any other that whippings leave a profound effect. They merely fail to recognize it. *Every person who was beaten as a child shows the marks of the blows in his character.*

The typical result of the whipping in childhood is either the servile, timorous individual, who usually is at one and the same time cringing and crafty, or the arrogant and objectionably self-assured person. Almost everyone who was beaten in his childhood has a tendency toward brutality. He may become a very capable person; his hardness and harshness may make him particularly well fitted for success in business or some profession. But he is wanting in genuine gentleness, warmth, and the capacity for intimate contacts. It is not that he is incapable of deeper feelings; he simply cannot rid himself of distrust. Basically he may always fear a recurrence of the humiliations and abasements that he experienced as a child, and as a result he is callous and unfeeling.

Mr. F. was a child who received constant whippings. His parents loved him greatly and were indulgent toward him in many respects; but whenever they were at a loss as to what to do—as they often were—they gave him a sound thrashing. Mr. F. is an unusually successful business man, noted for his poise and self-possession. He has an attractive wife, who seems very much in love with him, and handsome children. Actually, Mr. F. has not a single good or close friend. He is more feared than liked, for he is overbearing and refuses to admit anyone as his equal. No one is reliable enough to suit him; no one except himself can possibly understand his business. Through his lack of consideration, which often reaches the point of tactlessness, he offends a great many people who might otherwise have formed a closer acquaintanceship with him.

He tyrannizes his family unmercifully. Only with difficulty has he been restrained from treating his children to the same beatings that he himself had received. But, although he has capitulated on this point, he lays great stress on being regarded in every respect as the lord and master. Everyone must jump when he cracks the whip. He allows his wife no freedom at all, is extremely jealous, and dictates when and where she may go and with whom she may associate. He often takes pleasure in embarrassing her before strangers. Any sign of disagreement or opposition drives him into a tantrum. He storms and shouts and swears, or becomes sarcastic and acrimonious.

We can plainly recognize that behind his seeming superiority lies fear. He safeguards himself against rebuffs, against symbolic blows from everyone with whom he has dealings. Thereby he has made a host of enemies and estranged his wife and children. He neither understands nor wants to understand that people who ostensibly yield to him, actually deceive and trick him whenever possible. He senses, but does not want to admit these facts to himself; terrible will be the awakening when he has to face them. And no less terrible would be the shock if he should ever suffer a reversal in his business—a contingency that he dreads and which often disturbs his sleep. For that would mean the end of the material superiority on which he has built his prestige and his power.

Yet the method of corporal punishment continues to be employed, although its uselessness, absurdity, and downright harmfulness should be apparent to everyone. This mystery finds its explanation in the fact that it is mostly the whipped children who, as parents, advocate the theory that whippings are indispensable. They believe that they are following their good sense when they deal out blows, whereas actually they are following only a strange inner urge. They want to give their child a vivid and drastic demonstration of *their own superiority;* they fear that otherwise they will be unable to subdue his resistance; and they do not realize that the use of brute force plainly betrays an essential weakness that has no other resource at its disposal. Nor do they admit to themselves how much *cowardice* is implicit in such a procedure. If a boy strikes another child who is much smaller and weaker than he, he is regarded as unfair and cowardly. Is there any difference when an adult whips a weak, defenseless child? Since this is neither necessary nor productive of the desired effect, you should seek in your own character the causes of your impulse to strike your child if you ever feel this compulsion. Then you will come to the realization that you have a certain tendency toward violence; that you like to demonstrate your power and superiority; and that, above all, you cannot bear to admit the limitations of your authority. Then, perhaps you will recognize that at the moment when you raise your hand to strike, you feel weak and helpless in relation to the child. This sense of impotence is the source of *your desire to show by any available means which of you is the stronger one, even by bringing into play your physical superiority and brute strength*. So strong is this desire that you may not stop to think whether what you are going to do is beneficial or even fair.

In the attempt to refute these facts you may believe that the child "needs" whippings. Or perhaps you fall back on the old standby, the so-called "weak nerves," that you "lose control of yourself." But in this case, too, the situation is the same. You know that you should *not* beat your child; but, in your helplessness, you may resort to violence despite your sense of wrongdoing, and afterward salve your conscience with the lament of "nerves."

The sense of social solidarity, which is of such importance to the child's satisfactory development, is inseparably bound up with the *inner* acknowledgement of the social order in which he lives; and this sense of social solidarity is never advanced but only retarded by disparagement. The individual who was humbled and repressed as a child is never a real *social* being; he remains a half-tamed animal. Therefore, a method of training which aims to make the child an active member of society must avoid any expedient that tends to suppress and humiliate him.

Chapter 5

Specific Training Situations

V ARIOUS EXTERNAL situations in the child's life pose specific problems. If not handled properly, they may have far-reaching, pernicious effects on his later development and thus become the starting point for subsequent difficulties. Under such circumstance hidden conflicts not infrequently may come into the open with bewildering abruptness.

If you have the proper attitude toward the child and observe the basic principles of conduct, you will have no trouble in determining what to do in each new situation. But it might be well for you to acquire more knowledge of the child's requirements at the successive stages of his growth. Modern mothers prepare themselves for infant care through courses and practial exercises, especially so far as *physical* care is concerned. But care of the baby requires also an understanding of other needs—in regard to his activity, play, and interests, and these needs change with each passing year. To describe them in detail would exceed the scope of this book.[1] In this section we shall touch on the psychological aspect of the problems arising from certain important situations.

[1] We recommend for your careful study, the following books:
Gesell, Arnold. *The First Five Years of Life.* New York: Harper & Brothers, 1940.
Gesell, Arnold and Ilg, Frances L. *The Child from Five to Ten.* New York: Harper & Brothers, 1946.
Spock, Benjamin. *The Common Sense Book of Baby and Child Care.* New York: Duell, Sloan and Pearce, 1945, revised edition, 1957.

Prenatal Adjustment

You (mother and father) are confronted with your first educational task when you expect the baby. Your attitudes and anticipations before his birth establish a relationship long before the child is actually present. At this time you can make all the characteristic parental mistakes discussed in the previous chapter. Fears, overanxiety, excessive expectations, and over-activity are possible and frequent pitfalls. Beware of them! The period of pregnancy should be utilized deliberately to build up your morale, your courage, your self-confidence. It is advisable to study, through books or classes, infant care and child psychology. But be careful of the effects of such studies. If you become discouraged or apprehensive because of the amount of information and advice, you derive no bene-fit from your studies. If you permit yourself to become afraid of your ability to raise your child, you undermine your strength and resourcefulness, on which you will have to rely for adequate functioning.

First Experiences

The first experiences of the infant with the people around him are of greatest importance. Much labor and care are nec-essary to correct his pattern of behavior once he gets wrong impressions and, as a consequence, develops wrong answers. Long before the child can understand words, he responds to his atmosphere and senses human relationships. The mood of other persons is strongly perceived and answered.[2] Anxiety and concern in the parents induce timidity and nervousness in the infant. Calmness and casualness are conducive to quiet and peacefulness in the child. There is no doubt that the vicious circle which disturbs the harmonious relationship between mother and child may be first stimulated by the child. Prema-ture birth, serious illness or disturbance in the development of the infant will understandably upset the mother; but her frame

[2] See Chapter 7, "Crying."

of mind then in turn affects the child and inhibits his adjustment, thereby continually provoking new agitation in the mother. Or the vicious circle may start with upsetting conditions independent of the child, disturbing the mother and consequently affecting the child. Even after the cause of the original difficulty has ceased to exist, the disturbed relationship between mother and child continues to upset both alike. Therefore, you cannot be too careful in maintaining your own emotional equilibrium. That is always true, but it is especially important during the first few weeks and months of the baby's life.

It is understandable that you should try to protect and aid a human being as weak and helpless as an infant. However, the child cannot develop sufficient courage and self-reliance if he experiences from the start the favorable consequences of helplessness. It takes enormous self-restraint to refrain from helping the child in every little predicament, but great is your reward; first, in the child's increasingly successful efforts to gain control over his body and in handling difficult situations, and later in the child's courage and independence. Pity and fear are motivations for wrong actions that will disturb not only the child's development, but what is more important, his relationship to others. Parental ambition and vanity are other causes leading to abuse or oppression of the child.

From his first day of life, the infant is an independent human being who has to fit into the social order of his community. Although he requires help and assistance in certain functions, he is perfectly capable of adjusting himself to life *with his own resources* and he is entitled to this experience.

Nursing

When he is suckled the child has his first adventure in cooperating with another person. The same is true when he is bottle-fed. Hence, from the first day of his life the necessary training for regularity can begin. Once he is used to it, *order will come to be a pleasurable experience.* Regularity of feeding from the beginning has two advantages. It exposes the infant to order and regularity, which is an integral part of social living; regularity in the intake of food is also in accordance with biological order, as all physiological and especially the vegetative functions are characterized by a definite rhythm. The sooner the child can establish a natural rhythm in his functions, the better will be his physical and social development. Periodic elimination can start very early, too, following the rhythm of food intake; but a training in elimination must wait until the child can control his organs for deliberate action. Food intake, on the other hand, does not require the control of an organ. When the child is exposed to regularity, his stomach adjusts itself without any special control.[3]

The establishment of a feeding schedule requires consideration of the needs of each child. You should consult your pediatrician for setting up a proper schedule. A four-hour interval has been found to be the best for the average child. However, if the child is especially frail or sick he may require another timing. As he grows, the schedule may be revised. But at all times you should have a definite plan.

Most of the errors in feeding result from the parent's unwarranted anxiety. Overanxious parents are afraid that the child will not eat enough. They underestimate the strength of a living organism. As long as they do not interfere with the child's appetite, he will take care of himself. If he eats less one time, he will make up the next time. There is no reason for worry if he falls asleep during the feeding. And neither is there a reason to be swayed by his whimpering when he wakes up hungry, or to disrupt the regularity and to feed him ahead of time. If you do give in, you prevent the child from enjoying the benefits of regularity.

However, there is a danger of using a feeding schedule as a new source of anxiety. You should not regard it as a sword hanging over your head all of the time. A few minutes earlier or later make no difference. It is all-important that you be

[3] See Chapter 4, "Spoiling the Child."

quiet and calm when you feed the baby. The infant responds very strongly to tension and anxiety which disturb his vegetative functions. Whether your anxiety is caused by your concern over the temperature of the bottle, the amount or quality of the food which the child takes, or the exact time of the feeding, it makes no difference; your anxiety is more detrimental than any slight deviation from the requirements.

Weaning

Weaning is another difficult problem of child training. If the time for weaning has arrived, you should again follow the planned routine and not allow yourself to be diverted by the child's objection to giving up a comforting habit. Your strength is purely and simply of a passive nature: *Just do not give in.* You can let the baby's hunger work for you without resorting to any coercion or pressure. If you can control your own concern, your anxiety and sympathy, you will remain calm and friendly, but firm. Then the baby will not get the notion that you are more interested in his feeding than he is himself.

As he was accustomed to a purely liquid diet, he may push away in disgust any food in which he detects a solid body. If he is *forced* to take such nourishment, his loathing is only increased. If the child refuses a certain dish, he should not be given a substitute. In this way he eventually will accept food which he at first disliked.

Early Motor Activity

The child has a natural desire to pull himself into an upright position. When he is strong enough, he will sit up of his own accord and later will get up on his feet. You should not try to drive him beyond his ability, and never should you show anxiety. In standing and walking, the child not only learns to use his legs and move about; much more important is it that, through this exercise, he has *his earliest experience in self-reliance.* Giving too much help impedes his learning to walk and hinders the growth of self-reliance.

The child must also learn to fall. When you console him afterward or take him in your arms, you put a premium on tearfulness and self-pity. But by being unimpressed with his lamentations—for, after all, he rarely hurts himself seriously —you can gradually harden him to more severe pain. Children of anxious parents cry easily and often; they try by this means to secure immediate compensation for their hurt.

The self-reliance of the child in drawing himself upright and taking his first steps is respected when he is left wholly to himself in a play-pen. If he is taken by the hand and dragged along, the process is made unnecessarily difficult. He should not have to depend on others when he learns to walk, or else he will be unsure of himself whenever he lacks assistance.

Toilet Training

Toward the middle of the second year the child can be trained to be clean, depending on his development. A good indication for the right time to start is the child's ability to stay dry for two hours. Again, the sense of order grows out of punctuality and system. He will learn the benefits of the toilet if he is put there at regular periods, whether he needs to relieve himself or not. The more casual the procedure, the better. Regardless of what he does, you should never scold and become peevish. Conflict and anger are wholly superfluous. It is not advisable to wake up the child during the night to put him on the toilet. Such procedure induces him to perform his function half asleep. He may appear completely awake, but generally is not.

This procedure should be continued until he asks to be taken to the toilet or goes by himself. If he relapses at a later period in his cleanliness—occasional "accidents" can be overlooked—you should again resume the routine. It is the natural consequence of his disregard of his obligation. But you should always investigate the reason for his relapse, and try to remedy the situation. Perhaps he is jealous of a new baby and tries to be a baby himself. In such a case it often helps to put on diapers if he cannot take care of himself. Whatever you do, whether you put him again on the toilet regularly or use diapers, you should do it always only for one day and give him a chance the next day. But if he again starts to wet his pants, he has to be put on a daily schedule of two-hour intervals which may be increased to hourly intervals if he proves refractory, especially when he is very young. You should not let him stay on the toilet more than a few minutes regardless of whether he urinates or not. This routine must bε maintained, however, with as little talk as possible, to avoid the gratification of attention. Do not say you have no time for such a routine! The training of the baby requires time. If you do not take the necessary time for this task, you will be much more occupied later on, in a more disagreeable and upsetting way.

First Independence

The pitfalls of early training are your anxiety and indulgence. Be especially careful from the very beginning not to become the victim of your natural inclination to spoil the baby! Watch out for and sense his attempts to gain undue attention and to put you into his service and fortify yourself to resist his schemes. His crying and exaggerated helplessness are his weapons. You can learn to distinguish between the various forms of crying and whimpering—whether they indicate actual needs, pains, or discomfort, or whether they are merely attention-getting devices. We are all inclined to underrate the baby's ability to take care of himself in difficult situations. If he hurts himself, he does not need your sympathy and consolation, but a word of encouragement to go on. This may sound like cruel advice; but your comfort at the time is even more cruel as it makes his pains worse, when he learns that through suffering he can receive attention and affection.

It is natural for a child to cry—that is his way of informing you that he wants something from you—but your assistance is timely only when he really needs help. It is amazing to what extent children can learn muscular control, how well they can overcome physical obstacles—even during the first year of life—if left to themselves, if you permit them to find their own solutions. What they need most is stimulation, not protection. If they discover that crying will not bring them help, they will look for more adequate solutions and learn to take care of themselves, and, what is most important, they will suffer less and be happier.

Karen was eight months old when I watched her become all tangled up in her play-pen, both legs protruding from the bars and her body twisted. She could not extricate herself. Mother sat nearby. Instead of helping her, she said in a calm voice, "You can get yourself out by yourself—go on, Karen." The baby certainly did not understand the words; but she got the meaning. She stopped crying, and soon her legs were freed and she showed a definite expression of accomplishment.

The following episode occurred when Karen was fifteen months old. She liked to climb chairs and had just learned to slide down safely. Presently she began to practice climbing and getting down. During this practice she became so excited and exuberant that suddenly she jumped from the chair and fell flat on her face. She was bleeding from her nose and crying frantically. Her mother picked her up calmly, led her quietly back to the chair, and said, "Now try it again, Karen." Hesitantly the child climbed up again, still whimpering. "Now go down again." The child was frightened, although no longer crying, and held out her hand to get help. Mother said reassuringly, "You can do it by yourself, Karen." And down she went, carefully sliding down. Again mother suggested that she climb the chair; and this time the child went down quickly, no longer showing any fear. Her little face was swollen for a few days, but no psychological scars were left after the accident—scars which otherwise would have remained for a long time, affecting not only the courage and the sense of security of the child, but the whole relationship with the mother and other potential helpers.

The sooner a child learns to rely on his own strength and abilities the deeper his sense of security, the greater his comfort.

Living in the World of Grown-ups

It may be considered "unnatural" for a child to live in a world designed for grown-ups who are giants in the eyes of the child. But this is reality, and we have to face it. We can understand the efforts of Montessori and others to scale a world to the size of the child for the purpose of helping him to function efficiently. But while an overprotected and discouraged child may need such arrangements to gain courage, self-reliance, and independence, it is more advisable to let the child develop these qualities within our adult environment in which he must live anyhow. For the same reason, it is inadvisable to confine children to their own rooms, arranged for their needs and away from those rooms where they could do damage. They must learn to behave properly wherever they are— whether in living room or in kitchen.

Many parents are puzzled about how to achieve this. Can one explain to a baby what he may touch and what he may not—what objects are breakable or even dangerous? It is true the baby may not understand words and complicated sentences. But he does understand meaning and can register experiences. "Now then," you may ask, "is not this the occasion when you must slap the baby's hand when he touches what he should not?" Certainly not. There is no need even to speak in a harsh voice, threatening with "no, no." One can calmly make the child understand what he is not supposed to do by taking him away. Little babies have no difficulty in finding out what is wrong for them to do. It is not their lack of knowledge which makes them destructive. On the contrary, they behave in this manner because they know that such conduct is forbidden. And most parents have trained them systematically though unwittingly to do the wrong things. Watch all the excitement and commotion which a little baby can cause by breaking something. He literally gets a "bang" out of it. Why then, should he deprive himself of a repetition of such an enjoyable experience?

The first time the infant throws down an object is the time to watch yourself. You may be inclined to pick it up. Such early experiences are dangerous. You may think that the child does not notice what is going on. He notices it, but you do not. You may consider it "cute" when he pulls the curtain down or empties your drawer. After all, it may be the first evidence of his muscular strength and you may heartily enjoy it as such. How can the child realize that a few months later you will get furious at similar activities? But what should you do? Simple enough: when he touches something he should not touch, when he pulls or throws objects, you just calmly put him in his play-pen, accompanying your action with soft words expressing your regret. Very soon he will find out which acts deprive him of your company. Children are too intelligent not to draw the right conclusion. He must accept the requirements of the surroundings; otherwise he cannot have freedom to roam around. But when he is removed, he should get a new chance immediately when he is ready. (When he is so small that he cannot express his readiness, you can give him this new chance in a short while.) This kind of training does not require spanking, harsh words, or violence. It is a quiet expression of a necessary order. A well-trained child can adjust himself to the objects around your house without danger to himself or to the objects.

Throwing things may require some consideration. It is "normal" for a child to throw things down while seated on a highchair, on your lap, or in his crib or buggy. It suffices in such instances not to retrieve the object, but either to ignore his action entirely or simply to remove the object.

The child recognizes danger naturally and automatically by observation and experience. However, it is necessary to train the child systematically to become aware of certain dangers which are too harmful to be realized through haphazard experience. For instance, handling sharp objects, running into the street, lighting matches, touching hot objects, or similar actions require a special training. It is not sufficient just to remove the child or the object. You can and must take the time to experiment with the child until he understands the dangers involved. Words, explanations, and preaching are insufficient and even detrimental when they imply prohibition. The child needs practical demonstrations. You can take a knife or scissors and show the child how it hurts. You can show him your bleeding finger and express your pains when you have cut yourself accidentally. When you invite the child to touch a hot stove under your supervision he will remember and learn his lesson. The effects of a lighted match can be learned in the same manner. You can teach him not to run into the street by himself, by training him how to act on the street. Permit the child to walk with you without holding hands until you come to the curb. Then you take his hand while crossing, explaining that crossing the street is done in that way. You may take time to repeat this experience as a game until the child accepts the procedure.

Play

Play is the child's proper occupation. Whatever he does, whatever he learns is a game for him. But this play is a serious matter. His whole development, his mastery of himself and the world, are dependent upon it. In children's play, repetition is not a purposeless quest after pleasure, but the process of training, necessary to self-education. If a child does not have time and opportunity for play (in keeping with his age), his development will suffer.

The child's play is at first *function play*. He acquaints himself with his body and the use of his various limbs, but soon he learns to know the objects about him and embraces the world with the revelations of his sense organs. Later on, his play becomes work play. With building-blocks, dolls, colored balls and cubes, or other toys, he creates something new. Through *work play* he learns little by little that he must subject himself to certain rules before he can produce anything. He acquires a sense of duty toward self-chosen objectives.

In *group play* he is trained to adjust himself to the rules of the community. In the latter category belong the early simple games with his mother, in which he first experiences the nature and importance of a person other than himself. From work play grows work itself, when the delight in sheer activity changes into the satisfaction of achievement.

The one important principle to observe is that the child must have abundant opportunity for undisturbed play, that he be allowed to follow his own inclinations, and that he be given serious recognition for his achievements. His toys should be as simple as possible, so that his fantasy may be stimulated and have room to unfold. The more primitive the object with which he plays, the more suitable it is, especially in early childhood.

Extremely pampered children cannot play, either alone or in company. Some children are unable to accommodate themselves to group play; they can play only by themselves. Hence, by observing a child's play, you can keep check on a great many disturbances in his development that you should promptly attempt to remedy.

It is absolutely necessary for the maintenance of a proper relationship between parents and child that the parents spend some time playing with him. Reading to him or taking him for. a walk is not sufficient. True enough, on such occasions you can feel close to the child, but there is not enough mutual participation, no give-and-take, unless you really play with the child. Unfortunately, many parents are not prepared to play; they just don't know how. As a consequence they do not find time for it, or they fail to realize how important such play activities are. They have more than enough to do to keep the children fed, clothed, clean, and out of mischief. If all this is accomplished they want to rest. Many parents, especially fathers, are not interested in playing with children. They are bored if the child asks them to play with him. And if they find interest in a toy, they play for themselves, relegating the child to the position of a spectator or of a servant who has to stand by when they need something. Any prospective parent should learn to play with little folks as an important preparation for parenthood.[4]

Playing with his parents is extremely important to the child. Only those people have influence over him who can arrange pleasant activities with him. In your playtime you establish your relationship, maintain your influence, and prepare orderly cooperation. During playtime you can observe the child, direct him toward taking on responsibility and contributing to a common goal, teach him to take part actively in common endeavors, and to become a good sport and a good loser. Especially if you have several children, playing with all of them together is obligatory. In such pleasant, organized activity they can learn to regard each other as friends instead of competitors. Their feeling of belonging together is best stimulated through common play activities in which each member of the family participates.

Dressing

The functions that the child must undertake become progressively more complicated. They will be learned more easily if you encourage self-reliance and exert less pressure and compulsion. All the child's pursuits are by nature pure play. You can make use of his play instinct until he is far into school age. If his duty is presented as play, he will take real pleasure in his tasks. The reason why the idea of duty is so repugnant to many people is that during their training all the enjoyment was taken out of their work. The simple word "must" is often sufficient to make the most pleasant occupation distasteful.

The child will make a game out of learning to dress himself if this achievement is presented as enjoyable. He will enter into your plans with enthusiasm when you propose the amusing

[4] The following books may be helpful in acquainting yourself with games which you could enjoy with your children: *How to Play with Your Child* by Ruth Zechlin, and *Two to Six* by Rose Alshuler. The National Recreation Association, 315 Fourth Avenue, New York, N. Y., has published various pamphlets on the subject, for which you may send.

game of pulling stockings on and off, or putting on shoes and tying the laces. (This "game," naturally, is no less serious than the other forms of children's play.) And if after a time he is given *permission* to try dressing himself completely, he will set about the task with vim and may even reject offers of help when he runs into difficulties. Of course the game is at an end when you begin to exert pressure or find fault with his clumsiness. If you take a special delight in dressing him and treating him generally like a doll, he will never learn to dress himself, even when you finally decide that it is time for him to do so alone. And if, to cap the climax, you begin a conflict, the line of healthy development will be definitely broken. Through awkwardness and slowness the child can force you to help him incessantly, and his own abilities are superseded by his power over you.

Speaking

It is a great mistake to talk baby talk with the child. You should avoid using only those words that he already understands and you should not imitate the baby's pronunciation. In addition, you should make no special effort to understand him when he speaks indistinctly. If you make it too easy for the child to make himself understood, he will have no reason to enunciate clearly. Perhaps you even pride yourself on the fact that only you can interpret his utterances. In this case, your pride hinders him from speaking properly.

If you want to help him, you must speak slowly and carefully yourself, and he will learn to form his sounds correctly. You need not hesitate to use more difficult words but you should *not* correct his faulty efforts to reproduce them. When he speaks indistinctly, you should not criticize or scold. The only successful method of correcting him is your reluctance to understand what he means.

Washing

Quite similar is the development of physical cleanliness. Why do boys tend to run around with dirty hands and faces more often than girls? This is not due altogether to the girls' "natural feminine instinct" for primping and making an attractive appearance, but to the fact that boys are more pampered by their mothers. They sometimes consider it a requirement of masculinity to abhor cleanliness and tidiness, and regard washing, brushing the hair, and cleaning themselves as equivalent to being a sissy.

Thus, while the boy may express his superiority by refusing your demands to wash himself, he on the other hand may be very well pleased to convert the washing process into a personal service which you have to furnish. A dirty neck and dirty ears are, therefore, either an expression of defiance or a plea for attention.

Washing, too, can be made a pleasant game. But coercion spoils the sport and readily leads to one of the two extremes—self-neglect or overfastidiousness. The natural consequence of untidiness is the refusal to associate with a dirty child, either at meals or at play.

Eating Habits

Mealtime is more than just eating. It is one of the few occasions where the whole family is together, occupied with a common activity. The atmosphere around the table and the orderliness or disorder during the meal reveal the whole structure of a particular family. As soon as the child can feed himself he should eat with the others, thereby becoming a full-fledged member of the family. As long as he must be fed he can sit in his highchair at the table, but should have his meals separately, as any preferential or differentiating treatment of one member disturbs the whole family relationship.

You, as parents, are responsible not only for the atmosphere but also for the maintenance of order during mealtime. This is the time when the child gets an impression about what you think and how you feel. Pleasant conversation is part of good eating habits.

Order requires that each member eat in the manner prevailing in the community. It is also part of proper eating habits that the child learn to eat everything. Otherwise it is impossible to maintain a balanced diet.

No child should get away with any infringement of the order. If he does not behave properly, he cannot eat with the others. (Do not threaten, but act when the order is badly disrupted.) Next time he may join the family group again. If he does not come to the table on time, there is no place for him after the others have started and he misses his meal. (The rigid observance of these suggestions is only necessary when you notice a laxity in the behavior of your child. A harmonious family may not need natural consequences to maintain the cooperation of each member.)

The following principle should, however, be rigidly observed, otherwise you are headed for trouble: whether a child eats or not is his own affair. No one has the right to coax, advise, reprimand, or threaten. On the other hand, if he does not eat properly, plays with the food, or dawdles and has not finished his plate with the others, nobody should wait for him and his plate should be taken away. It is only natural that a person who does not feel well enough to finish his plate should not get anything else served at the meal. (Naturally, you make allowances for the taste of your children. They can have a second helping or a smaller helping.) No word should be spoken about eating, no attention be paid to a slow or poor eater who must experience the consequences without previous warning and exhortation at the moment.

Helping about the House

Children should be drawn at an early age into active participation in domestic life. This promotes their social interest and their capacity for cooperation. Moreover, it strengthens their self-assurance and starts them on the way toward useful accomplishment. The child's willingness to collaborate is easily secured by presenting his tasks in the light of play. Also he can be easily managed by appealing to his ambition and pride. He feels big and grown up when he is *allowed* to help, and proud of what he can already do. Small, recurrent duties, commissions, and errands of every sort offer abundant opportunity for usefulness. But if you make brusque and impatient demands for his help, you arouse an antipathy toward work. It is also a mistake to use promises or threats, rewards or punishments in the effort to get him to perform a task. This makes the work itself merely a disagreeable adjunct, the reward or the avoidance of punishment becoming the real issue.

The child acquires the right outlook only when his collaboration is an end and a satisfaction in itself. This is the same attitude that a child takes toward play. Only under this condition is he prepared to assume his tasks willingly and gladly, even when they are unpleasant or difficult. The development of such preparedness is of the greatest importance to the child's subsequent progress, to his success and happiness in life.

"Dethroning" the Child

One of the most difficult situations for both child and parent results from the birth of a younger child. In the lives of a great many people this is an event of the gravest importance —an occurrence that has influenced their whole development and molded their characters. Up to this point the child has been the youngest of the family, or an only child. Now he sees himself ousted from his position. The detachment from the loving and attentive mother takes place suddenly, and the unkindest cut of all is that it is brought about by a strange intruder. Frequently, therefore, the hostility toward a new baby is very pronounced. The indignation of the older child has been depicted humorously in numerous poems, stories, and cartoons.

But often the situation is far from amusing. The child may advise that the baby be given back to the stork, or suggest in all seriousness that it be tossed out the window or thrown into the furnace. And it is not uncommon for him to pass from words to actions. You may sometimes have to protect the infant from the attempted violence of the older child. Occasionally the attempt is hidden behind a pretext of awkwardness; but when we hear that he has spilled the baby out of his carriage or let him fall off the table, we have a pretty fair indication of the hostility felt by the "dethroned" older child.

In this moment he needs particular consideration. It would be absurd to become indignant at the brutality and crudity of his statements and actions. He has no conception of death, and his feelings toward the baby are those toward an inanimate object, a toy perhaps. It is true that his attitude betrays an objectionable tendency to occupy the limelight, but the blame for this rests with the parents and their pampering. Hence you should not hold him too strictly responsible. You must now realize that every sharp reproof only increases his sense of neglect and thus intensifies his active resistance.

He may try by the most devious means to regain the attention that he fears is lost. In this situation many children are deliberately troublesome and naughty or in some way deficient. Accordingly, you must take special pains not to respond to their intentions. Only too often you may be provoked into using drastic measures that may permanently alienate your older child.

There is only one way to help him out of his predicament. You can point out the advantages of his superior age and win him as a partner in the care of the younger child. This can be done by emphasizing his valuable insight, judgment, and strength. He can be shown convincingly that the mere curtailment of the time that you can now devote to him does not imply any reduction of your love. In this situation you, the father, may perhaps be able to give more attention to the older child. You, the mother, naturally, are occupied with the younger; but if you observe the principle of allowing the baby as much rest as possible, you will have plenty of time for the other child. In no event, however, should you attempt to deal with the annoying, provocative methods that he employs to attract your interest. You can afford to overlook these, toler-

antly and understandingly, if you pay attention to him outside of the sphere of conflict. You should make special efforts
to arrange for pleasant experiences and common activities
with the dethroned child.

In your effort to give each child his due, you may be constantly tempted to equalize the rights of the rival children. You
wish to do justice to both; but this sometimes leads to a peculiar form of competition. I have seen a case where a mother
actually had to weigh chocolate and fruit so that neither child
would receive more or less than the other. The result was
that the mother became the children's slave. If you want to
treat both children fairly, you cannot allow bickering as to
who gets more than the other. It is not important; and neither
of the children will care if "getting less" does not imply "having less value."

Peaceful cooperation between the two children presupposes an abatement of the jealousy which causes one to be
constantly on the alert for signs of favoritism. Jealousy is
a trait that can never be wholly eliminated from anyone's
personality. But children are jealous only when they feel
neglected. Some parents have a fatal gift for making *all* their
children feel slighted. They make a point of putting each
child in the wrong and playing them off, one against another.
This policy sharpens the rivalry among them. It is a result of
the oft-discussed tendency to educate by humiliating. You can
make each child feel that you love him and that it does not
detract from his personal worth if a brother or sister happens
to be able to do certain things better than he. Given the proper
recognition of his individual abilities and attainments, he will
not find it necessary always to be measuring himself by another's standards.

There is no denying the difficulty of striking a balance between two children. This is the heaviest burden imposed on
parents by the two-children pattern. The child who fails is
either the one against whom the parents have for some reason
acquired a bias, often because they failed to understand the

struggle arising from his sense of neglect, or the one who is more pampered and, as a result, discouraged. When one child loses courage and gives up, the development of the other child is also jeopardized. The apparent proficiency and excellence of the one are too often built on the victory over his competitor. If later in life the successful child fails to rise with equal ease above his adversaries, or if, through some stimulating influences, the other child eventually becomes more successful, the whole structure of capability and decorum collapses and the fear-generated conflict which even the seeming victor secretly wages is brought out into the open. In order not to provoke this situation, be very careful not to compare one child with the other. Your belief that this may stimulate the failing child is completely mistaken; it invites only hopelessness and discouragement on his part, leading to the relinquishing of every effort to compete, and it endangers the victor, who becomes convinced that he, too, will be lost if he ever stops excelling.

The frequent fights and quarrels growing out of competition and the desire to be superior can be arrested only if you carefully avoid taking sides with either child. It is unimportant who starts the fight and who is right or wrong. A great deal of the conflict between children is directed toward securing your attention. Your attitude should be that regardless of who is right or wrong, the children must learn to get along with each other. If they are noisy or disturbing, *both* should be sent out until they have finished their quarrel. It is dangerous and completely futile to interfere with their struggles and fights; interference only prolongs and incites them. If one child appears with a complaint, he must be told that it is too bad that he cannot live in peace with his brother or sister. After all, each story has two sides! And the culprit of today may only be trying to avenge his injury of yesterday. Any misbehavior or disturbance of one child should be thrown into the lap of the whole group of children. They must learn to take care of each other.

The feeling of belonging together and the mutual cooperation between competing children can be stimulated best if you arrange many common and pleasant activities, by playing with them, taking excursions, sharing exciting experiences together. During these activities, any scolding of one child must be carefully avoided. If one child misbehaves, you should withdraw completely from both. That will help to make the children aware that they depend upon each other for their fun and pleasure. Only this awareness will bring them together in mutual respect and consideration.

The Child's First Society

In preparation for the timely and gradual loosening of the ties between mother and child, the child should join the company of other children at the earliest possible age, that is, after his third year. In other words, he should attend nursery school and kindergarten. The necessity for this type of group activity and the problems connected with it were discussed in some detail in Chapter 3. Here we shall make only brief mention of some problems arising from the child's entrance into nursery school.

The spoiled, timid child who is greatly attached to his mother, may offer strong resistance to the society of other children. He fails to find among them the indulgence and solicitude that he has come to expect. He may use a variety of methods to avoid going to kindergarten. He whimpers and cries, and perhaps even develops nervous troubles. The purpose of his behavior is obvious. If a mother lets herself be deceived she not only obstructs his adjustment to the group, but also sets a dangerous precedent when he sees that nervous disorders and complaints can get him somewhere—that they can help him evade unpleasant situations. These children try to undermine their parents' resolution by creating a reaction of anxiety. They scream in the night, and may suddenly begin to cry without motivation. They are afraid of the "bad" children and complain of the latter's aggressiveness, in an effort to prejudice the parents against the group. And, simultaneously, their own peculiar conduct arouses the ill will of the other children. If you sympathize with the child and intercede for him, or go to the extreme of withdrawing him from kindergarten, he will never learn how to get along with people. You had better be firm when the child tries to shirk the society of other children. You must suppress your own anxiety and your pity. Kindly persistence without harshness, but also without excitement and fuss, generally helps to overcome the child's resistance within a few days.

Starting School

In earlier times the first day at grade school was a most momentous experience of childhood. Today its impact is somewhat mitigated by the prevalence of pre-school programs in kindergartens and nursery schools, and, in many countries, by the blending of work and play in the first grades. Nevertheless, school still represents an entirely novel situation for the child. He can win recognition only by his achievements. His society is no longer a play group, but a work group.

You should endeavor to give the child the right preparation for school. He must be capable of working. Negligence or spoiling retards the child's intellectual growth. He may be unable to speak correctly or in other ways be inadequately prepared for school. Teaching the child to read and do simple sums before he is of school age is no advantage to him, and only lessens his interest in reading and arithmetic when he enters school. He is denied the satisfaction of progress and growth if he knows his letters and figures in advance. It is much more important that he be able to dress and wash himself, and overcome difficulties without assistance. But these are the very qualities that are so often neglected by parents.

Also it is an essential part of self-reliance that the child learn to cross streets by himself and watch out for traffic. It does not help his position among his schoolmates to be escorted to and from school for too long a period. He gets the reputation of being a "mother's boy" and usually is ashamed of such attentions.

It is a serious mistake to assist the child with his lessons. The supposed assistance is generally a trial and a deterrent to the child, for your anxiety may make you irritable and impatient. You may discourage the child even further, and stir up more opposition. You should leave the child's progress to his teacher, and give him a helping hand only rarely, when he asks for some information. If you do work with him, you should never lose your composure, or you will make learning a torment and incite resistance that may render him permanently unfit to acquire formal knowledge. For this reason it is questionable whether teachers should ever ask parents to supervise the homework of their children. A child who has bad working habits and fails in school or refuses to do his work reveals thereby that he has been improperly handled by his parents. As they have not been able to manage him adequately before, how can one expect them to help him now to acquire better working habits?

Actually such suggestions generally indicate an attempt to shift responsibility, teachers and parents blaming each other for the resistance of the child. Teachers should realize their own inadequacy if they cannot sell their merchandise to the children. Many teachers could learn a great deal of practical psychology from salespeople who are not permitted to blame the customer if he shows sales resistance. Inadequate supervision on the part of parents is certainly deplorable; but the supervision should not extend to the work which a child has to do for school.

It is wrong to keep the child out of school after he has reached school age, for the importance of school does not lie solely in the information that he accumulates. A good tutor could impart this knowledge equally well. The really valuable element that no tutor can supply is the *joint work in the society of other children.* The child learns to adapt himself to a group and to a rigid order of functions. Accordingly, his difficulties are multiplied if he does not enter school until the second or even the third grade; he is likely to become stand-offish, a "queer duck" who finds it hard to make friends and never feels at home in a crowd.

Temporary Illnesses

All children pass through a series of illnesses and all parents are anxious to guard them against these normal eventualities. However, much greater than any physical dangers are the emotional consequences of serious or repeated illnesses. The child may, for example, get the impression that mother loves him more when he is sick than when he is well. His will to be well may be impaired if he gets such mistaken notions, especially when, into the bargain, his sickness exempts him from disagreeable duties, from going to school perhaps, or assuming responsibilities at home. After recovery, children often try to retain the privileges that they enjoyed during their illness. They cause difficulties at mealtimes, complain of the slightest malaise, and may finally turn into hypochondriacs. It is a well-known fact that pampered children maintain the characteristics of whooping cough much longer than children who are not interested in being sick.

During an illness the child needs special care, but a certain order must be observed even for the duration of the disease. One should not humor him too much. He should not get too much attention or unusual demonstrations of affection; not too many gifts or the satisfaction of all his whims. Your sympathy for him is understandable; but you certainly do not want to add to his temporary physical suffering a lasting maladjustment such as a refusal to live his later life without equal pampering. If you make illness too simple or pleasant, he may come to regard it as a desirable state (and we know how easily one can get sick if one wants to).

Adversities

It is, of course, impossible to list all the occurrences that may prove injurious to the child. Illnesses represent one type. But there are many other events that make him a special object of compassion: the death of one or both of his parents, family misfortunes of various sorts, sudden impoverishment, etc. The danger of such situations may be many times increased through extreme indulgence and sympathy. The child may need help, certainly; but friends and relatives should be careful lest their good intentions hamper his development. He must learn to surmount difficulties through his own resources. Assistance will be much more valuable if it induces him to find the right way of his own accord than if it merely smooths the way for him externally. Pity can be extremely harmful.

Changes in the External Situation

Another type of potentially harmful experience is analogous to the situation at the birth of a younger brother or sister: a change of residence, of school, or even of teachers. If the child feels incapable of adjusting himself to an alteration in his circumstances he gives up trying. His failure to re-acclimate himself indicates that he is badly discouraged and that his previous scheme of action no longer fits. He then needs your assistance, not pressure. You must try to discover wherein his difficulty really lies, and you will find that the new turn of events has brought into the open certain defects in his previous life plan. Your attention should now be devoted to these defects, not to his present discomfort. You must not be blinded by the external provocation. The fault lies deeper. Perhaps the child has played first fiddle up to now and no longer finds it easy to maintain his old status; he may have been too much indulged and be unused to opposition. He may previously have been relieved of all responsibilities and decisions, and now is suddenly thrown on his own resources. Decisive changes in the external situation act, therefore, as a touchstone of the child's ability to adapt himself to the needs of social living. Hence the resultant difficulties should provide an occasion for amending the defects in the child's earlier preparation for life.

In the case of smaller children in particular, a change in external circumstances can be used as an opportunity for establishing better conditions for the child's development. The very necessity of adjusting himself to a new environment makes the child more amenable to a change in order and requirement. This is especially important for the acquisition of new habits. Hence it is quite possible to establish a new order from the outset especially when faulty methods of training or the child's resistance have previously prevented the maintenance of order. Under new conditions you will find it easier to correct the results of earlier pampering or to improve the child's attitude toward you and toward other children.

In short, here is a chance to create a new and more advantageous setting for the whole process of training. You must see to it, however, that from the first day the new regime is enforced with absolute consistency. This cannot be done through conflict, of course. The new order must be distinguished from the old by finding better forms of cooperation to replace the old combative methods. In a new situation you have an opportunity to gain the interest of the child and to win him over, since he feels a greater need of friendship and intimacy. If you set the stage by not indulging and giving in, the child may follow suit and fit into the order which you establish by your own behavior.

Mishaps

Significant for the child is his inclination to be discouraged through reversals, whether at home, among playmates, or elsewhere. He must learn to live with his failures. If you, his parents, are unable to bear his misadventures, your excitement will discourage him rather than help him. When you scold and become angry, he takes the reversal as an indication of further and more serious failures. Whoever throws up the sponge because of one reversal is faultily prepared to cope with the normal difficulties of life. He should, instead, respond with a redoubling of his efforts and a concentration of all his energies. Failure can, therefore, become a valuable incentive to new achievements. Hence, your reproaches, aspersions, or expressions of despair may dangerously weaken the child's power of resistance. But it would, of course, be equally wrong to make the situation too easy for him—to comfort him unreasonably or even relieve him of the consequences. This is what many parents are inclined to do when, for instance, they take the child out of kindergarten if he does not get along well. They may even console him with presents or special treats. This is no way to teach him to bear up under adversity. He must learn to fight his own battles. The part which you have to play is to fortify his courage and self-confidence. You can do this most easily by expressing an unshakable belief in him and giving convincing proof of your genuine interest and friendship. "Next time you will do better!" But first you must actually have faith in the child—for this faith is the inexhaustible source from which he can draw strength, even when he meets with rebuffs that might otherwise sap his courage.

Family Strife

Unfortunate environmental conditions may make training especially difficult. They may cause despair in parents who in other respects are admirably suited for their task, but are thus rendered incapable of giving their child the support and guidance that he needs.

One can well sympathize with you, the mother, when your husband, your mother, your in-law, or some other dear relative continually interferes in the rearing of your child, interposing on all occasions and finding fault with everything you do. Although such a person exercises an obviously unfavorable influence through spoiling or harshness, nagging or inconsistency, he may be utterly impervious to reasoning. The one thing that you should *not* do is allow yourself to be led astray by others' conduct. You cannot hope to balance or mitigate the mistakes that others make by doing the opposite. This would only increase the damage already done, adding your mistakes to theirs. You, at least, can be a constant factor in the child's life—an element of complete reliability. If you maintain this status, he may even learn to tolerate extraneous influences without being harmed. Naturally, your position is not easy when, through great indulgence and copious bribes, some other person tries to alienate the child from you. Adverse influences put your courage and reliability to a test. If you avoid discouragement you will find still better means of winning the child back—through friendliness, playing and talking together, storytelling, stimulating the child's abilities, and recognizing his accomplishments. In the long run, the proper attitude toward the child will always prevail over the pseudosuccesses achieved through indulgence or bribery.

There is a great temptation to employ the child as an ally against other adults, especially when the others try to use him in that manner. When you play this game you forfeit your objectivity toward the child, and soon become a ready tool in his hands. What is most important, you become indiscriminate in censure and praise, lose the right perspective in your expectations and moods, and appreciably unbalance the human relationship between the child and yourself. Your attitude toward the child should remain untouched by the conflict and strife, competition and spite that may exist among you and other members of the family. Only then are you in a position to rear the child properly and exert a beneficial influence on his development. This you *can* do, no matter how many dangers and detriments may threaten from other quarters.

The same is true of other handicaps arising from the child's environment—undesirable living conditions, poverty, lack of time on your part, sickness or other calamities. Your duty can be only this: to do the best you can for the child in a given situation. The worse the situation, the more necessary is your adequacy. If you yourself become embittered and despondent, the child will lack your help. Your defiance and rebellion, your animosity and your quest for scapegoats may be very understandable; but for the child they mean an aggravation of the external circumstances—an increased burden which, after all, might well be spared him. If you back him up, which cannot be done by indulgence, the external distress and oppression may perhaps serve as an impetus to extraordinary achievements, to a concentration of all his powers. Through your understanding and your ability to give courage and self-confidence, you can help him open the way to a better future.

We can hardly ask that all members of the household, relatives and servants, have pedagogical ability, but nevertheless their influence as educators should not be underrated. What can and should be expected of them is a quiet, friendly attitude, the avoidance of coarse or indecent language, and the observance of the proper forms of conduct. In his own home the child has his first experience with social living, and consequently his relations with the various members of the household are significant factors in his development. However, if the persons around the child do not behave properly, you should concentrate—not on changing them—but on doing the best *you* can.

"Silent Partners"

Great is the number of persons (apart from those already mentioned) who may exert some influence on the child's behavior and who may be called the "silent partners" in education. Among them are all the friends of the family and occasional visitors, the grocer and deliveryman, the neighbors and the child's playmates, and later the writers and actors who make lasting impressions on him through the media of books, theatre, radio, and movies. It is impossible and unnecessary to censor all these influences. You cannot prevent a child from seeing and hearing things which are not good for him. The only adequate method of preventing damage is by increasing his resistance to wrong influences. You can, by watching the child, recognize the influences to which he is exposed. You can moderate the less wholesome and encourage the more beneficial. This is not done by merely forbidding. Experience proves that forbidden fruits are the sweetest, and curbing increases curiosity. You can maintain your own influence only by winning the child to your point of view. The child is eager and willing to listen if you discuss the problems with him intelligently and reasonably. The child, like any human being, dislikes being told what is good and what is bad for him. Preaching and moralizing shut his ears.

It is one of the most distinguished functions of parents to give their child moral values, to help him to discriminate between good and bad, so that he may find his way in a world made up of both. Wrong attitudes of neighborhood children or the dreaded influence of the radio with its horror stories, of certain comic books and other trash, could be regarded not as a danger and annoyance but as a welcome opportunity for interesting and friendly discussions to convey a wholesome point of view to the child. If, instead of turning off the radio when the horror story begins, you would listen with the child, explaining how the various noises are produced and how unthinking people are induced to fear and excitement, the child will learn to find these programs just as silly as an intelligent adult does. If the children in the neighborhood swear and Johnny comes home proudly displaying his newly acquired knowledge, you might discuss with him why the children swear. It is not enough to point out with disgust how "bad" these words are. The child knows that, anyhow; that is why he uses them. But he can discover that he does not need to resort to these means to make an impression, to feel big and important. He might even gain a new kind of strength in refusing to behave like the unfortunate boys on the street who may not have other opportunities to get attention and recognition. A sheltered child who is prevented from experiencing such challenges and dangers is likely to face real life as a defenseless stranger.

Sexual Enlightenment

You may feel embarrassed and helpless when your child shows interest in the sexual functions. You reveal thereby your own apprehension about sexual problems. This is in part the result of your parents' inhibitions regarding sexual enlightenment. Here, again, we can see the persistence of false attitudes and methods in education through generations.

This is not the place to go into the deeper, social causes of bashfulness in regard to sex. Our objection to prudery should not be viewed as an encouragement of shamelessness. But one must realize that parents' false modesty regarding the natural processes is often a serious drawback to the development of the child's emotions and may actually impair his later love-life. Moreover, it leads with logical certainty to a break in the child's confidence in his parents. If you are incapable of giving simple and natural answers to your child's natural and ingenuous questions, sex becomes a mysterious, forbidden, and dreadful secret. But that is not all. To satisfy his curiosity the child will appeal to other, often highly dubious sources of information. In any case, he will conceal his thoughts and speculations on the subject from you, and you may never be able to regain his lost confidence and implicit trust.

Yet sexual enlightenment is by no means as difficult and embarrassing as you may imagine. You may be afraid of two possibilities: first, that the child will ask questions that are beyond his understanding; and second, that you may have to give him answers that would offend your own sense of propriety. Granted the right attitude, however, both apprehensions are unfounded. It is true that the child asks his first questions on sexual matters at a very early age, perhaps between his third and fifth year. But if you observe some general principles, you will find it easy to answer all questions adequately. The child expects a *literal*, plain answer. By answering just what he asks, you remain within the bounds of the child's comprehension and, at the same time, can avoid all awkwardness.

The parents' dread of such direct answers is ordinarily due to the fact that they look forward with terror to the additional questions which—so they imagine—will immediately ensue.

In reality this is not the case. The child is completely satisfied with one simple and accurate response; and it will be some time, perhaps years, before he raises his next question. This, in turn, will again correspond to his intellectual progress, and will require an equally plain and definite explanation. The value of allusions to reproduction in the plant and animal kingdoms seems to be much overrated. In most cases they are sure to exceed the very young child's grasp, and they call his attention to processes in which he is not yet interested.

Quite different is the child's own observation of animals. It is very advantageous for the child to have the opportunity of making these observations (on the farm, for instance). We know that each person assimilates from his observations only that which is within his power of comprehension; similarly, the child will learn from such observations only what he can understand. Hence they will automatically regulate the progress of enlightenment. In such cases, the child needs no specific explanations until the age of puberty. At that age he will require thorough instruction in sexual matters. This, however, is not necessarily your job, if you feel too modest—or perhaps too ignorant.

In general, the child's interest develops along these lines: In very early childhood he may ask, "Where do babies come from?" You need not hesitate to answer, "From the mother," for there will be no further queries for the time being. Not until later will the child be curious to know where the baby was in the mother. The answer again is quite simple, "Under her heart." And still later he will want to find out how it got there in the first place—"From the father." Finally you may be confronted with the question you may dread most: "How did the baby get from the father into the mother?" But what he wants to know is much simpler than you may believe. At his age the child has no desire to learn the mechanical details;

explanation of this matter would be premature and wholly out of place. He will be quite content if you respond truthfully, "It happens when the mother and the father love each other." In most cases he will not query more searchingly until he arrives at puberty.

These stages in the growth of curiosity, it must be added, are characteristic only of the sheltered child who has not been exposed to other sources of information. In his case alone can premature explanations offend his modesty or disturb the development of his emotional life. If the child has already been "enlightened" through outside experiences or influences, an attempt to treat him as innocent can be only ridiculous in his eyes and will only force him into hypocrisy. This very common situation is rather neatly described in the following anecdote:

Grandmother has taken Johnny and Mary to the zoo. They are standing in front of the stork's cage, and grandmother is explaining that this bird had brought the children to their parents. Suddenly Johnny turns to Mary and says, "What do you think? Should we tell grandma the truth or shall we let her die stupid?"

Every untrue answer to a child's question endangers the child's confidence in you. Hence the myth of the stork has no justification. No less wrong is the answer, "That's none of your business. You wouldn't understand it anyway." Such responses—not to speak of actual rebukes—impel the child in an undesirable direction. They lead him to attach an undue importance to his questions, and his overstimulated curiosity will tend to bring him under influences that may prove harmful.

There is one exception to the rule that you should answer your child's questions truthfully. You must make sure that he does not ask just for the purpose of getting attention. If his motive is attention, his questions should not be answered logically. Otherwise, new ideas for which he is not ready may be instilled in him, especially when he happens to ask about sexual subjects. We will discuss later the distinction between a sincere and an attention-demanding question. You must be careful to distinguish the purpose of the child's question, especially if they relate to sex.

Your greatest difficulty will come from the child who is already mature mentally though not physically. If you feel incapable of talking with him candidly about everything, you can send him to a child psychologist or a doctor; or you can give him one of the many good books designed for the enlightenment of children.[5] This is advisable in any event. But it would surely help your friendship with the child if you would overcome your modesty and, so far as your information permits, attend to his complete sex education yourself. No harm is done if you find it necessary to admit that you are not too sure about some of the answers.

Even more important than the enlightenment on the physical functions is the discovery of the social differences between the sexes. The child learns to distinguish between boys and girls, first by their clothes, then by hair, stature, skin, and voice; but soon he realizes the different role that each sex plays in life. His early impressions of these differences may be very significant. If a child comes to regard his or her own sex as inferior, an impairment of his social integration may result. He may rebel—without prospect of success, since sex is immutable. The assumption of the superior role of the male not only incites girls to protest, but also boys to fear that they may not be able to be "real men." This "masculine protest" leads to the evasion of the "natural" functions of either sex as being either degrading or too difficult, or to an exaggeration of them in an attempt to assert superiority. The girl may rebel

---

[5] We can recommend the following books:
For Children: *Growing Up* by Karl De Schweinitz; *Being Born* by Frances Bruce Strain; and *The New Baby* by Evelyn S. Bell and Elizabeth Faragoh.
For adolescents: *Life and Growth* by Alice Keliher; *My Body and How It Works* by Dorothy Baruch and Oscar Reiss; and *Step by Step in Sex Education* by Edith H. Swift.

against femininity, escape from the duties attached to her sex, and imitate the boy who, for his part, tries to demonstrate his supposed superiority by senseless, often asocial acts and manners. This struggle of the sexes, aggravated by the heightened competition of our time, begins in childhood and thrives on the notions and prejudices that each child acquires regarding his own sex role and the threat from the opposite sex.[6]

The proper instruction of the child, therefore, cannot begin too early. Later fears of sex, love, marriage, responsibilities, and functions can be avoided only through early and careful enlightenment. Here, too, overanxious parents may stir up conflict. You make the child discontented with his sex if you say to a daughter, "You're just like a boy!" or to a son, "You behave like a girl." The mother should never give her child reason to believe that she herself would prefer to be a man. It is fatal for the child to realize that the parents had wanted a boy instead of a girl, or vice versa. In reality—despite the social and legal preferences shown the male (which have become less pronounced in our day, but still are far from being eliminated)—each sex has its marked advantages and disadvantages. The important fact is that every individual, whether man or woman, can find in his own sex the appropriate means to happiness and success.

Treat the Child According to His Age

The treatment you accord the child must be related to his age. This requisite is self-evident, yet parents frequently fail to comply with it. As in the case of any deviation from the rule, transgression may tend toward either of the extremes. The treatment of the child may lag behind his age or forge ahead of it. In either event, this error on the part of the parents hampers the child's development, disturbs the growth of necessary abilities, heightens his sense of inferiority, and impairs his proper social adjustment.

[6] I have discussed these problems in greater detail in *The Challenge of Marriage*.

The mistake arises from an inadequate observation of the child and a faulty understanding of his situation. He does not exist merely to satisfy the wishes and expectation of his parents; he is a human being in his own right. He has his own needs and requirements to fulfill, and these are in large part determined by his age. In many cases the successive stages of the child's development are not taken into consideration. Vain and overly affectionate parents would like to prolong the first years of babyhood. Since the child is delightfully "cute" and "cuddly" at this age, they want him to remain a baby always. So they try to imitate his earliest lisping, and speak to him in an unnatural, childish manner, which they think is the only proper medium for conversation with children. They are unaware of the extent to which this impedes the child's speech development. For years to come they continue using "cute" language, talk of "granny" and "nursie" and "going bye-bye" until long after the child has started to school, and they cling to the shifts and alterations of sounds that characterize the child's earliest language. Through the maintenance of speech habits and other peculiarities, children of four or five sometimes remain in the atmosphere of two- or three-year-olds.

Often, too, the child is freed from the responsibilities of his age. Some children of school age are washed and dressed daily by their parents and sometimes are actually kept from attending school. Until they are seven or eight they are treated like infants under the tender care of mother and family. Frequently they are denied the right to make decisions of their own until they pass the age of puberty.

Many parents find it hard to realize that their child has grown up. They cannot see him as anything but their "baby" and are unable to conceive that he has become a free agent like themselves. This sometimes gives rise to grotesque situations. I once knew two women, one about sixty, the other about forty—mother and daughter. The daughter was submissive to the mother in every way. When she went shopping she was admonished, "See that you don't stay out too long," and "Watch out that nothing happens to you on the street." And the forty-year-old woman always answered politely, "Yes, mother." Fortunately, children will rarely stand for such nonsense; but if parents had their way it would be much more common than it is.

The period in which the child develops into maturity is, for these reasons, especially critical. Unfortunately, girls and boys alike have to overcome great difficulties within themselves during puberty, and these troubles are badly aggravated if the parents are unwilling to admit that their children have changed and suddenly become grown-up men and women. Young people, who in appearance and mentality are completely grown up—though naturally not yet settled and mature—are treated like the children they actually were only one or two short years ago. Painful reprimands, curtailment of individual freedom, personal disregard and disrespect—these are the characteristic results of failure to understand the child's development. The transition from responsible parent to friendly comrade and fellow-being should be accomplished gradually, starting at the time the child enters school. But most parents have a hard time bringing themselves to make this change.

The opposite attitude, strangely enough, often leads to a similar retardation of the child's development. Here we see evidence of the planlessness that results from pursuing one's own interests instead of considering the child's needs. Accordingly, parents often require perfectly impossible achievements of a very small child. These consist usually of activities that are less conducive to the child's development than they are subservient to the vanity, ambition, and comfort of the parents. Thus many children before they enter school are already taught to read and write, since the parents are thrilled by these premature, and hence seemingly exceptional abilities. But the same children may still be incapable of dressing themselves or going to the bathroom without assistance. If the child displays no abilities that the parents can boast of, they become indignant and consider him backward. Many parents attempt to make a prodigy of their child by artificially cultivating certain pseudo-achievements for which he has no real talent. This does not serve to encourage the child. His quite under-standable distrust of himself may subsequently lead to total failure, to a complete breakdown. Thus the overrating of the child's aptitudes is often quite as retarding in its effect as the disparagement of his abilities. It is disastrous for small children to be treated like adults.

Seven-year-old Marc took part in all his parents' conversations. Whenever guests were present, he was allowed to sit with them at dinner. He went to bed late in the evening, at the same time as his mother and father. At table he—like his father—had to have his newspaper in front of him! His parents were proud that he was so "grown up" and "clever." But, on the other hand, he gave them a great deal of trouble, for he absolutely refused to obey. He became violent whenever his desires were not immediately grati-fied and went so far as to raise his hand against his mother. He never ate what was set before him, he had no friends, and, because of his forward and aggressive ways, was unable to get along with anyone. The connection between his faults and his (seeming) merits is quite obvious. His parents were equally responsible for both.

Moreover, children cannot be expected to make decisions for which they lack the necessary insight. Here, too, the faulty consideration of their child's development may lead the par-ents to regard him at one moment as more stupid and unrea-soning than he really is, and in the next to expect from him an intelligence and discernment that are out of proportion to his age. Sometimes the child is even drawn into personal conflicts or business problems of which he cannot possibly have any understanding.

Frequently a child astounds us with his keen perception and judgment. In many respects his thought processes are more natural than ours; he reasons immediately and objectively, and not, like an adult, according to set social patterns. But still, there are certain associations of ideas that are unintelligible to him and which he must gradually learn to grasp. Conversations and analyses of situations and problems must, therefore, be adapted to the child's comprehension. You must never underrate your child's intelligence to the extent of refusing him an explanation that he requests. But neither should you overburden him with your own worries. You should study his reactions to the problems of life, and should not misinterpret any expression of the typical child mentality as obtuseness, tactlessness, or brutality. Misunderstanding of the young child's power of comprehension may easily arise in the case of problems that are impossible for practically every child to grasp—the problems of death and dying, of business interests, and of social or political matters. It is not always easy, but it is nonetheless necessary to appraise correctly the various stages of the child's growth toward intellectual maturity.

Puberty

The period of sexual maturation is fraught with many potential dangers. The world appears suddenly in a different light. This is the result not only of the child's increased size, but also of his changed glandular functions. Both factors make him unsure of himself. He must re-learn the use of his body and orient himself in a wholly new situation. He experiences sensations that irritate him. He tries to integrate himself into society as a whole, and to find his place in a confused and confusing world. At this age the growing boy and girl need, and eagerly seek, help and guidance; but they rarely receive them from their own parents, who still regard them as little children and treat them accordingly. The ensuing violent conflict of the generations destroys the germs of fellow feeling and cooperation. This is a trying time for the parents—when the child grows rapidly, and assumes the appearance of adulthood although he is still a child in years. Many boys and girls between twelve and fourteen seem completely grown up; hence they are treated as adults by strangers, and naturally rebel against being looked upon as children by their own parents. The disparity between social maturity and physical development requires a high degree of understanding and insight on your part. You will gain little by referring to your parental authority. Your influence depends upon your ability to win and preserve the child's friendship and confidence. If you fail, from want of sympathy and good will, or if you destroy the first steps toward a new fellowship by stressing your authority, the child will be tragically estranged at the very moment when he is starting to lead a life of his own and is ready for friendly cooperation on an adult level.

The development of girls is quicker and more obvious. The glandular changes in the female produce a more marked and more pleasant change in appearance than in the male, and this transformation leads to an easier social acceptance. This is the reason why girls seem to "mature" earlier than boys. However, the girl should be prepared in advance for the events of maturation, or else her first experience of the sexual functions may be unpleasant and painful, leading her to regard the entire sex life as embarrassing, repulsive, and despicable. It does not matter at what age sexual maturity occurs. You need not be concerned whether it comes too early or too late. Only in cases of exceptional retardation (as late as the fifteenth or sixteenth year) will it be necessary to consult a physician. If a girl suffers from such a delay because she likes to "appear" grown up and therefore envies her friends who have matured earlier, she must be shown that the external signs of womanhood are relatively meaningless and irrelevant. In this period of transition between childhood and maturity, young people tend to assess *semblances* too highly. They want to pass for something that they are not yet sure they really are. The more you emphasize his childishness, the more your youngster will be inclined to imitate the mannerisms of adults. Thus you may impede his *inner* maturation by undermining his self-confidence as an adult-to-be.

BEYOND WORDS BOOKS

03/11/95 13:57 I 0 5299

1 @ 10.00 BOOKS $ 10.00
1 @ 1.75 CARDS $ 1.75
SUBTOTAL $ 11.75
SALES TAX @ 5.00% $ 0.59
TOTAL $ 12.34
TENDER Credit $ 10.50
TENDER Cash $ 2.00
CHANGE $ 0.16

RETURN POLICY-STORE CREDIT W/IN 30 DAYS
WITH RECEIPT-NO CASH OR CREDIT CD REFUND

From the parents' failure to understand and appreciate the sensations and the difficulties of the period of puberty arises the *defiance* that is so characteristic of adolescence—a defiance not only toward the parents and educators, but toward the world at large. The rebellion in both boys and girls, and the attempt to cover up a sense of puniness and frailty with arrogance, make the "flapper" overact and the adolescent boy go to extremes when they feel uncertain and insignificant. But the tendency toward presumptuousness and exaggeration is not alleviated by disparagements and slights. These lead to an increased feeling of inferiority, and thence to still more inadequate compensations. The desire to be important and significant is more easily satisfied through antisocial behavior than through socially recognized activities. Often it is *ambition*, not recognized or properly channeled by parents, school, and church, that drives boys and girls toward delinquency and crime. It is so much easier for an ambitious girl to receive recognition and admiration through sexual adulation than through academic achievement. When parents and teachers scold and criticize, the admiration of an infatuated male may provide her with the only opportunity to feel wanted and accepted. The ambitious boy who cannot successfully compete with the excellent student, may feel big and heroic by being truant, by gambling and drinking, and by taking out girls. He may become a hero only by smashing windows, stealing, or even worse acts of violence.

During psychotherapy, a patient complained that her sixteen-year-old daughter had become completely unmanageable. She ran around with boys, came home late, did not help around the house, was untidy and impertinent. No words, no promises, no punishments seemed to make any impression on her. At my request the daughter came to see me. She was very pretty, intelligent, well poised. I asked her how she felt, how she got along with mother, whether she was happy. She answered cheerfully, that everything was fine. Q. "Don't you sometimes fight with mother?" A. "Oh, mother is sometimes irritable, but she does not mean what she says, and everything is soon fine again." Q. "And you don't suffer from the scolding and nagging?" A. "Oh no, it does not bother me."

Then I became quite earnest. I told her frankly that I knew her mother very well, and understood how difficult she must be to live with. The girl looked at me in utter amazement. Her eyes began to fill with tears—and then she let loose. First she cried so hard that she could not speak. Then the words came, slowly, haltingly. "Everybody thinks I am a bad girl, and mother is an angel. She has no good word for me; whatever I do is wrong, only my little brother is good. I am always bad. I want to please mother, but she does not even see it. What I get is only scolding, never a good word; no praise, no appreciation."

That was her story. It was the first time an adult had heard it. Her defiance was mere self-preservation and natural pride. When I told her mother what had happened, she would not believe it. Nobody had ever seen the girl cry, nobody had ever broken through the impenetrable indifference behind her happy-go-lucky manner.

Whoever wants to aid these youngsters must get beneath their megalomania and recognize the discouragement that lies at its roots. Yet, how few parents of half-grown children succeed in recognizing it! Adolescence is the stage of life when young people are least sure of themselves, most conscious of their lack of social status, most eager to feel significant, willing to function within the adult community if it would bring them acceptance and equality. But there are so few opportunities open to them for appreciated contributions. They are eager to receive guidance and support; but there are so few adults with whom they can talk frankly because they feel understood and appreciated. Only in the rarest cases do parents show sufficient respect and appreciation to penetrate the mask of stubborn cocksureness. Consequently, their children are almost driven into the arms of more or less questionable friends and leaders who give the impression of understanding them better simply because they accept them as equals.

Loosening the Parental Ties

The goal of training is to render itself superfluous. The loosening of the ties between child and parent is a natural and gradual process that begins very early, really with the weaning of the baby. His introduction into new groups, at kindergarten and school, leads to further significant stages in this process of dissolution, which approaches its end with puberty and the child's entrance into college, business, or professional life. The parents as such will remain their child's closest intimates, if they have not estranged themselves from him. As educators, however, their function is concluded. But this does not prevent the continuation of respect for their wishes and opinions that is always observed between good friends. If the function of the parents as educators is retained beyond its natural measure, disturbances or actual flaws in the child's development may result. Mothers and fathers often try to rescue themselves from superfluity by attempting to keep their children permanently under their thumbs; likewise the children, from a dread of personal responsibility and despite their apparent striving for independence, may retain their childish helplessness even after they marry.

The necessary loosening of the ties offers difficulty only to parents who fail to acknowledge in their child a new personality with his own rights and requirements, who expect from him the satisfaction of their own desires, and in whose eyes, accordingly, the child is not a free agent, an end in himself, but a personal chattel. They cannot conceive of him as independent. This is not a new problem arising only at puberty, but one that extends throughout childhood. For the child does not "grow up" at a fixed date; he begins to grow away from his parents in his earliest infancy, if they do not learn how to establish and maintain friendship with him. If they fail in this when he is small, they must take the consequences when he is older and not complain of his inconsiderateness or callousness if he lives as a stranger under their roof, and loses all intimate contact with them when he leaves home.

The proper dissolution of the parental ties is the crowning achievement of your work as educator. The genuine human relationship between you and the child outlasts time; it cannot be destroyed by distance, by occupational and social differences, or by the setting up of separate establishments. But your day will pass and you must make way for the new generation. Those who today seem small and weak are the mainstay of tomorrow. Only a profound human bond of union can transcend the flow of time and change. The child must stand firm in life after you retire from the scene. There should be no need, even when he is small, for the futile question: "What will he do when I am gone?" You should learn, rather, to step back while you are still here. Make the child independent now! You must have the courage to surrender him *today* to life, to other people, to the whole community of mankind. He must begin today to build a relationship of equal to equal, of man to man, for his success in this relationship will later prove whether or not you have been good parents, whether you have reared the child as children should be reared.

III. THE DIFFICULT CHILD

Chapter 6

Understanding the Child

IF IT were possible to rear children properly from birth on, if parents were faultless and the atmosphere in which children grew up were completely harmonious, then extreme misbehavior, violation of order, and maladjustment would probably not occur. But since these favorable conditions rarely exist, children cause an infinite variety of difficulties. It helps little to talk of what should have been done from the beginning to avoid the predicament; it is necessary to guide parents and children to a solution of their *existing* problems.

We have attempted to show you the methods which are effective in child training and have pointed out the mistakes which most parents inevitably make. This may give you a chance to train yourself to avoid previous errors, and to employ methods heretofore not attempted. However, you cannot expect to achieve immediate success. The child has by no means abandoned his antagonisms. You may even expect the child to become worse, as a first reaction to your change of approach. He is still adjusted to conflict, and if you break off the struggle, he may redouble his efforts to force you back into the old relationship, to which he has adapted his conduct and for which he is prepared. In order to extricate him from the conflict situation you must be steadfast against his provocations to force you to continue your former mistakes.

Abandoning previous methods is only the first step. You cannot help your child unless you understand him. This complete lack of understanding is one of the tragedies of contemporary parent-child relationships. Most parents have not the slightest idea of why the child misbehaves; they are completely ignorant of the causes and purposes of his actions. In the following cases we will try to demonstrate why and to what end a child behaves as he does. You will perceive the concept on which he has built his existence. This may help you to recognize the life plan which guides his actions. Then you may realize the difficulties that confront *him*. So far you have probably been impressed only with the difficulties which *you* have had with him. It is only when you have an appreciation of his conflicts that you can really help him to resolve them.

In order to be able to exert a constructive influence on your child you must learn to observe him objectively. This you can do only if you take his misbehavior less seriously. You must stop regarding his faults as a moral issue. The child who misbehaves is not a "bad" child. He is only unhappy, misguided, and discouraged, and has not found the right answer to the social problems which confront him. Every misbehavior indicates an error of judgment in his efforts to find his place within the family and to meet the demands and pressures to which he is subjected.

As parents rarely understand his concept and judgment, they are puzzled by the way in which he tries to solve his problems. Often a mother recites with complete bewilderment and moral indignation the various misdeeds, deficiencies, and transgressions of her child. "How can he do that? Look what he did again!" Her account cannot be interpreted intelligently at its face value; the child's behavior makes sense only when one knows the counterpart played by parents or other leading figures in his environment. Action and reaction are completely logical on both sides and equally faulty in a psychological sense. The real issue is not a moral one but a question of personal interrelationships. The moral note is raised by the parents merely as a tool to defend their defeated authority (a misinterpretation which society as a whole is prone to make).

Thus the intrinsic, disturbed relationship is veiled and the problem is diverted to one of judgment, which is supposed to be objective. Such an attitude makes the educational problem static and unsolvable.

Every action of a child has a purpose which is in line with his effort toward social integration. A well-behaved and well-adjusted child has found his way toward social acceptance by conforming with the rules governing the social group in which he lives. He senses the requirements of the group and acts accordingly. He is active when the situation warrants it and passive when need be; he talks at the proper time and knows when to be quiet. He can be a leader or a follower. A perfectly adjusted child—if there ever was one!—would reveal little individuality; he would merely reflect the social needs of his environment. Only in the slight deviation from perfect adjustment, through the characteristic approaches which he has found and developed for himself, does a child manifest his individual personality.

In this sense, all individual activity implies a slight deviation from absolute conformity. We cannot consider this deviation as maladjustment because the needs of any social group are not static. The social group itself requires improvement, growth, and evolution. The individual who imposes his ideas on the group is the impetus for its development. If his ideas are beneficial for the group and his method constructive, he is still—and only then—well adjusted, although not completely conforming. Thus, mere conformity can be an obstacle to social development and thereby can become an expression of social maladjustment.

Maladjustment can be defined as behavior which disturbs the functioning of the group and its evolution. The psychological dynamics underlying maladjustment in adults are very complex. It takes time and great effort to unveil the variety of factors at work beyond consciousness, and the mask of adulthood. Adults have the same fundamental attitudes which they had as children; but in the process of adolescence they learn for appearance's sake to cover up and to accept the pattern set by society. The successful masking of one's intentions and motivations is then called maturity. The child has not yet reached this stage of development; although he, too, is not aware of his goals and intentions, he demonstrates his attitudes openly. It is possible, therefore, to recognize the goals of a child's behavior merely by observation.

All disturbing behavior of the child is directed toward one of four possible goals. They represent his ideas about his relationship to others in the group. He tries to: (1) gain attention; (2) demonstrate his power; (3) punish or get even; (4) demonstrate his inadequacy.

A child's goal may occasionally vary with circumstance; he may act to attract attention at one moment, and assert his power or seek revenge at another. It is usually possible to tell by the child's behavior whether his predominant goal is attention, power, or revenge, or whether he is trying to evade any action and responsibility by demonstrating to the outside world, and proving to himself, his inadequacy. He may resort to different techniques to obtain his ends, and the same behavior pattern can be used for different purposes.

The attention-getting mechanism (A.G.M.) is operative in most young children. It is the result of the method in which children are brought up in our culture. Young children have very few opportunities to establish their social position through useful contribution. There is so little that they are permitted to contribute to the welfare and the needs of the family. Older siblings and adults do everything that has to be done. The only way a young child can feel accepted and a part of his family group is through the older members of the family. *Their* contributions give *him* value and social status. As a result, the child seeks constant proof of his acceptance through gifts, demonstrations of affection, or at least through attention. As none of these increases his own feeling of strength, self-reliance, and self-confidence, the child requires constant new proof lest he feel lost and rejected. He will try to get what he wants in socially acceptable ways as long as possible. However, when he loses confidence in his ability to use socially constructive means effectively, he will try any conceivable method of putting others into his service or of getting attention. Unpleasant effects like humiliation, punishment, or even physical pain do not matter so long as the main purpose is achieved. Children prefer being beaten to being ignored. If a child is ignored and treated with indifference he feels definitely excluded, rejected, and without any place with the group.

The desire for attention can be satisfied through constructive methods. The child is naturally inclined to be constructive as long as he feels able to succeed. However, if his requests become excessive or if the environment refuses to meet his demands, the child may discover that he gets more attention by disturbing. Then the struggle starts. For a while the parents may succumb to the provocation without getting too angry and annoyed. Pleasant and unpleasant episodes are held in balance: the child's desire to occupy his parents with himself is met and a workable equilibrium is maintained. However, there may come a time when the parents decide to subdue the child, to stop him from being annoying and disturbing. Then the child changes his goal and he and the parents become deadlocked in a struggle for power and superiority. The child tries to impress upon the parents that he can do what he wants and that they are powerless to stop him. Or he may demonstrate to them in a passive way that they cannot force him to do what they want. If he gets away with it, he has won a victory; if the parents enforce their will, he has lost; but he will come back the next time with stronger methods. This struggle is more fierce than his fight for attention. The child's maladjustment is more obvious, his actions are more hostile and the emotions involved more violent.

This battle between parents and child for power and dominance may reach a point where the parents resort to every conceivable means to subjugate the culprit. The mutual antagonism and hatred may become so strong that no pleasant experience remains to sustain a feeling of belonging, of friendliness or cooperation. The child moves then to the third goal: he no longer hopes for attention, his effort to gain power seems hopeless, he feels completely ostracized and disliked, and finds his only gratification in hurting others and avenging his own hurt. That seems to him the only alternative. "At least, I can make them hate me," is his despairing motto. In groups where he can still gain personal superiority and power he may act less violent and cruel than in those where he has lost every status. Children of this type are the most violent and vicious; they know where it hurts most and take advantage of the vulnerability of their opponents. No display of power and force impresses them any longer. They are defiant and destructive. As they are convinced from the beginning that nobody likes them, they provoke anyone with whom they come in contact to reject them. They regard it as a triumph when they are considered horrible; that is the only triumph they can obtain, the only one they seek.

A passive child will not move in the direction of open warfare. If his antagonism is successfully beaten down, he may be discouraged to such an extent that he cannot hope for any significance whatsoever. Similar conclusions may be reached by a child who considers attention-getting or power as essential, and finds himself unable to obtain it. Then he gives up in discouragement and refuses participation and functioning. There seems to be no sense in doing anything if it will bring only defeat and failure. This defeat, then, looms as the greatest danger, and the child tries his best to avoid it, by proving his inadequacy to himself and others. He uses his inability as a protection so that nothing should be required or expected of him. In this way he tries to avoid more humiliating and embarrassing experiences.

Maladjusted children may be either active or passive and in either case they may use constructive or destructive methods. The choice of method depends on the child's feeling of being accepted or rejected by groups of people: his antagonism is always expressed in destructive acts. This feeling of belonging or the lack of it is a decisive factor for the switch from constructive to destructive methods. Active or passive behavior indicates the amount of courage the child possesses. Passivity is always based on personal discouragement. The combination of the two pairs of factors leads to four types of behavior patterns:

1. Active-constructive
2. Active-destructive
3. Passive-constructive
4. Passive-destructive.

The sequence as presented is based on the actual progression of maladjustment. Many parents and educators are inclined to regard an active-destructive child as much worse than a passive-constructive one. However, this is not necessarily true. If the child's antisocial attitude has not developed too far, as in cases of attention-getting, he can be induced with relative ease to change his destructive methods into constructive ones; but it is extremely difficult to change a passive child into an active one. The passive-constructive child is less unpleasant, but needs more assistance for the development of self-confidence and courage.

Attention-getting (goal 1) is the only goal that can be achieved by all four behavior patterns. (For this reason, the various behavior patterns which serve for attention-getting will be divided accordingly, while the other behavior patterns will appear only under the heading of goals 2, 3, and 4, without division into active and passive methods.) Active- and passive-destructive methods can be used for seeking superiority (goal 2) or revenge (goal 3), while the display of inadequacy (goal 4) can naturally use only passive-destructive methods.

A short discussion of the four types of attention-getting mechanisms may help to clarify the point. The *active-constructive* A.G.M. resembles a very cooperative and conforming behavior. The difference is that in this case the good behavior of a child exists only for the purpose of getting attention and recognition: it will turn into misbehavior if the child does not receive the desired attention. Then he may try *active-destructive* methods. This type of behavior may resemble that used to achieve the second or third goal, and distinguishes itself from it only by the lack of violence and antagonism. The child still seeks only attention and the fight stops when this goal is achieved. The child who wants to demonstrate his power is not satisfied with mere attention; he wants his way.

A very interesting group is that which uses *passive-constructive* methods for attention-getting. Many parents and teachers do not recognize the actions of children in this group as misbehavior. Their pleasantness, charm, and submission cause the observer to overlook the discouragement behind their passivity and dependence on others. In the masculine culture, passive-constructive behavior patterns are almost demanded from women. For this reason, the passive-constructive A.G.M. is found more frequently in girls than in boys. We have already pointed out the mistaken tendency to overlook the greater discouragement of *passive-constructive* children as compared with the *active-destructive*. The passive-constructive child is less unpleasant, but needs more assistance for the development of self-confidence and courage. A child who seeks attention with passive-destructive methods may very well end up in the fourth group of completely discouraged children.

This chapter will be devoted to an *understanding* of the child's problems, but a few general principles for treatment of the various groups and types can be formulated. Children who drive for attention must learn to become independent by recognizing that *contributing* and not *receiving* is the effective instrument for obtaining social status. Within the four groups of A.G.M., the attempt should be made to help all children to become active and to change destructive methods into constructive ones, until the child is able to overcome the need for any special attention. Children who drive for power and superiority should not be exposed to power and to pressure against which they have successfully rebelled and still rebel. Acknowledging their value and even their power is essential for making them self-confident so that they may no longer need their power drive. They must learn that power is less important than being useful. Children who want to punish and to get even are usually those who are convinced that nobody likes them or ever will like them. Helping them involves a long process of demonstrating that they are or can be liked. Children who give up in discouragement have to be brought back slowly to the realization of their abilities and potentialities.

The various behavior difficulties which children present do not necessarily indicate the pursuit of one and the same goal. Laziness, for instance, can well be employed for all four. It can serve either to get attention and assistance, or to establish superiority by refusing what has to be done, or as revenge against an overambitious parent who thereby becomes personally hurt. Or it can be used as an excuse when it seems hopeless to gain anything by trying.

In the following discussions the various behavior problems will be arranged as accurately as possible according to the one goal for which they are most frequently used. But the fact that a given problem appears under one heading need not mean that it could not show itself in other circumstances or for other purposes as well.

The main emphasis of this section will be placed on the clarification of the relationships between the child and his parents and siblings as the basis for the understanding of his behavior. For the purpose of convenient reference, some of the material will be repetitious, especially in regard to possible techniques in dealing with each problem, which will be indicated only briefly; these short suggestions will necessarily be similar for those problems with similar psychological mechanisms.

A. Attention-Getting Mechanism
Active-Constructive Methods

The "Model" Child

Many children who are the sheer delight of their parents and teachers are actually not so perfect as they seem to be. They merely try very hard to display their "goodness" to gain praise and recognition. Their lack of genuine goodness becomes apparent under certain circumstances. They often have a poor social relationship to their own age group; if they cannot shine, they feel lost. Their desire to be perfect, to be correct, to be superior is often stimulated by overambitious and perfectionistic parents who encourage such traits, sometimes in playing this particular child against other siblings. Competition with a sibling often leads to the development of this striving for applause. In order to maintain his superiority over a younger brother or sister, or to match and possibly exceed an older sibling, the child tries to become good, reliable, considerate, cooperative, and industrious, seeking and accepting any possible responsibility. Little do he and his parents realize how his excellence affects the other sibling, driving the latter into discouragement and maladjustment. The virtue of the model child is only too frequently achieved at the expense of the problem child.

Nine-year-old Billy was a wonderful little boy. He had lost his father four years ago, and he managed to be a great solace and help to his mother. Very early he assisted her not only in housework, but also in taking care of six-year-old Marilyn. Even at his tender age, mother could discuss any problem with him, and he actually assumed the function of the "man of the family." The only area in which Billy did not do so well was at school. He had few friends and was not particularly interested in schoolwork. That is not surprising when we consider that in school Billy could not attain the extraordinary position which he enjoyed at home.

One can easily imagine what type of child Marilyn was. She was so unruly that mother no longer knew how to manage her and asked for help. She was untidy, unreliable, noisy, disturbing, and annoying, a real "brat." Mother could not understand how the two children could be so different! It was hard for her to realize the connection between Billy's goodness and Marilyn's deficiencies.

We had the following discussion with both children together: First, we asked Marilyn whether she thought mother liked her. As could be expected, her answer was a shaking of the head. Then we explained to her that mother loved her very much. But because she, Marilyn, did not believe it, she acted in such a way as to make mother constantly angry with her. Perhaps she thought mother would pay attention to her only when she misbehaved. If she would try to behave differently, she would learn that mother loved her, too.

We then asked Billy whether he wanted Marilyn to be a good and nice girl. He immediately shouted, "No!" We asked him why and he became embarrassed, groped for an answer, and finally said, "She won't be good, anyhow." Then we explained to him that perhaps we could help her; and he could help her, too. Together we might succeed in making her a good girl. Would he like that? Somewhat uncertainly he said, yes, he would like it. I told him frankly I did not believe he meant it seriously; I was sure that his first "no" was more sincere and accurate. But why didn't he want her to be good? Perhaps he could tell me. He was thoughtful for a while. And then it came out—"Because I want to be better."

Such children do not enjoy being good if they are not recognized as being better than others. And they actually stop being good if they cannot be better, as happened to Billy at school. If we succeed in helping the difficult child, the so-called good one generally becomes troublesome, sometimes for the first time in his life. For this reason it is not sufficient to adjust the problem child. The whole relationship must be improved. Billy needs as much encouragement as does Marilyn. He, too, is not sure of his position and is afraid of losing it. His desire to be so good is simply a compensation for the fundamental doubt in himself.

Frequently a younger child makes up for his deficiency in age and strength by using his goodness as a tool for superiority to gain the interest and favor of his parents. Sometimes girls compensate for the privileges and prerogatives of their brothers by becoming extremely considerate and responsible, to the detriment of their male competitors, who become more unreliable and selfish as they cannot keep up with the goodness of their sister. Such "goodness" of a girl may endanger her own happiness and ability to get along with others, because—without being aware of it—she makes others feel like a heel; she may make herself a door-mat for everybody willing to step on her. That gives her a peculiar glory of moral superiority. In this way she may become a martyr, always blaming her own misery on the deficiencies of others. Because her maladjustment is seldom recognized in time, no efforts are made to help such a "good" girl.

Exaggerated Conscientiousness

Overconscientiousness is often employed as a technique to gain approval and to demonstrate one's moral superiority over other children. Behind exaggerated conscience lies the strife for special attention—generally hidden from everyone, and not realized even by the child himself. As long as attention and recognition are obtained, as long as parents submit to the child's demand for constant approval and reassurance, conformity is maintained. But sooner or later the child's method will be challenged, either when the parents refuse to submit any longer to his exaggerated demands, or when siblings or playmates revolt against the special consideration which he gets.

This extreme conscience may then be used in an active-destructive way, and is then used for the purpose of getting more power and superiority, even over the parents. Unusual ambition and a great ability to rationalize can move a child to cloak his striving for superiority and power as overconscientiousness. He does everything asked of him, but in such a way that the opposite is accomplished, with the result that the parent, against whom the conflict may be directed, flies into a helpless rage. Yet everything is glossed over with affection and good will. He drives his parents to distraction with his immoderate and compulsive efforts to do everything outstandingly well. He is not unclean—far from it! He washes his hands thirty times a day, and thus dawdles away his time. He is late to meals for the same reason, has to interrupt his studies, and is tardy at school. The excessive love of order conceals a struggle *against* order. He is not lazy—on the contrary, he works the whole day long, so that he has to be stopped or sent to bed. And if you take him from his studies and put him to bed, he is naturally unprepared the next day and fails in the test. Like any form of hidden antagonism, this attitude favors the growth of a neurosis.

You should not be deceived about the hostile nature of the child's behavior or let yourself be drawn into conflict with him by attempting to intervene forcibly in his affairs. Urging and admonishing, not to speak of threats, are either without effect or only intensify the struggle for power. It is necessary to recognize the causes of the hostile attitude and of the child's rebellion. For the most part, they have their origin in extravagant pampering and/or high pressure on the parents' part. The child has no faith in himself, nor in the people around him. Thus he stresses his good intentions and excuses his defects.

Eleven-year-old Mary is an overconscientious child. Her parents, extremely loving and anxious, were always fretting over their only child. They studied her moods, anticipated her every desire, dogged her footsteps, and took elaborate care that she should not overtax herself. It was only natural that she, from a healthy instinct, should rise up against this extreme solicitude. Idolizing her parents as she did, she could not give open expression to her revolt. But she caused them a great deal of unhappiness by taking everything in deadly earnest and regretting deeply each of her own slips and errors. And as a consequence, she made far more mistakes than could be explained by mere ineptitude. Whatever she was asked to do became a problem; and soon her parents were wary of asking anything of her.

Parents may become irritable and perhaps even harsh if they rebel against the exaggerated moral values of the child. In this event, the child will not yield to pressure nor give up his moral convictions and good will, but will increase his inner defiance to a point of complete inner isolation. In his behavior he may then resemble a highly stubborn and defiant child, distinguishing himself from an openly rebellious child only by the maintenance of his "good intentions."

Bright Sayings

A good many children are conspicuous because of their ability to express themselves in a striking and amusing way. Whatever they have to say is charming. The parents tend to brag about their offspring's "bright" and "cute" remarks to their acquaintances, usually without considering whether or not the child is present when they boast about him. He, naturally enough, rejoices in his prowess and starts to turn out bright remarks on a big scale. While the child is small, his utterances may have a certain charm, if only through the quaintness of his speech and the unspoiled power of observation that children evince. But gradually pertness may become a plague, and amusement yield to dismay. Now, instead of helping the child out of the difficult situation in which their own awkwardness has involved him, instead of bringing him around in a friendly fashion and diverting his desire for recognition into other more acceptable channels, the parents begin to chide and scold. It is most disastrous to label him as a "jabber-jabber," a "chatterbox," for his development will become definitely fixed in this direction.

The urge to talk arises from a striving for recognition. It reveals anxiety. Naturally the tendency is most pronounced in those who find it hard to assert themselves more constructively. The greater volubility of women is probably owing to this cause. Tattling, a specialized form of the same fault, likewise serves to raise a feeling of personal prestige. It is very difficult to keep small children from blurting out confidences, for they know all too well that they can be sensational by saying precisely that which should be left unsaid. You must understand this temptation and not blame the child too severely for his transgressions. But you may easily train him to discretion by presenting it as a high attainment, a proof that he is already grown up. By this means the child may discover silence as more desirable than talking. Mere exhortations, however, and especially reproofs, will never touch the fundamental reasons for talkativeness.

Active-Destructive Methods
Showing Off

Ambitious children who are discouraged in the field of tangible, useful achievement, may use the most bizarre means to put themselves in the foreground and attract attention.

Eight-year-old Irving had a sister three years older than he. She was energetic and capable, learned easily, and at eleven already looked quite grown up. The boy was delicate and small, but very aggressive. He always had the last word and was constantly showing off. At school he was extremely restless and inattentive, and disturbed the class with his antics and gesticulations. How did the parents react to this tendency to attract attention? They regarded him as vain and difficult to please, and usually attempted to suppress his obvious striving for recognition. Such efforts, naturally enough, were in vain, for the child was really discouraged, and disparagement only strengthened his poor opinion of himself. He gave the appearance of being unambitious, since he made little effort to learn, and accepted punishments or censure at school with apparent indifference. In reality he was highly ambitious; but his ambition was not directed toward useful attainments. This approach was blocked for him by his sister. She had crowded Irving into the background.

Irving must realize that he does not always have to be the center of attention to compensate for his sister's superiority. His exaggerated opinion of her importance and doubts about his own position are further confirmed by the dissatisfaction that he arouses through his misguided attempts to assert himself. He must, therefore, be shown that he is not only esteemed for what he can do, but also that he is loved. Hitherto he has experienced his importance only when he succeeded in shocking people. This practice can be stopped. Occasional experiences of an inexorable order are as necessary when he misbehaves as attention and interest when he behaves well.

Obtrusiveness

Innumerable are the tricks by which children try to impress others. The weird ideas that occur to them are often astounding and amusing. Innocent parents who have no conception of the reasons behind such conduct are often completely bewildered—when, for instance, their four-year-old boy (the youngest of the family) takes a notion to cut his soup with his knife! The child's tendency to attract attention frequently takes the form of "bedeviling" the grown-ups. In this way he makes his presence felt and keeps his family on edge. He interrupts his parents' conversations; he refuses to let his mother talk with acquaintances.

Eight-year-old Gertrude—a second-born, spoiled child—would not allow her mother to pay attention to anyone else when she was around. If the mother wanted to talk with someone else, Gertrude put her hand over her mother's mouth or yelled so loudly that conversation was impossible. Between screams and protests she clung to her mother's neck and kissed her profusely. Her wildness and turbulence made her the terror of nursemaids. At school, however, she worked so hard that her diligence seemed to justify overlooking her less estimable traits. She was the "teacher's pet" and the best student in the class. She knew that at school she would not succeed with her tricks.

The "Walking Question Mark"

A child may annoy not only with persistent and unwarranted displays of affection; he may also make himself conspicuous through questioning. You can easily determine whether he asks for information or only in order to call attention to himself. You should not refuse to answer truthfully an honest query; but it is entirely out of place to discuss sham questions. The latter are clearly characterized by the way in which the child puts his questions. He pays no attention, and sometimes does not even wait for a response before asking a new question. Parents often fail to notice this game. They do not even catch on when the same questions are frequently repeated. When their patience is exhausted they brusquely scold the child, who is amazed at this sudden turn in the conversation and really hurt.

Once at the home of a friend I watched the following scene. The mother took her little three-year-old daughter on her lap and read to her from a picture book. On each page the girl stopped the mother and asked "What are these people doing?" and "Why is this dog here?" And each time the mother answered patiently. After a few pages I broke in and asked "What are these people doing?" and the little girl answered correctly! I kept quiet while the next page was being read and the child asked one or two questions, which the mother again answered patiently. This was the sequence: during the reading of one page I asked the questions and the child answered; during the reading of the next page the child asked and the mother answered, and so on. After the mother finished the book, I remarked that I had enjoyed the game. The mother asked in astonishment, "What game?" She had noticed nothing at all of what was going on.

This episode is less humorous than deplorable. It shows how little parents are aware of the tricks of their children and thereby encourage false attention-getting mechanisms. This little girl called three or four times after she was put to bed; for water, toilet, a running nose, and a forgotten item—and the parents complied until they became irritated. This is the usual sad end of such a game.

You should not let a child get away with *thoughtless* questions. By listening carefully it will not be hard to distinguish these from serious inquiries. But you must realize that children sometimes enlarge their mental horizons with startling abruptness, and then they actually have a great store of sincere questions. However, it is still possible to differentiate between a thoughtful and a purely mechanical spinning out of questions: the latter is often marked by the stereotyped form or the general senselessness of the queries. The eternal "Why?" of children may spring from a real thirst for knowledge; but more often it shows only the desire to attract attention. Even when you have determined that the latter is the case, you should not react with reprimands. You can remind the child that he cannot possibly be in earnest with his queries.

This can be done in all friendliness. He will soon stop his tedious questioning when it fails to bring the desired result. If you answer such questions at all, your reply should not be logical—as the child already knows the answer. You may play a little game with him. It often works when you agree to ask questions alternately, first the child, then you; or, you can shoot questions at him in the same way he does; or you may make up a fantastic story to answer a simple question. But all such games should be introduced properly, explaining to the child why he asks the questions, and expressing your willingness to give him your attention if he wants it. If you have no time at the moment, you can say that you will give him your answer later. You do not save time if you answer logically to keep him quiet, or say "I don't know"—which is not true; or if you shout at him and try to stop him. All such responses will only stimulate him to bother you further with his questions.

Once more we must emphasize that questions arising from the child's need to expand his knowledge should never be ignored or ridiculed. Disparagement leads to forfeiting the child's confidence and drives him to other sources of information. Or it may hamper his intellectual development. A child who asks a question objectively and seriously is generally capable of grasping a simple reply. You should never tell him that he is too young to understand. You must take the trouble to discover the real gist of the question; and if the answer is limited strictly to the question, it will not exceed the bounds of the child's understanding. An adult may perhaps regard a child's question as unanswerable, and believe that it passes the child's power of comprehension merely because he, the grown-up, thinks at once of the additional questions that would arise from an exact reply. The child, however, queries no deeper than he can think. (This, of course, applies only to serious questions.)

In addition to objective and obtrusive questions are the so-called rhetorical questions: "Is that right?" "Is that what you really believe?" "Do you mean it?" "Do you think so?" Any reply to such queries is, at best, inept, and in any case unwarranted. But, nevertheless, critical, scolding parents often use such questions as an occasion for harsh or at least unfriendly comments.

"Enfant Terrible"

The ability to say or do something at exactly the wrong time characterizes the "enfant terrible." His purpose is to draw attention to himself under every circumstance, and he succeeds in the simplest way: by breaking the unwritten laws of tact and convention whenever he can. Often these children are especially attractive because of their intelligence and wit, and the charm with which they dramatize themselves. Their strategy is to do nothing that is expressly forbidden but to carry the permissible to extremes.

Eight-year-old Francis was an "enfant terrible." He had lost his parents and was being reared, with more determination than good sense, by two older brothers and an older sister. He was pulled back and forth between their sympathetic indulgence and their helpless severity. But he knew how to attract everyone's attention. Once his brother scolded him severely for telling a lie and delivered an extemporaneous sermon on the necessity of truthfulness, with astounding results. The following day a distant relative paid a call; Francis informed him at once that the family spoke of him in no complimentary terms. He answered the subsequent reproaches of sister and brothers with the ingenuous comment that after all one must always tell the truth. And henceforth no one could rid him of this hyper-veracity. His family trembled whenever a guest arrived; they knew that Francis, with uncanny skill, would dig up something embarrassing but true to tell.

Naturally, an "enfant terrible" who is worthy of the name does not limit himself to embarrassing remarks. He plays his tricks in infinite variety and with remarkable inventive faculty.

Once in our Child Guidance Center, I became the victim of my own gullibility. A little girl, about five, appeared for the first time during our consultation hour. The mother told of the child's pranks and of her own efforts to influence her through pleading, which of course remained fruitless. Meanwhile the girl sat on a bench and played perilously with the inkwell. Her mother warned her and pulled her hand away, but it did no good. Now I was eager to show how it should be done; so I said, "Go ahead and put your hand in the ink. You'll just get your fingers dirty, and it won't look very nice. But go ahead and try it if you want to." As I had expected, the child was taken aback by my words and stopped playing with the inkstand. But suddenly, after some ten minutes, I heard a sharp cry from the mother. The girl had thrust both her hands into the inkwell and proudly and exultantly held up her little fists dripping with ink.

It is plain to see that the "enfant terrible" is not easy to reform, for the simple reason that he is sly and clever. Yet the consequences of his conduct in later life are rarely as bad as distracted parents are led to fear, for these children are shrewd enough to calculate when and to what length they can venture a prank. Nevertheless, one should try to deal with them. Naturally, this cannot be done unless parents call off the conflict with them and win their understanding and sympathy, for these children are intelligent enough to recognize the purpose of their behavior. It is not so simple to let them experience the natural consequences, since they themselves—as we have just seen in the case of Francis—are sufficiently adroit to use the unpleasant consequences of their acts to their own ends. Yet suitable opportunities for logical consequences can be found.

In the first place, the child is too often permitted to succeed in his maneuvers. Parents scold him, but they laugh at his tricks; and this, of course, spurs him on to bigger and better achievements of the same sort. Visitors or other outsiders who are only occasional, amused witnesses of such scenes exercise a particularly harmful influence. Hence it is a good idea to deprive the child of the opportunity to show off before guests. You need only say to the child: "Do you think you can behave today when Aunt X comes? Shall we give it a try?" And if he does not act properly, you can keep him out of sight the next two or three times when you have guests. Later you can give him another chance. But in the meantime efforts must be made to win the child over. Above all, you must understand the entire situation, which perhaps involves rivalry with an older brother or sister. You must also avoid paying undue attention to the child or stimulating his ambition to satisfy your own vanity.

Instability

This trait, too, has a definite purpose.

Fourteen-year-old Lil is in constant agitation. She is perpetually changing her clothes, her friends, her activities, her interests; and she is soon satiated with everything. For a short while she excelled in mathematics; then she turned to history, devoured one fat volume after another, and tossed them aside. She is continually showing how gifted she is—what she *could* do, *if*—if she could only stick to one thing for any length of time. And this is the principle by which she acts.

Lil stands in the shadow of a very capable and conscientious elder brother. Ostensibly she is the more talented of the two. But he accomplishes more and is dependable. So Lil *tries to suggest what she potentially could do*. She has no faith in her ability to fulfill her promises. Not only does she fear disappointments, she actually provokes them. She arranges them everywhere—in her personal relationships, as well as in books and interests. She does not realize that the disillusionments do not come from outside, but grow within herself.

An unstable child puts no stock in the value of persistence. His ambition, too, does not lie in the direction of attainment even if he believes or wishes to believe that he will succeed. As his courage is limited, he gives up easily and turns to the next project. His first exaggerated enthusiasm reveals his pessimism. He cannot take his time, as he is sure that time will prove his deficiency.

There is no reason to assume that his instability is innate. Such an assumption is an excuse that the child himself has manufactured, incited perhaps by miscalculated reproofs from family and associates. Help will come only from insight into the child's scheme and an alteration of his life plan. You can talk the matter over freely with older children; but in the case of a young child the transformation can result only from your understanding of the situation. You must give him new courage and help him to change his aims. The child is not interested in *doing*, but in *getting* as much as possible with the least effort. Instead of his drive to excel or to get easy and quick results, he must discover the satisfaction which lies in work and effort, regardless of the outcome.

Passive-Constructive Methods
The Clinging Vine

Children, especially when they are small, find many pleasant methods of getting attention without effort. They just have to look, and everybody stretches their hands out toward them. They adore and admire, and everybody falls for their tricks. They use their weakness and helplessness to put others in their service; but they do it so charmingly that nobody resents going out of his way to do everything for them. They never disturb or annoy, because then they would lose their power. They may tend to become scheming, and are actually completely concerned with themselves, while they appear to be interested only in others.

The tendency to lean on others sooner or later leads to disturbed relationships. As long as they can please, all is well; but when a situation does not permit pleasing, their good manners end. They may first become destructive in order to attract attention. If that fails, they may easily move into the third group of children whose exaggerated desire to be liked may lead, then, to the assumption that they are not liked at all. Many dependent children turn into hostile and even cruel beings when they find out that their charm no longer works; for instance, when they are dethroned by a new sibling.

Vanity

Children who are admired just for what they *are* and not for what they can *do* are invited to become vain. Vanity springs from the ability to attract admiration without doing anything to deserve it. Vanity is encouraged by remarks of adults who praise the child's appearance. If such recognition is considered by a child to be the basis for his social position within his family group, then his vanity becomes firmly entrenched. It is a danger of beautiful children that they learn to rely more upon their appearance and the impression they make than upon their achievements and efforts. The evolving lack of confidence in their own abilities makes them only more dependent on the approval of others and increases their vanity. This in turn eventually leads to conflict, as they demand more and contribute less.

The elimination of extreme vanity is a most difficult task. Whoever does not know that an exaggerated striving for prestige arises from strong feelings of inferiority will merely try to rebuff the seemingly vain and conceited child by disparaging him. However, this will only heighten the child's sense of inadequacy and increase the impulse toward presumptuousness or other forms of self-display. Vain children cannot bear to yield precedence to anyone, and therefore sidestep any situation in which they cannot excel. Hence, in the event of pronounced discouragement, the vain child may recoil from any activity in the presence of other people. Thus every vain child is timid whenever uncertain of success. You must learn to see through the masks of conceit—as through those of indifference. A boy may learn nothing at school, but still be ambitious. And, similarly, the complete neglect of clothes and personal appearance by no means excludes vanity. Such children have simply stopped trying to make a good impression. They are not interested in looking just neat, like all the others. If they cannot impress with their glamour, they don't care; or they may even try to impress with their sloppiness. Such "carelessness" is plainly dictated by vanity. The child would respect the conventional standards of appearance, if he were not concerned with the impression he makes.

How can we overcome vanity? Chiefly by not fostering it. Most parents stimulate vanity in the children by putting so much emphasis on "what people will say." Many parents expect the child to scintillate, either through his attractiveness or his charm. They dress him up, make a great to-do over his clothes, and rejoice in his "success." But the admiration which he receives is not sufficiently supported by his sense of his intrinsic worth. Through showing off he gives exaggerated weight to the opinions of others at the expense of his own estimation of himself. If he fails to impress, he feels his own importance questioned. But even his success does not give him real self-confidence; the ease with which he can win recognition through his external appearance often leads him to minimize productive achievements. He does not need to learn, to be industrious, to have any special abilities. Even when vanity is combined with useful and valuable activities, even then it unmistakably reveals a feeling of inadequacy. No one desires notoriety unless he believes that otherwise he is of no worth. And whoever wants to be the first will be ceaselessly tormented by the thought that sometime perhaps he may not succeed and someone else may outstrip him. Parents who require their children to be exceptional implant in them the dread of failure. The vain child is intent on making impressions only because he lives in constant fear of being unable to do so.

This apprehension—namely, the feeling that one acquires importance only through other people—is equally present in bashful and in conceited children. Both fear ridicule as the greatest of all possible misfortunes; but the vain child still has the courage to use constructive means against this danger, while the timid one desires only evasion and strives for recognition only by means of weakness and deficiency. In both instances the child must be educated to attach less importance to the opinion of others, to find his true worth in himself and his attainments. He must recognize the merit of useful contributions as contrasted with external impressions. He suffers from a false notion of human values; his ambition ought not be repressed, but directed into the proper channel.

Passive-Destructive Methods

Bashfulness

Ten-year-old Tess is a bashful child, just the opposite of her brother, three years younger than she. He is spirited and resolute, ready to tackle anything; she, easily embarrassed and reticent. When asked a question, she is speechless. She likes best to stay at home with her mother, and never goes out without her. At school, too, she is retiring, and has only one good friend. Very characteristic is the mother's attitude when anyone speaks to the daughter: "Why don't you answer the doctor? Don't look down at the floor! Stand up straight!" When the girl is asked a question, her mother answers for her. It is simply impossible for her to wait for the child's response. Big as the girl is, she tries to hide behind her mother's skirts. What is the meaning of this conduct?

Tess is strongly competing with her younger brother. She feels that she is slighted on his account—and not only because he is a boy. He is quicker and more vivacious, more clever and capable. The boy had been encouraged by his parents to surpass his older sister. When he was small, the girl was urged to give in to him. Everything he did was "nice" and "cute." She, who previously had been spoiled as an only child, became sulky and obstinate. She soon learned how to use her dependence and maladroitness as a means not only of evading further responsibilities in the care of her brother, but also of forcing her mother to show a greater interest in her. There was a drawback, it is true; for she had to put up with continual preaching on her awkwardness and inability. But, after all, she did succeed in concentrating her mother's attention on herself.

Many timid children follow the same scheme. (We must, however, distinguish them from those who have been cowed or, so to speak, intimidated.) Through their behavior they force other people to be concerned with them and help them. To get an answer from them takes time and effort. Their conduct is unpleasant and annoying; yet one cannot be indifferent to them. No doubt they make themselves conspicuous—by merely doing nothing. Their discouragement may be combined with ambition, otherwise these children would no longer try to get attention, but give up completely and resign themselves to complete and dull inactivity. Bashful children dread ridicule. With the aid of their timidity they strive to evade any situation in which they may have to play an active role. Still they demand and expect everybody to pay attention to them. This technique sometimes leads to serious neurotic symptoms, as, for instance, to a fear of blushing (erythrophobia). Individuals suffering from this neurosis evade all social duties, but by means of their blushing still contrive to feel that they are the object of general attention.

Tess's mother demonstrates how one should *not* treat a bashful child. The girl certainly invites constant supervision and tutelage—for this is the purpose of bashfulness. But one cannot afford to accept her invitation. The child's fear of activity and obligations can be overcome only by systematic encouragement. This process is highly complicated in the case of children who hide behind their pretended inadequacy in order to escape the requisites of living. If they are praised they either refuse to believe or are flattered, but dread all the more a future failure. It takes considerable time for such a child to regain his lost faith in himself; and it requires *systematic* work. Even encouraging and commendatory *words* are not enough. The child needs more substantial evidence of trust and recognition.

Dependence and Untidiness

Dependent children—who are often untidy—give a great deal of trouble. They always need someone to tell and remind them what to do and, finally, to *do* everything for them.

Children become dependent if forcibly deprived of their natural desire to be independent. A want of faith in the child's abilities, a desire to relieve him of inconveniences, or perhaps the parents' need to gain personal importance through their protectiveness, can lead a child to give up all desire for self-reliance. The more capable the mother, the more she tends to assign to herself all the domestic duties and responsibilities, the more likely will her child become dependent.

You should never do anything for a child that he can do for himself. If he is used to being catered to and waited on, then this procedure must be stopped. Naturally you should not be impatient. If the child is awkward from lack of practice, it will take time until he can develop skill. Meanwhile you can encourage him and spur him on, but never should you relieve him of any obligation, either from impatience or a misdirected sympathy.

It is not always the parents alone who are responsible for their child's lack of self-reliance.

Eight-year-old Trudi can do nothing for herself, or, if she does manage to finish a task, it is wretchedly done. She goes about everything the wrong way to invite constant assistance. When the family goes for a walk, she lags behind and has to be called and finally fetched. She can dress herself, but none too neatly. Even her food is cut up for her. When she pours water she usually misses the glass. She is flighty, untidy, and indolent. In short, she needs someone to look after her and play servant to her. And she has this someone! Her mother, a business woman, has little time for her; but Trudi has a sister, four years older than she, who nurse-maids her abundantly. Twelve-year-old Anne is earnest, intelligent, and capable beyond her age. She manages not only her own affairs—since no adult pays any attention whatsoever to the children—but also those of her sister. And she refuses to be relieved of this additional burden. Once, when the two of them were together at a camp, Anne could not be stopped from practicing her pedagogy on her younger sister. She wanted to be around her, fretting and nagging all day long, as she was accustomed to doing at home. Thus the well-bred and diligent girl disturbed the whole atmosphere of the camp, at least as much as her ill-behaved and clumsy sister.

You can see why Trudi developed as she did. The rivalry between the two sisters led to a peculiar distribution of defensive and offensive weapons. Anne may be victorious as the more capable of the two, but more attention must be paid to Trudi. One child tries to win recognition actively, through useful accomplishments; the other passively, through ineptitude. It is not enough merely to encourage Trudi. This must be done, it is true, if better accomplishments are to be expected of her. But she will avoid accomplishments because they will deprive her of the means of holding her own with her more capable sister. Improvement can be obtained only by influencing *both* children. Their strong rivalry must be toned down; only then would it be possible to reduce the A.G.M. on both sides. They must learn to work *with*, not against each other. For both are wanting in social interest. (It is characteristic, and very understandable, that Anne, too, is unsuccessful in her relations with other people. She has no real friends, since they refuse her the superior position that she desires.) Thus, both must learn to play their proper roles in life.

It is not always necessary, however, to transform the whole life plan in order to break the child of a single undesirable trait. A certain sense of order can be instilled in any child. The only requisite is that we allow no carelessness. The human organism is by nature attuned to regularity and system. Untidiness is first developed as a trick or device. The child recognizes the advantage of not getting up on time, failing to wash and dress himself, being late for meals, refusing to put away his toys, or not going to bed at the set hour. In these ways he wins his victories in his struggle with mother and father, and thus secures the attention that he wishes. In order to wean him away from such habits, it is necessary to avoid conflict and bring the natural consequences to bear.[1] But parents themselves must observe order, or else the child will soon use their own failing against them.

Lack of Concentration and Stamina

A child's incapacity for work is often blamed on a supposed mental or physical weakness that keeps him from paying sustained attention to a task for any period of time. This assumption of a "lack of energy," of an impairment of "nervous energy," is utterly erroneous, though it may seem to be confirmed by the experiences of anxious parents and timorous individuals. Such people tend to attribute their own failures, or those of their children, to nervous debility or some other constitutional weakness. This, like the ready assumption of

[1] See Chapter 3, "Natural Consequences."

congenital feeble-mindedness in each case of seeming stupidity, leads in turn to an aggravation of the complaints.

Fifteen-year-old Fran is a nervous, "weak" child. She is attending high school and has much difficulty, although she is bright. She tires so easily that after school she often spends the remainder of the day in bed. It is even hard for her to pay attention in class. And when she has some unusual assignment, or faces the prospect of an examination, she goes completely to pieces. The night before, she cannot eat or sleep. Sometimes she gets so ill that she has to stay in bed when she should be taking a test. Even in elementary school she could not bear to sit quietly and hold her hands still. In her earlier years she had to repeat a grade, and for this reason it was at first decided not to send her to high school, but, by weeping and wheedling, she succeeded in getting her way, since all her friends were attending. However, she keeps up with her work only with the greatest difficulty and she needs continual help.

Parents and doctors assumed a constitutional weakness. But what was the real cause of this condition? Until she was four, Fran was well developed, energetic and lively. But at this age she changed completely. She is an only child. Her mother lived on very bad terms with her father, and devoted little time to the child, whom she left to a nursemaid; but still she was very ambitious for Fran. The girl was never pretty enough to suit her. She bought her the most attractive clothes and dressed her like a princess. Fran set great store by her appearance. She would cry and pout for a day if she got a pair of shoes that failed to please her. She was generally pitied because her father treated her and her mother so badly and eventually deserted them. Her relatives bought her whatever she desired. When she passed a shop window and saw something she liked, she stopped and cried until she got it.

Yet on the whole she was very well behaved, and never *directly* imposed her will on others. She had different means of getting what she wanted. Until she was ten the maid had to dress and undress her. She was very compliant, and by accommodating herself to everyone she succeeded wonderfully in making everyone her servant. Today she still plays the "cute little girl" and runs about in socks and hairbows. No one is hardhearted enough to refuse her anything. She always selects either older children or very young ones as playmates. And even the younger girls immediately mother her, which she graciously permits. But she much prefers to play with grown-ups. Her mother dissuaded her from becoming intimate with other girls, claiming that they would only teach her bad habits. Hence she likes best of all to play alone.

From her fourth year on, she used her weakness systematically as a means to get service. She had to be urged to eat—and promptly lost weight. She became exhausted on long walks. Once, in the country, when she was so big that her relatives could no longer carry her, they had to hire a man to transport her home! She could not do housework; everything was too hard for her, and she always steered clear of the kitchen. She was never apt at handiwork—she tired too quickly. She always wanted to make something for her mother, but could never get it done.

Fran's mother paid no attention to her unless she was ill. And in the last few years she became ill very often. An impending test at school, as we have seen, was enough to send her off to bed. To what extent her good behavior is only a show and a means of making an impression can be seen from the following detail. The desk and shelves in her room are littered with schoolbooks—and a hodgepodge of other books. She never reads them, except when somebody enters the room; then she seems deeply engrossed in some lesson or self-set task that she will never complete.

Here you can plainly recognize the devices employed by an ambitious child who finds it hard to win recognition by useful accomplishments. Fran's boundless ambition is surely obvious, though no one around her suspects it since she never attempted any real achievements at school or elsewhere, but strove to avoid them. Her seeming "constitutional weakness" proved to be her most effective alibi; and, what is more, it also served to support her in her demands for being nursed and mothered.

Like Fran, many children try to take refuge behind frailty and use it as a means of making their parents their slaves. Then they are exempt from responsibilities out of consideration for this "weakness." Yet if you try to *force* them to conformity, you will soon find out that this weakness is stronger than your strength. No violence or pressure can move the child to co-operate. His ambition, the whole trend of his endeavors, must be turned in a new direction. The previous pampering must be superseded by a systematic program of joint *work*. Hitherto the child has been the *object* of solicitude, and he has taken full advantage of this fact. Now he has to become a fellow worker.

Self-indulgence and Frivolity

Fifteen-year-old George is a flighty, unrestrained boy who lives only for the moment. He is an only child, who, in his first year, was entrusted to an aunt because his parents had no time to care for him. This aunt had a daughter three years older than George, but favored the boy in order to make him forget the lack of his own home. He always got a bigger helping of pudding and more than his share of candy. Later he had more pocket money, and was allowed to sleep longer than her own daughter. She was given only bread and butter for her school lunch, while George always had meat in his sandwiches. Only George was helped with his homework. Until he was eight, his aunt washed him, while her daughter had to wash herself when she was little more than a baby.

Despite this preferential treatment there was no open conflict between the two children. The girl adjusted herself to the situation; a certain independence and capability compensated her for the neglect that she experienced. She tried to mother George, too, for he had by now developed a peculiar faculty. He was an attractive child, and knew how to ingratiate himself (passive-constructive A.G.M.). No one could resist him. He exploited to the limits all the persons with whom he came in contact, and had a charming way of "pumping" relatives and acquaintances for money, which he promptly spent on candy. At school, too, he crept into the favor of his teacher, and became her acknowledged pet. He got into a great deal of mischief, but no one could stay angry with him, and his pranks were always forgiven. When he entered high school he encountered his first real reversal. His usual methods were ineffective. Honest work was required and he was unprepared. At elementary school he had made a straight record of A's; he barely passed the first grade of high school. At this time he shifted from passive-constructive methods to passive-destructive behavior.

It is obvious that George's whole personality was conditioned by his childhood situation and the way in which he tried to master it. There would be no value in singling out his frivolity and greediness and making them the subject of a campaign to reform him. He is very ambitious but his aspiration is *to get as much as possible out of other people*. Only when he succeeds in this does he feel important. Work is burdensome to him. He has no desire to control himself because then he would have to relinquish his demands upon others and upon life. He has not discovered the joy of active achievement. Success through accomplishment presupposes a long period of exertion, and this is something that George has never tried. He does not plan for the future; he wants everything *immediately*. Hence he cannot stand tension or suspense, but uses these as a means of securing greater momentary advantages. He runs away from home if anything chances to displease him, and incurs debts from friends when his family refuses him the money he wants. Through his insidious helplessness he makes other people reap what *he* has sown. With his lack of restraint or discipline he extorts whatever he wishes.

The greatest obstacle to diverting George from his course is his relatives. His readjustment depends upon whether they can be induced to adopt a more reasonable attitude. When an attempt was made to put him into a foster home he ran away and was promptly reaccepted by his family. Thereupon he made life miserable for everybody; there was no one to make him bear the consequences when he brazenly flouted the established order. And yet this is the only means of finally opening his eyes. From the attitude of his environment George must naturally conclude that he has found the right methods for asserting himself. And, if his family cannot bring themselves to stop yielding to his wishes, they will begin a desperate struggle, with threats, affronts, abasements, and coercion, which in turn will only increase his resistance and his rebellion against order. He no longer seeks merely at-

Steadfastness on the part of the family, and a continued process of encouraging George[2]—these are the methods that may mark the way to a transformation of his life plan.

Greediness characterizes persons who aim at cheap momentary success because they have little confidence in the future. Whatever they cannot get at the moment seems to them highly uncertain of attainment. This lack of faith in the future is typical of greedy children. They are unable to save. Why should they? Tomorrow will be unpleasant enough without ruining today. Hence it is of no consequence to them that to-day's enjoyment brings tomorrow's discomfort. They take this as part of the bargain. They are children who feel threatened by more successful brothers and sisters or are pampered by inconsistent parents. Naturally a certain amount of defiance is involved when the child tries, against all orders, to obtain "treats." The candy bought on the sly, the jam pilfered from the pantry, the chocolate bars consumed at one sitting that should have lasted a week—these not only taste good, but signify easy triumphs over the adults, without requiring work and effort. Greediness and discouragement are always closely associated. Thus the greediness of a child shows that his psychic equilibrium is upset and that he needs help. But once again: help is not synonymous with indulgence.

Anxiety and Fear

In the earlier discussion of extreme conscientiousness we mentioned the problem of neurosis. At the center of all neurotic phenomena is fear. But whereas deep fear in the adult is considered pathological, fear in children is considered natural. It appears occasionally in every child. Only when it becomes severe is it regarded as unusual.

Fear is the expression of helplessness. Whoever feels that he is weak dreads not only real, imminent dangers; his anxiety seeks out vague and unknown menaces. In man, and perhaps

[2] See Chapter 3, "Encouragement."

in all living beings, the fear reactions are the innate recollections of a more primitive mode of life; for the aboriginal peoples are actually under constant threat of dangers, some of which are unknown, others incomprehensible to the primitive mind. Civilized man, under normal conditions, lives sheltered within his social community. But still the child feels his helplessness, and this feeling takes form in his susceptibility to fear; and as we sympathize with his helplessness, we respond to his fear.

Here is the crux of the problem. The child learns *to use his innate fear reactions to achieve his personal goals*. The more impressed the parents are by the child's anxiety (whether from excessive love, from sympathy, or because they suffer from their own fears), the more readily they succumb to his scheme of action. Through fear, the child may make himself a tyrant who lives beyond the pale of all order and system.

A timid child dreads solitude and darkness, and through his fear reveals his characteristic weakness and its cause. Only a spoiled child will react in this way. He thinks it the worst of all fates to be left alone, because he feels incapable of existing without the aid of adults. Nothing is more terrifying than to be alone, for then he has to depend entirely on himself. And, similarly, in the darkness he is completely dependent upon his own resources. Sometimes the parents themselves provide the child with arguments that he can use against them; they resort to solitude as a punishment or use the spectral "bogyman" or ill suited fairy-tales to paint the horrors of darkness and night. The typical childhood fear is often developed through the child's refusal to go to bed. Many children object to being sent to bed; either they are unwilling to give up, even temporarily, the warmth and solicitude of their parents, or they resent the slight implied in not being allowed to stay up as late as the grown-ups or older brothers and sisters. Hence going to bed, with the correlated necessity of staying alone in the dark, becomes a subject of resentment. And in this case fear proves itself to be a weapon that few parents can resist.

The degree of dependency to which parents can be brought by this device is often absurd. The child will not go to bed alone. The door must be kept open, or there has to be at least a slit to admit the light that symbolizes contact with others. Gradually the requirements may increase: the door to the adjoining room must remain open; a lamp must be left burning; a grown-up must stay in the room until the child falls asleep; the mother must sit by his bed and hold his hand; if she lets go, he immediately sets up a howl; even after he has fallen asleep, he senses his mother's attempted withdrawal, wakes up, cries, and keeps her at his bedside until deep in the night. Children who have accepted the necessity of going to sleep by themselves may still find it possible, through nightmares and nocturnal spells of fright, to creep into the parents' bed and escape the dreaded solitude.

In the daytime, too, fear proves itself effectual.

Twelve-year-old Paul uses his fearfulness to dominate his entire family. He is a late-born child, with two adult siblings. Everyone pampers and indulges him; but he lives in constant anxiety. At night the door must be kept open. In the evening he cannot stay alone in a room. He evades every situation in which he would be left to himself. He dreads schoolwork, is afraid when the other boys fight, cannot swim or participate in gymnastics. Whenever his mother attempts to leave, violent scenes follow. And so his family always tries to comfort him, to help him, and to smooth the way for him.

His mother came to consult me, but not because of concern about the child's anxiety. She asked for a certificate excusing him from swimming class—the poor boy could never sleep the night before! That he might learn to stand on his own feet, trust in his own strength, and cope with his own difficulties—this was a possibility that had never entered her mind. And never would Paul have attempted it of his own accord; for he likes the sheltered atmosphere he lives in, though he pays for it dearly with his fears.

Paul, however, is still rather conservative in his choice of methods.

Fourteen-year-old Ernest has done a better job of training his parents. They must tell to the minute when he can expect them home, for the suspense is unendurable. He conceals his imperious egotism behind a much-stressed love for his parents. He lives under the incessant fear that something might happen *to them*. And that is why he insists on punctuality. If they stay out longer than they indicated, they must phone at regular intervals to assure him of their continued well-being. And no one realizes that what Ernest wants is to make his parents show attention to him.

What steps can be taken against the exaggerated fears of children? Force, naturally, is useless. The best course to follow is to *ignore anxiety*. The child naturally will fight this policy by every means, and stir himself up to all sorts of "states." While he is still small, he can simply be allowed to spend his fury and quiet down. You must give him the affection, love, and concern which he wants and needs, but not under the pressure of his fear. In difficult cases it may be necessary to call in a pediatrician or a psychiatrist.[8] Sometimes, too, it is possible to succeed in obviating anxiety by stimulating the child's ambition and sense of pride—by representing fear as a natural device of little children which is beneath his dignity to employ. Above all, you should not focus your attention on the *symptom*, but seek the deeper *causes*.

The child's helplessness usually springs from his sense of dependence upon adults. Accordingly, he must be granted the opportunity to acquire a greater degree of self-reliance. The observant parent will see that the anxiety becomes more pronounced when the child is faced by a problem. Hence he must learn to contend with difficult situations. *And here the parent's anxiety is more dangerous than his own.* Also his tendency to make himself the center and get his own way at any price must be corrected. Less indulgence is the best means to this end, as has been repeatedly stressed. The fact that the child's anxiety is based on undue indulgence becomes obvious, as he loses his

---

[8] See opening pages of Chapter 7.

fears completely in strange surroundings where no indulgence is shown him. Yet severity can only heighten his sense of helplessness. In this case the necessity to repress his fears may lead to deeper disturbances, usually of a neurotic nature.

Eating Difficulties

No child will become a feeding problem if his parents do not try to make him eat. Eating difficulties begin when mother or father attaches an inordinate importance to the child's eating. This may occur very early if the mother is overanxious about his weight, or if the child is sickly or has lost weight during illness. Then he is exposed to a pressure which at first may be only mild but eventually may develop into force and finally into violent coercion. Being urged to eat disturbs one's ability and willingness to accept food. It upsets the normal functioning of the stomach and makes eating repulsive. Furthermore, a child exposed to pressure reacts in general with resistance. If this resistance is directed against the intake of food, the parents, already overconcerned with the eating procedure, increase their pressure. Their desperation may grow by leaps and bounds, but will never improve the child's feeding. Moreover, it gives the child the impression that eating is not for his own interest, but for his parents' sake. Thus eating becomes a ready weapon to be used against them, especially if the child feels neglected or slighted. Such may be the case if a new baby arrives, or if the child has recovered from an illness and the parents stop their special attention.

A two-year-old girl resisted any food offered to an extent that worried not only her mother but the family physician. The child developed tantrums at each meal, and went for days without food if left on her own. It was possible to trace the beginning of this aversion to food to its origin. The mother was advised to keep the child on regular feeding hours (which was good advice), but what methods did she use? When the child was asleep at the hour of feeding she awakened her. When the child refused to take the bottle, she did not—as she should have done—let the child go until the next feeding time; instead, she forced the bottle into her mouth. When the child refused to take her first spoonful of fruit juice the mother took an even more drastic step; she held the child's nose, waiting until the child opened her mouth to breathe, and then put the spoon into the gasping mouth. Is it any wonder that this child developed such an antagonism against food?

All eating difficulties vanish within a few days or weeks if parents permit the child's natural impulses to exert themselves. These impulses are present *in every child*. Let him go hungry, and after a while he will ask for food. If you provide this food at regular times he will automatically adjust himself.

Instead of following this simple procedure, parents who have difficulties with their children's eating habits behave generally in a way which would make every normal child a food problem. First, they try persuasion. Mealtime becomes a tragic farce. The mother warns the child of the dire consequences if he does not eat. She feeds him and coaxes. She tells stories or gives good advice. She offers rewards or threatens punishment. Eventually she becomes angry; she begins to scold or to shout and even uses violence in stuffing the food into the child's mouth. Such a mother can become a fury out of sheer love, never noticing how the child twists and writhes until he finally throws up the food so laboriously forced into him. Now she either gives in and lets him go without food or she prepares special foods according to his preference. There are mothers who spend a large portion of each day planning a menu that the child will like and accept. Or the mother becomes determined and decides—"just to get him used to it"— to give him the same food at the next meal that he refused at the last, naturally with the same results. And yet, both parents and child could so easily be spared these agonies.

In the first place, the child's eating is no subject for discussion and no reason for commotion. Parents should trust the child's healthy instincts. He will not starve if you refrain from meddling, which only serves to stifle his instincts. With your concern you provide him a satisfaction much greater than his physical satiation. Think of all the attention he gets from you! He is even in a position to overpower you, to render you completely helpless, just by not eating. These social gains are more desirable than physical comfort. No child, left to his own resources in the midst of plenty, could develop malnutrition and dietary deficiencies to such a degree as children frequently show whose parents worry about their physical development and force them to eat. The first step in correcting a child's eating habits is to let him alone. No word should be spoken, no comment be made about finishing his plate or hurrying. But it is not enough to keep quiet. An anxious mother can speak eloquently without opening her mouth. If you sit at the table staring at the child, expressing all your tension, apprehension, despair, and fury, you give him just as much undue attention and provoke his defiance.

Secondly, the child must experience the natural consequences of his refusal to eat. If he does not want to eat what is set before him he should be granted the privilege of rejecting the food. But you should not indulge him and, out of pity or fear, give him something else to eat. When he does not eat his meal he must wait for food until the next meal—no snacks, no candy or bread and butter, not even a glass of milk outside of the set routine. And at the next meal he should be given the same food that the rest of the family is served.

Pampered children may "condescend" to eat those dishes which "taste good." If they get away with such demands, the parents either do not understand the importance of order or are helpless to stop their overindulgence. We have already explained why it is so important that the child learn to eat everything.[4] It is not difficult to induce a child to eat even food which he dislikes, unless his aversion is based on organic sensitivity (allergy). If he does not finish his serving with the rest of the family, the plate should be removed and he should be given nothing more during this meal. If you wish to train him to eat a certain food, you can arrange to follow it with his

[4] See Chapter 5, "Eating Habits."

favorite dessert. He should know what is coming but you must be careful to mention it in a way that is neither a reward or a punishment. Such threats as "If you don't eat your spinach, you won't get your ice cream" are entirely out of place. A casual attitude is imperative. But you must be firm and resist all promises, temper tantrums, or other tricks with which he may try to impress and weaken you. You must express your sympathy with him but must not give in. You should not be impressed even when he strives hard to eat what does not appeal to him but cannot get it down. As soon as he gags and struggles with his food, you just remove his plate and tell him that apparently he is not hungry and that he should not force himself; but the consequences must take place just the same.

Little Fred was invited to a party. Apparently he was a very poor eater. All the rest of the children had finished, but Fred still had almost his whole cup of cocoa and chewed away on a sandwich without noticeable effect. His grandmother who was with him remarked that it often took him an hour to finish his milk. She tried to persuade him. "Aren't you ashamed, Fred? All the others have almost finished; hurry up." The hostess asked her to leave the room and then turned to the boy. "At our house you don't have to eat if you don't want to. Give me your cup and your sandwich." And she made a gesture of taking them away. At once Fred grabbed them with both hands and took a huge bite of the sandwich. Now he had both cheeks full, but he could not get the food down. His training was against him. So she persisted. "No, Fred, that won't do. I can tell you are not hungry, so I will just have to take the food away from you if you don't want to eat it." Nothing more was said. In five minutes the cocoa was gone and the sandwich consumed, to the great amazement of the grandmother who could not understand how the feat had been accomplished.

Another case—and one of the worst in my experience—was that of little John. He was seven years old when his mother brought him to my summer camp. He had just recovered from whooping cough. He coughed and vomited not only when he started to eat, but also whenever he became excited or exerted himself physically. He had lost so much weight that he was down to skin and bones. The frantic parents had hired a nurse who fed him several times during the day. Each feeding took hours. The nurse had literally to force each bite into his mouth. The result was that a small amount of food did get eaten, but most of the time it did not stay down.

I was willing to accept the boy on the condition that the parents would not visit him for two weeks and would not inquire about his gain or loss of weight. The parents had already tried everything else; they had no alternative. The boy ate actually nothing for a few days. When food was placed before him he just looked at it. Nobody made any remarks; after a little while the plate was removed and, according to the rules, nothing else was offered to him. He took only milk and fluids at the time when they were served to all children. It was difficult to watch this child starve himself without doing something about it—but it was the only way to cure him.

Toward the end of the first week, John started to put some food into his mouth. The way in which he did it may best be described in the following anecdote: We had taken an excursion into the surrounding mountains. I encountered John on top of a hill and asked him how he was. He did not answer. This was puzzling as he was generally very friendly and conforming. I tried to find out what was troubling him but was unable to get any response. Finally I asked him to open his mouth. He obliged. There was his roll which he had taken at breakfast, one hour ago. He had put it in his mouth but had neither chewed nor swallowed it. It took two weeks of patient waiting before he started to eat normally. But then all difficulties were gone and he picked up weight very rapidly.

I observed another characteristic episode in a summer camp. A boy of fourteen had suffered from some abdominal tumor and had undergone several operations during the past few years. At the time he was physically well but could not eat. He vomited as soon as he took food. He was extremely underweight and in danger of starvation.

On this first day in camp, at dinnertime, he did not like the soup which was served. It was explained to him that he did not have to eat but he would not get anything else for this meal. Still he refused to eat. Then, when the meat was served he "became hungry" but he was not given anything. He said in amazement, "But I want to eat!" Apparently he had never experienced refusal when he was ready to eat. He was told in a friendly but firm manner that he had our sympathy, but that the rule could not be broken. At this point some other children intervened. They saw how undernourished he was, and when he started to cry, they begged that he be given some food. Everybody felt badly about it. But giving in to him would have meant losing the battle. He did not get anything on this day, but after a few days he ate everything and his vomiting stopped. This verified the diagnosis of the consulting physician, that the eating difficulties and the vomiting were of a psychogenic nature and probably the result of the overconcern and coaxing of his parents whose apprehensions and fear were only too understandable.

Speech Impediments

Occasional slight speech disturbances occur normally during the child's development and should not be regarded as pathological. So-called natural stuttering may, however, lead to more serious disorders when the parents intervene with warning, admonishments, and reproaches. Thus speech, too, may become the core of a conflict in which the child wins his victories against all parental efforts. Stuttering is directed specifically against contact with people; it impairs association with others. The child demands special assurance for making contacts. Stuttering often appears in the presence of persons whom the child fears. Sometimes, however, excessive ambition lies at its roots. The child does not so much fear the people themselves as he fears the possibility of disgracing himself. Stuttering is a symptom of anxiety and of fear of failure; but at the same time it signifies opposition, producing concern and special attention.

Stuttering may require professional treatment, yet the problem is less one of speech exercises than of general readjustment. Parents can help by not paying attention to the disturbance and—what is still more important—by applying all possible methods to reduce his antagonism and lessen his feeling of inadequacy.

One particular speech disturbance definitely results from extreme indulgence and pampering. This is a kind of pseudo-muteness. The child acts like a deaf mute without being one. Sometimes it is difficult to determine whether he is actually a deaf mute or not. He never talks or listens. He does not find it necessary to say anything, since his family grants all his wishes, which he indicates with gestures and facial expressions. Appropriate treatment *of the parents* always leads to the removal of the muteness, thereby permitting a final diagnosis.

Similar mechanisms produce inadequate speech in smaller children. They talk very indistinctly so that nobody except the members of the family can understand them. Their lack of participation in communicating with others is in line with a general "laziness." Such children make no proper efforts in any direction. They successfully demand that others do everything necessary. They walk slowly, dragging their feet; they do not dress themselves and have to be fed—all similar devices for getting attention in a passive-destructive way. They may seem dull and apathetic but actually they are clever enough to realize that they need not do more, as everything is done for them. Why should they exert themselves unnecessarily if they get so much comforting attention by doing nothing? If one succeeds in restraining an overprotective mother—or an older sister who gains status by her management of the "baby"—the "baby" soon grows up and assumes all the activities which he refused even when exposed to violent force.

Inarticulate speech is only one symptom of artificial babyhood. If you wish to improve the child's pronunciation, you should ignore whatever he says if it is not clearly expressed. It is inadvisable to correct his pronunciation or to get him to repeat a word correctly. All this is undue attention which will stimulate the child to continue his defects rather than to give them up. He will improve his speech only when he finds it beneficial to himself to do so. The advantage of speaking correctly will appear if he is unable to make himself understood otherwise.

B. Striving for Power

Whenever the child's efforts to gain social status by attracting attention fail, a new phase of social relationships begins. In most instances, it becomes a struggle for power. By being able to do what he is not supposed to do and refusing to do what is required of him, the child challenges your power and tries to make himself a potent force within the group. The idea of power is, of course, not the child's invention. He realizes from his observation of parents, relatives, and acquaintances that power gives social status and settles issues. Whoever can overpower the others gains triumph, is considered smart and superior. The whole atmosphere of our contemporary family, as part of our society, favors the mutual struggle for dominance and power. When other methods of trying to be a part of the social group fail, the contest for power looms as the next attempt for social recognition.

Disobedience

Disobedience is a characteristic tool of the child's struggle for power. This struggle disturbs cooperation and the necessary order. Whenever the question of power arises, the child stops conforming. Thus, disobedience is the most frequent and universal expression of the child's revolt. It occurs in conjunction with a great variety of other "faults." It must be remembered, however, that every healthy child offers occasional resistance. Children who always obey implicitly are not well-bred, but cowed children. In their case, resistance does not come out into the open; their faults are of a different nature.

A child is not disobedient merely because he does not do everything exactly as he should. It is when you need to enforce order that the child reveals the extent of his reluctance to obey. Some children do the opposite of what they are asked to do, as a matter of principle.

Six-year-old Jack is a great trial to his mother. When he is supposed to be dressing he runs around naked, and at mealtime he refuses to leave his toys. He pays no attention if asked to do something, and when told to come into the room he is bound to go in the opposite direction. His mother is completely nonplussed.

Jack is an only child. His father is a "weak" person who makes the mother's life miserable by his nervous complaints. She is a diligent, capable woman, but even she cannot stand the nervousness of her husband. In the end she always gives in to him, and maintains household discipline only through great effort on her part. Her attempts to instill orderly habits in Jack meet with violent opposition from her husband, who is extremely attached to the child and wants to relieve him of every inconvenience. He always takes the boy's part against the mother. If the little fellow expresses any wish, his father grants it at once, regardless of the mother's objections; and Jack has learned to take advantage of this situation. He does whatever he wants to do, for he is under his father's protection; and whenever his mother tries to insist, he immediately takes refuge with the father. The mother feels that she should counterbalance her husband's indulgence with severity, but this serves only to increase the child's resistance.

The life plan of this boy can be understood from his position between two warring despots. By allying himself with the one and defying the other he strives to win his position in the family. He knows no other triumphs than those over his mother's authority. His ideal is not ability and personal worth, but victory through resistance. And he turns on this potent disobedience as often as opportunity permits. Even when his mother asks him to do something that he might like to do under other conditions, he will do precisely the opposite. His fundamental error is his belief that defiance alone can secure power and prestige. He is far behind in useful accomplishments. He can dress himself only with difficulty; he is disorderly and lacks self-reliance; and he frequently stutters.

The greatest parental deficiency is naturally the incredible indulgence of the father, although the mother's efficiency may play a part in the deficiency of both her husband and her son. Disobedience often occurs in connection with spoiling, for an act of disobedience presupposes an inexcusable compliance on the part of the parent. Undoubtedly mother spoils and overprotects Jack, too—perhaps out of consideration for the ailing father and his excitability, or perhaps because she likes to take on too much responsibility. In any event, the boy has never yet experienced his mother's ability to enforce her wishes. Instead of attempting enforcement, she gives new orders: "Jack, do this, go there, let that alone!" And when Jack shows not the slightest inclination to obey these commands, she repeats them. As this does not help, the mother begins to scream at the boy, or she slaps him. Finally, she lets him have his own way since she does not want to bother with him any longer.

This attitude on the mother's part is characteristic of the development of disobedience. We can observe it again in a similar case.

Fred is a willful boy of eight. His mother died when he was quite young, and he has been living with his grandmother. The household includes several uncles and aunts and a sister who is almost ten years older than he. He is always getting into mischief, and is a typical "enfant terrible," the perfect "brat." Never under any circumstances does he behave. He is always fidgeting or prowling about; he never sits still for any length of time. He invariably has something in his hand, usually some breakable object that he will eventually drop on the floor with a resounding crash. Day in, day out, he is admonished, "Fred, hold your legs straight, don't drum with your fingers, let the bowl alone, stay in your chair!" The whole family takes part in this edifying chorus of remonstrance. But Fred ignores them. Only when the shouts become deafening or when he is slapped will he stop one nuisance—merely to begin another. No one knows what to do with him. At school he behaves in the same way. He is fidgety, always chattering and disturbing the class. He writes a wretched hand, and spells accordingly. Yet he is an intelligent, bright boy, who often so disarms you with his responses and remarks that you have to laugh—and let him do as he pleases.

What is this boy's life plan, and how did it originate? He is the youngest and smallest in a family of adults. His sister, the only other sibling, is already quite grown up and was always his superior in ability, inasmuch as she promptly took over the functions of the deceased mother and became very capable. Ever since his mother's death, Fred has felt sorry for himself, although all his relatives, out of pity and because of his lovableness, pampered him greatly and gave in to him in everything. Quite early he must have come to the conclusion that he could assert himself in this family group only by making the others concern themselves with him. He was unable to see any other way of confirming his importance. So he became dependent and failed in his schoolwork. By these means, and especially by his trick of making himself conspicuous, he compelled the others to pay constant attention to him. As they became increasingly annoyed and attempted to subdue him, Fred's A.G.M. turned into a struggle for power.

By now it should be clear that any attempt to rear Fred properly is doomed to failure unless we succeed first in changing his opinion of himself. He believes that he is of no importance, and that there is no other way of holding his ground than by making a spectacle of himself, attracting everyone's attention, and having his own way. If we want to help the boy, we must make him see that he, too, can win recognition and esteem through useful contributions. It will not be easy to impress the value of real achievements on the mind of a child who is so terribly discouraged; but such encouragement is essential. Above all, we shall have to show an interest in him in those rare instances when he is not in mischief and when he really contributes something. The alteration of the life style is the most important premise of improvement. Disobedience in particular remains unintelligible unless we know and understand the *entire background* of the child's conflict.

In addition to spoiling, certain purely technical errors in

training play a part in the development of disobedience. We shall briefly recapitulate here a few of those that have previously been mentioned: inconsistency in giving orders; indecisiveness of tone; violent, offensive or humiliating approaches and expressions; and impatience that does not even wait for the execution of a command. The most drastic error, however, consists in the repetition of an order. Every command with which the child does not comply increases his general disobedience. It is necessary to give specific commands only very rarely, when compliance is absolutely essential. But when something has been said *once*, it must not be repeated a second time; for the *words* are of no avail, and *actions* must take their place. It is self-evident that these should not consist in the application of *force*. Whenever the child does not respond to an order, you can and must allow the natural consequence of his behavior to take full effect.

This can be done quite peaceably. Especially in the case of a very willful child must you delay a command until the proper time arrives—a time when you are prepared to answer nonresponse with a logical consequence. Such occasions are more frequent than parents who evade reflection can imagine. In any event you must avoid the heaping up of commands and injunctions. The child must first of all learn to mind. If he has found in two or three instances that you are in a position to enforce your orders, he will be more apt to heed your words.

A youngster of two or three is standing in front of a display window and refuses to budge. His mother and father have gone ahead and are shouting at him and coaxing him. But the boy refuses to leave the spot. The parents are desperate. The father comes back and speaks loudly and sharply. The child pretends not to hear. Finally the father's patience is exhausted. He grasps the boy and begins to drag him off. And now the real show begins. The child resists fiercely; he howls and screams and throws himself on the sidewalk. Mother and father tug away at him in great excitement. A crowd gathers and takes sides with or against the parents, until the father picks the boy up bodily and retires with him from the battlefield, not at all a radiant victor.

And yet it is so easy to bring a child like this to his senses! There is no need for uproar and turmoil. If the parents had been wise they would have told the child after his first refusal to move on, "You want to see the display window, do you? Well, we're sorry but we haven't the time, so you'll have to stay by yourself and we'll be going on home." And if the boy had seen that they were really in earnest and were actually leaving, he hardly would have failed to follow. But suppose that he has previously been treated so laxly that he does not take his parents seriously and is convinced that now as always they will give in to him. In this event they need only turn the next corner and cautiously watch him from their vantage point. When they have disappeared, he will probably trot after them.

There are situations in which it is not easy to find the logical consequences. First of all, the time of company is not the proper time for training. (But on the other hand, you must not, from dread of a row, let the child have a free hand, or else he will take advantage of your fear of embarrassment.) When the proper time arrives, you can give the restless child the choice of sitting quietly or remaining alone in the room, since you simply cannot stand his company under such conditions. Similarly, when he fails to be quiet at mealtimes and does not conduct himself properly, there is no choice but for him to eat alone, either at a little table of his own, since he is still unable to act grown up, or perhaps even in the kitchen where he can eat as he chooses. It can be seen that it is unnecessary to exhort and command and run the risk of having him do as he pleases after all. But you should never *threaten* with consequences, only *apply* them!

In the case of unruly *older* children it is sometimes very difficult to see that an order is carried out without using brute force. Here it is best to introduce negative consequences. Refusal to submit can be maintained against even the strongest boy. If he does not arrive punctually for meals, all his violence cannot succeed in getting him a special serving. If mother leaves the room, he cannot prevent her from doing so. If he follows, she can leave the house. It would, of course, be a mistake to try to send *him* out of the room if he refuses to behave suitably. This could not be done without force, and probably not even then. Much depends, therefore, on how you construct the situation from which a child is to learn obedience.

Since the child's disobedience indicates rebellion and defiance, the hostile atmosphere must be cleared before the fault can be repaired. In the case of Jack we have clearly seen the serious error that the mother committed. She made scarcely any effort at all to win the boy over. Naturally it was no easy task to compete with the fawning indulgence of her husband. But she could certainly have found ways of interesting the child and gaining his confidence if she had not felt constrained to compensate the father's weakness with special severity on her part. Hence, when a child refuses to mind, you must first avoid arousing a conflict. Instead, you should devote more time and attention to the child in moments when he is in a good frame of mind and ready for friendly cooperation. By this means you will succeed best in obstructing the sources of his resistance.

Stubbornness

Stubbornness is a variety of disobedience. Hence much that was said in the previous section is equally true here. What should be your attitude toward the child when he has a spell of stubbornness? Persuasion, threats, and promises, even the application of force, are usually futile. The child sulks and refuses to be moved.

Twelve-year-old Joe has occasional attacks of stubbornness. Sunday the family had planned to go to a restaurant for dinner, but instead they were invited to the home of some friends. Joe was furious. When they arrived, he stayed outside in the yard and could not be persuaded to go into the house. The parents sent his older brother out to fetch him, and the children of the house did their bit to convince him; but all efforts were wasted. Joe later told me how much it pleased him to have everybody entreating him—it was worth missing the dinner. But his fury really started when they finally gave up urging him and went back inside. Then at last he began to regret his mulishness.

Life had been no bed of roses for Joe. He was completely overshadowed by his elder brother. In his own opinion, nothing useful and worth while that he could do could compare with the attainments of this brother, whose superiority was constantly impressed upon Joe. Solely through his frequent attacks of stubbornness could he make himself the absolute master of his family, who were at a loss to know what to do with him. In these moments even the brother was insignificant, and he, Joe, became the hub and axis of the household.

Obstinate children use their behavior as a means of provoking people to fight with them. And most parents fall neatly into the trap. Stubbornness is one of the many devices by which children who feel abused or neglected try to attract attention and to demonstrate their strength. ("You can't make me do it!") The best answer, therefore, is to *leave the child to himself*. You can gradually break him of using these tactics if you take pains to understand his conflicts and relieve his anger by improving your relationship with him.

Temper Tantrums

Intensely combative and hostile emotions may create symptoms that appear almost pathological. Yet behind them is nothing but the desire for power and ascendancy. This is true of fits of temper. Some parents may assume an organic affection of the nerves, a nervous debility or a hereditary defect. Temper, however, is always curable through proper treatment; but parents who are afraid that a nervous disposition is the cause of temper give in to the child at the crucial moment.

You may be easily inclined to such an attitude if you or some other member of the family likewise suffers from a violent temper. In this event the assumption of an inherited predisposition becomes a foregone conclusion. Yet this person (let us assume he is the father) may also be a discouraged individual who feels an occasional urge to play the tyrant. Through the impressive spectacle of uncurbed violence he tries to prove that he cannot be tampered with. And if he seems to regret his conduct afterward, he is only masking his intentions from himself and others by his contrition and self-reproach. The whole family comes to respect his "weak nerves" and recognizes that in such moments all their own rights and prerogatives must be suspended. If the child observes outbursts of temper in his father, he may try similar expedients to compensate for a weak position; and he is encouraged to proceed in this direction when the other members of the family, horrified at his morbid "heritage," give in to his fits just as they do to his father's.

The mother of a four-year-old boy had a great deal of trouble with his fits of temper. She was firmly convinced that he had inherited this "affliction" from his father. The child was born after his father's death; hence he could not have acquired the trait by imitation. A more thorough inquiry into the circumstances revealed the following: The mother, deeply affected by her husband's death, devoted herself completely to the care of the posthumous son, her only child. In her love, she had given in to him ever since he was a baby. It was understandable that he should be indignant when finally a situation arose in which she could not submit to him. And he did what all children do in such cases—he screamed. Since his mother yielded, he became progressively violent and furious whenever anything was denied him. Then his mother realized with horror that he was "just like his father"; and as she had acceded to all her husband's pressing demands, so now she became the slave of her child's whims. With his fits of rage he broke down every resistance. Thus, as a result of her indulgent weakness, she had unknowingly brought up her child to use exactly the same methods which she, in her submissiveness, probably had fostered in her husband.

Attacks of temper may sometimes assume rather terrifying forms, as in the following example:

Four-year-old Frank, an only child, suffered from "respiratory spasms." After initial cries of rage, his breath suddenly gave out; he fell to the floor, became blue in the face, and his body drew up in a spasm. One can imagine the terror of mother and father, who then worked over the boy with damp cloths, picked him up, and carried him around until they were finally able to calm him down with caresses and kisses. These spells were always preceded by an altercation which ensued when the child could not have his way. Afterward, naturally, the parents promised him anything to quiet him.

Despite the menacing aspect of such scenes, tantrums never imply actual danger. They are merely a child's attempt to get his own way; and generally produce prompt results. If the child is left alone, if everyone leaves the room (however loath the anxious and terrified parents may be to do so), the child will recover very speedily of his own accord. If the child is older, he may follow, of course, but as long as nobody pays attention to whatever he may do, his efforts are in vain. An older child may threaten to break windows and furniture, or to throw things at you, a pattern that has been set by previous training. You must keep in mind that broken windows and furniture are not as expensive as a very disturbed child. You must take the chance and leave him alone. If necessary you may have to leave the house. Two or three demonstrations of the inefficacy of his device may be enough to "cure" the child of the dreaded attack. But, of course, we should not forget to mend the deeper injuries caused by previous spoiling, and rectify the derangements of the child's general life plan.

Bad Habits (Thumb-sucking, Nose-picking, Nail-biting)

Annoying habits are promoted by the nagging, spite-provoking attitude in parents that we have mentioned so many times before. Many of them are first evoked by this meddling;

others, like thumb-sucking, toward which the child is naturally inclined, are only reinforced and prolonged. The same
applies to all bad habits—which cannot possibly be enumerated
since they are as numerous and varied as are parents' demands.
It is always harmful when worried mothers and fathers call
special attention to some particular activity. "Sit up straight!
Walk straight! Turn your toes out! Don't put your knife in
your mouth! Don't put everything in your mouth! Don't
make faces!" (One can see that it would be impossible to list
all the variants.) These admonitions almost regularly lead to
a thorough *cultivation* of the denounced habit—a process in-
dicative of the child's rebellion against parental demands.

Once the habits are established, perhaps without your having
anything to do with it, you must consider how to deal with
them. We shall take up this matter in connection with the
habits that probably are most common and persistent—finger-
sucking, nose-picking, nail-biting.

Finger-sucking is by origin not a bad habit, but a natural inclination of the baby. Yet if it continues beyond the first year,
you must be careful. It is wrong to pull the child's finger forcibly out of his mouth or to slap him. There are more apt methods that even a baby can understand. You might put gloves on
his hands, and, if he has not become especially addicted to
sucking as the result of earlier interference on your part, such
a move may suffice to spoil his pleasure in the practice. If he
commences to put a corner of the bedclothes, or any other
available object into his mouth, then you should bear in mind
that *the less obvious attention you pay to bad habits, the easier
it is to correct them.* If the child is older and you wish to break
him of thumb-sucking, you can discuss with him freely his
inclination to indulge in easy pleasures. You can emphasize
that, after all, this is *his* problem, and not yours; but it may
produce deformities in his finger or his teeth and he might not
like it later. Such discussions must remain very rare incidents;
otherwise you are just nagging. Your main effort should be
directed toward helping the child to find better and more

wholesome satisfactions. It is either protest against the parents or lack of satisfying activity which keeps the child sucking his thumb. For this reason it is much better to let the child outgrow his finger-sucking instead of interfering in an inadequate way and thereby prolonging the habit.

Nose-picking, too, is among those practices to which all children naturally resort at one time or another. If the child is not refractory to begin with, it often is enough to have a friendly talk with him and point out how ugly and disagreeable the habit is. If you enjoy his confidence, he will believe you and follow your advice. But if you have missed this first opportunity and furthered the habit with exasperated words or actions—in this event you must await a favorable occasion for exerting any educational influence. If you are generally on good terms with the child you may find it possible to enlighten him on the habit in an intimate conversation, when there is complete harmony between you. Often he will agree not to do it any more, but still the practice continues. His defiance vanishes only for this one peaceful hour and may reappear as daily routine. Reproaching him with his inconsistency starts the conflict all over again. It is better to wait until the time arrives for the next friendly discussion. Then he will probably state that he would really like to rid himself of the habit, but simply cannot—he either does it unconsciously, when he is thinking about something else, or finds it impossible to control himself.

In these terms he describes the sham conflict within himself that we have already discussed.[5] This can be explained to him calmly and clearly, showing him that he apparently is still not ready to give it up. It is possible through such conversations to approach and solve problems that are of far greater importance to the child's subsequent development and the harmony of the family than the bad habit in and for itself. This technique, naturally, is easier with older, more mature children. In the case of younger children you will probably have to limit

[5] See Chapter 4, "Pull Yourself Together."

yourself to simple, encouraging suggestions. "I am sure you will learn to stop it, just to be polite," or because "it doesn't look nice." "Do you think that maybe you can keep your finger away from your nose all day tomorrow?" If he does not succeed the first day, he may the second or third. These attempts on the child's part should not, of course, be disturbed by inept meddling from other quarters.

As has been said earlier, in breaking children of bad habits you can make good use of *natural consequences*. These can be applied even in the case of a baby. You can tell a child, without offending him, that after he picks his nose you could not possibly let him hold your hands. And you might suggest that probably other people, too, will refuse to give him their hands if they see him pick his nose. Or when he does this, you can get up and leave the room with a remark to the effect that you don't like to watch him. Perhaps your creative imagination will devise still other, similar answers that can be regarded as unpleasant but logical consequences. However, such measures, once adopted, must be maintained and carried out consistently if they are to produce results. Hence it generally suffices to stick to only one of these consequences.

The situation is quite similar with nail-biting. Here again, instruction and natural consequences must supplement each other. This habit betrays obstinacy, rebellion, and tension, and hence occurs usually in combination with other faults. Children who practice it may be sullen, secretive, disorderly, or generally untidy about their persons; in other words, they infringe upon order at a number of points. It seems as though they vent their pent-up anger on their fingers. Sometimes this chronic rebelliousness is compensated, or covered up, in later years by a marked pleasantness; but it still reveals its presence in a variety of faults, or perhaps just in the maintenance of this particular habit. In nail-biting, therefore, particular stress must be laid on general revision of the child's attitude. You should be less concerned with breaking him of the one habit than with extricating him from the conflict-situation. You must try to discover its root—spoiling combined with extreme severity, a feeling of being neglected, or suppressed rivalry with brothers and sisters, and so on. You can accustom the child to order and cleanliness by diverting his ambition toward personal appearance.

However, shaming him about his unsightly fingers is not enough. An inner willingness to look after himself must be awakened. But this result cannot be achieved merely by pressure from without which only increases tension and rebellion. Direct influence, therefore, is of value only when it promotes an inner preparedness for reform. Hence you must pay close attention to the effect of consequences which you introduce, and must take care that they do not increase the child's stubbornness. You must clearly indicate your good will and desire to help. You may suggest, for instance, that he put on gloves when he goes walking with you or when you are to meet friends, because otherwise people might not offer him their hands. You may praise him when you notice that one nail is a little longer than the rest. Sometimes—especially with girls—it does good to have the child's hands manicured. But, first and foremost, every possible source of humiliation, every form of vexation and reproof, must be stringently excluded from the treatment of bad habits.

Masturbation

A separate discussion of this "bad habit" is justified only by the exaggerated importance attached to it by overanxious parents, who themselves are usually to blame for its development; for a child who is rightly treated will rarely engage in continual premature sexual activity. Boys who play with their genitals long before puberty generally have been exposed to two kinds of experience: first, to premature sexual stimulation by extreme demonstrations of affection on the mother's part, especially caresses in bed, kissing on the mouth, and close mutual petting (activities which may stimulate sexual sensations even in three-year-old boys); and second, to parental intervention whenever the child was caught manipulating his genitals. Thus masturbation serves to defy parental power, and sexual satisfaction becomes a triumph over restrictive order.

It is only natural that every child, in his effort to acquaint himself with his body, should devote considerable attention to his sexual organs. This absorption with his body remains uninjurious as long as it is not noted by the parents. If it is noted calamity begins. Their own misconceptions and fear of sexuality may induce parents to interfere with an activity which originally was harmless, but which they regard as reprehensible or even deleterious. Now the well-known cycle begins: exhortations and slaps lead to increased activity on the child's part; which increases the determination on the part of the parents; which again provokes stubborn adherence to the habit. Now—only *secondarily*, as a result of the conflict—it becomes a source of surreptitious pleasure. In this way the genital organs are prematurely stimulated to sensations that otherwise are reserved for a much later stage in the child's growth. And then, naturally, the parents' anxiety gets out of bounds and they resort to terrifying threats, which may seriously injure the child's emotional development.

The struggle against sexual bad habits usually expands later on into a general conflict. I have seen exasperated, despairing parents tie the child's hands together above the covers at night —without success, naturally, for he is cunning enough to circumvent any violent measure. I have seen attempts to render his genital parts inaccessible with bandages and appliances, even with plaster casts! Is it so strange, then, that his interest in the sexual functions is dangerously enhanced and becomes the focal point of his thoughts and emotions, sometimes for the rest of his life?

Such habits can easily be avoided if the parents follow a strict policy of non-intervention. But once the genital apparatus has been prematurely activated, this process can scarcely be terminated. Yet there is no need for worry. The theory of damage caused by masturbation has proved to be a false hypothesis. Such practices neither make the child neurotic nor impede his development. There is a relation between masturbation and later nervous complaints, but not as cause and effect. Both are the expressions of a poor attitude toward life and its responsibilities. Masturbation never gives rise to nervousness; but when practiced too early or in excess, it does indicate that the child is uncontrolled, pleasure-seeking, and unable to withstand temptation. These are the faults that require attention, not the incidental sexual play. Overemphasizing the habit provokes the guilt-feeling of the child. The resulting self-accusations and remorse about sexual interests and activities do not stop the child from continuing them, but cause inner tension and conflicts which are much more harmful than the original practices.

Untruthfulness

The problem of lying reveals similar mechanisms; an original harmless act can be made into a serious problem through the mismanagement of parents, who permit this fault to become a tool in the contest for respective power.

We must realize that children's "fibs" are not always faults. But they can become so permanent a habit that, for reasons which usually remain a mystery to parents, the deceitful child prefers lying to veracity. All children occasionally deviate from the truth. (Is it different with adults?) There are times when the child's lively imagination makes him unable to distinguish between true and false—that is, reality and fantasy. These phases occur almost regularly between the second and fourth year. Highly imaginative children with vivid daydreams may go through such a stage even later. The child fails to tell the truth either because he believes that his fantasies are real, or he is curious to see what will happen when he puts the fictions of his imagination to the test of reality. Such "lies" may even function as an A.G.M.

This, however, is only *one* source of the child's mendacity. There is no doubt that he also takes an example from the adults of his family and learns to lie when, for instance, he wants to escape punishment or evade a responsibility. Severe parents give abundant provocation for lying. These untruths, then, are simple methods of defense against the exercise of power. Forcible intimidation of children breeds falsehood.

Many parents are terribly upset when they catch their child in a lie. They interpret the child's lie as a serious threat to their power over him. Hence, the more insecure they feel in their authority, the more strongly a falsehood will irritate them. This is not a moral issue, because parents themselves cannot avoid some dishonesty in their own lives. Anxious parents, however, do not admit their concern for their authority, but imagine that the child will degenerate if they permit him to lie with impunity. Accordingly, they bring up the heavy artillery whenever they spot the slightest diversion from the truth. Not infrequently they brand their child as a liar, and thus lead him onto a dangerous road that he would never have followed of his own accord.

You should be careful not to take a lie too tragically. You need not be indignant; your authority is not so feeble that it can be shattered with a single blow. Lying does not make a criminal of the child. Naturally, you should train him to be truthful. But this will never be achieved by scoldings and threats. Vexation and anger only betray your weakness. Many children acquire a liking for falsehoods, since by this means they can baffle the parents. When the child has discovered the power he gains through lying, he lies whenever he feels the need to reduce his parents to helpless despair. His lying no longer springs from specific situations, but is an end in itself. Untruthfulness becomes an expression of the struggle for superiority between child and parent.

The same mechanism can be found in swearing. Children feel big and smart when they use "bad" words, especially when they realize the reaction those words will produce. The surest way to rob a lie of its potential effect is to let it appear as insignificant and trivial, as it really is. Then the child will soon lose his zest for repetitions. He must realize that it gets him nowhere. An understanding smile will make him feel ridiculous and ashamed of himself. But he can be shown that he himself has a vital interest in reciprocal good faith and veracity. *You can never rear your child to truthfulness unless you prove to him that truth is more practical than falsehood.* If he believes the opposite, then neither righteous indignation and sermons nor anger and chastisement are of any avail.

Sometimes a lie of your child may place you in a situation which you do not know how to handle. In all such perplexing situations it is best first to stop and think what you should *not* do (which is much easier to discover!). And simply refrain from any action you should not take; whatever else you do will be adequate. You may also be guided in perplexing situations by the principle of doing the opposite of what the child expects you to do. These considerations will always keep you on the right track. They will prevent you from getting angry, feeling lowered in your prestige, becoming alarmed and frantic. If your children occasionally show off with a lie, you can point out how easy it is to fool you; that if they need such cheap methods to feel important, it is all right with you and you will have to take it. This is a much stronger answer than demonstrating the deep impressions they make on you with a lie.

If they should not respond to such an approach, then you can either devise a game whereby everybody is free to say what he wants, regardless of whether it is true or not. And you, too, can fool them by calling them for dinner when the food is not ready, or pulling other stunts that they won't like. After a while you may propose to them that they might prefer reliability, i.e., trustworthiness. Or you can apply the "wolf! wolf!" story, when the child continues to fib; you just don't believe anything he says after a while. However, if he is untruthful only to escape punishment or disapproval, you must take it without resentment, for you yourself would very likely lie if you were sufficiently afraid of somebody. And if he lies in order to brag about his importance, you should develop his self-confidence by showing him appreciation and approval so that he will not need to resort to subterfuge to make an impression.

Dawdling

Dawdling is not an offense in itself; but it has a strong effect. It drives some parents to distraction when their child lingers, cannot keep himself busy or amused, and takes an eternity to get one thing done. Dawdling reveals itself as a potent weapon because of the strong reaction that it releases in others. It is an expression of defiance. Here we can clearly see the interplay of child and parent in the development of faulty conduct. For what do parents do when their children dawdle? They remonstrate, urge, become vexed—in short, run the whole gamut of expedients arising from the embittered sense of powerlessness, resulting in an increase of the child's defiance and the conclusive adoption of the habit in question. This is the genesis of time-wasting. It grows on the soil of a general passivity and thrives on misguided correctives.

Here again we can see the futility of parental action as long as the child is not understood in his motivation. Few parents stop and think why he behaves in such a way. When the child does not find anything to do and pesters them with questions of what he should do, or when he apparently tries to do something but instead procrastinates, is constantly distracted, or occupies himself with dissipating interests, the parents act on the assumption that he wants to do what he professes or is supposed to do. Consequently, they try to remind and press him to finish his job or to do something. But that is not what he desires. He may have first looked for their attention; but in the course of the struggle, of their pushing and his resisting, his dawdling becomes directed toward proving his own power, putting the parents into his service, and resisting all their pressure and authority.

What can you do about it? In the first place, the vicious circle has to be broken. No "flying off the handle"! No nagging! However hard it may be, you must learn to observe the child coolly, even when he provokes you. On occasion, you may simply let things pass. If your personal prestige is your main consideration, of course you will retain the old policy; but then you should not be surprised and complain if the child goes from bad to worse. Your first course then, is a negative one: you must avoid false tactics.

There are several positive methods at your command. Since dawdling is a manifestation of defiance and conflict, you would do well to relieve the situation, distract the child's attention, or disconcert him. If you refuse to become irritated and no longer nag him, that above all will set him back on his heels. It is no fun to be slow if nobody gets annoyed! By chatting with him, or arousing his interest in some way, his tendency to dawdle will be lessened. In any case it is essential that you reduce his general hostility by grasping the situation as a whole and helping him out of his difficulties. By such means timewasting can be transformed from a practically hopeless nuisance into a solvable problem.

C. Taking Revenge

The child who feels unfairly treated and defeated in the struggle for power will want to get even with the parents for what he thinks they have done to him. He has numerous methods which he uses unconsciously to punish and revenge himself upon them. They vary in destructiveness but have in common the amount of anger which they provoke.

Stealing

The horror and despair of parents at the theft committed by their child is easy enough to understand, for stealing reveals how little he regards the clearest and most convincing moral principle. The parents now fear that he will continue inexorably on the road to crime. Most often they try to influence him with severity, with threats and reprisals. They cannot conceive how ineffectual these measures are, or see that in many cases they only hasten and sometimes even give impetus to the dreaded development.

I knew a boy who reacted unusually to the repeated assertion of his mother: "You're bound to be a jailbird and end up on the scaffold." He had a bitter grudge against his parents and was incredibly defiant since he felt, with some reason, that he was slighted in favor of the other children of the family. And so, once when he heard his mother speak these words, he thought, "Not by a long shot! I won't give you that satisfaction!" Gritting his teeth he meticulously did everything that was asked of him, but not without cursing under his breath. He respected all the laws of propriety, but out of his secret antagonism grew an unusually severe compulsion-neurosis.

This reaction to such prophetic utterances is, however, exceptional. There is no surer means of driving a child into the arms of crime than to treat him like a felon and picture him as a future criminal. If we want to help him, we must first know how he came to lose the distinction between mine and thine. This never occurs without deepseated conflicts; but the incidental provocations to steal are various. One child steals because his frivolous nature wants to have immediately whatever his heart desires. He cannot wait. And he does not care about the consequences. When he was small he got everything he wanted, and he cannot see why there should ever be any deviation from this rule. Hence sporadic thievery is common in uncontrolled children who have been too much indulged. It shows an essential want of insight if, at this late hour, the parents stand helpless and terrified before the aberration which their own laxity has induced in their child.

The motives for theft may vary a great deal. Parents rarely detect the real causes. Their perplexity is due to their lack of understanding. The child does not reckon on understanding, since he himself does not understand the reasons for his acts, and so sullenly expects his punishment. When you ask a child why he has stolen you get either stubborn silence or a puzzled

"I don't know." It is generally true, the child really does not know why he did it. What he actually knows of his impulses —that he craved candy, fruit, spending money, or other desirable things—is no justification, and he looks for no clemency from admitting it. So he says nothing at all. He himself has not the slightest notion of the deeper motives behind his behavior. But if you want to help the child, you must track these down. You must recognize whether stealing served as an A.G.M., or as a tool for power or revenge.

Horrified and distraught, the mother of eight-year-old Helen appeared at the Guidance Clinic. This carefully nurtured, well-behaved child had, on a number of occasions and with the greatest cleverness, stolen different articles from a stationer's shop—blotting pads, pocket knives, pencils, and the like. She had not been detected until now, so adroitly had she executed the thefts. There seemed to be no reason for her acts. She was given everything she wanted by her mother. When questioned, the girl refused to say why she had stolen or how she had disposed of the articles. Only after we had calmed her fright and tension did we find out that she had distributed the stolen merchandise among her playmates and school-chums, who had no idea of how they were obtained.

Yet the mystery of little Helen was still far from being solved. Only after we grasped her whole situation, after we learned of the part she played as the youngest child of the family, and realized that she felt insignificant in competition with an older, more capable sister, did the clouds thin; and we saw the light at once. By handing out presents she sought to make an impression on the other children—to cut a figure. And she succeeded nobly. Since she always had some trifle to give away, they all wanted to play or walk with her. How could Helen, who was not aware of these causes and effects, explain why she stole? And can anybody imagine that reproaches and severity could in any way alter her behavior?

Quite different was the case of fifteen-year-old Robert. Here it was much more difficult to understand what moved this fine boy to take valuables and hide them at home. He neither sold them nor boasted of them. His situation, in brief, was the following: His father was very strict, and Robert, the eldest of three children, was particularly closely watched. He had a tendency to take life easy, and allowed himself liberties that his father could not condone. He took walks instead of studying, and failed to come home punctually. He smoked his first cigarette quite early. All in all, he was in obvious revolt against his father. The middle brother, two years younger than Robert, was his opposite. As could be expected, this brother was notably careful and painstaking, and thus became the perfect example of his father's principles.

Robert, too, was unable to say why he stole. His earlier misdemeanors had been rather simple and harmless, but they all evinced his desire to triumph over order and his father. Everything he did was under cover. It was like a secret compensation: "You see—I do what *I* want, anyway!" Nor was it so senseless that he allowed his stealing to be discovered, for each revelation defied anew his father's ideals. These principles had proved themselves powerless. And herein, apparently, lay the boy's secret aim in life—to demonstrate the futility of the coercion exercised by the social order through his father.

This propensity to snap one's fingers at authority lies at the bottom of a great many criminal acts. It is found even in healthy and respectable individuals. Many "honest citizens" delight in cheating the streetcar company out of the fare. The few pennies probably mean nothing to them, but still they childishly enjoy their "success." To get the better of someone —especially if he is the guardian of order—is not always regarded as dishonorable. This tendency explains many occasional thefts of children. In their eyes there is no essential difference between stealing an apple under the grocer's nose and ringing a doorbell, running off, and gleefully observing from around a corner the wrath of a beslippered paterfamilias. It is true that these are pranks that should not be countenanced, but great moral indignation is wholly out of place. It earmarks the childish stunt as a crime, and may exert a detrimental influence on the child's later development. The most natural consequence is to make the child return the articles.

Naturally, a large theft or the repeated occurrence of less serious acts gives reason enough for earnest consideration of what ought to be done. But so long as you are excited and outraged, you are incapable of helping the child; for then you are not the child's friend and are in no position to understand his situation. Also, it would be a mistake to hold him solely responsible for the trespass. A great part of the responsibility lies with parents, the family constellation, and all the other factors that combine to produce his life situation. In highly problematic cases it may be necessary to enlist the services of a trained outsider—a clinical adviser or a specialist in child guidance. The usual mode of disposing of such incidents—with an excess of anger or despair and feints at punishment—has, among others, the marked disadvantage that it leaves unchanged, or further aggravates, the real situation of the child.

In conclusion, I might point out that children do a great deal of stealing which fortunately never comes to the notice of their families. Although—or because—their parents can take no steps to correct the fault, these children do succeed in becoming respectable people. Is there any one of us who does not have memories of certain childhood transgressions? Even serious offenses need have no unfavorable consequences for the child's development if he is so fortunate as to have friends who use their sympathy and understanding to help him out of his muddled state.

The following example illustrates that stealing may have a great variety of motivations; it also demonstrates how difficult it is to win over a child who has given up hope of being liked and being loved.

Sixteen-year-old Dan was the terror of a social settlement house. Whenever some damage was done at a critical time, he was the instigator. He knew exactly how and when to strike to hurt the most. Once, before a theatrical performance, he ruined all the pianos, actually chopping them to pieces. On another occasion he cut the curtain the night before a performance. He committed endless acts of destruction to property and individuals. His family could not be approached. He was one of a large group of children and was completely ostracized at home. The family got into so many difficulties with and through him—in the neighborhood, in school, at home, with school authorities and police—that they no longer wanted to bother with him.

It was decided to assign him to one of our best and most understanding group workers. The young man made a special effort to win Danny and to get him interested in various activities. He let him help in stage-set construction, gave him responsibilities during the performances, and succeeded in gaining the boy's confidence and cooperation. For quite a while there were no complaints about Dan.

One day the young worker came in great excitement to discuss an episode which puzzled him. He and Dan had been working together when the boy took the worker's watch from the table and put it into his pocket. The worker saw the act but he was not sure whether the boy knew he saw it. At any rate he did not know what to do. He realized it would be a mistake to accuse Danny. So he pretended to look for the watch. Danny volunteered to help him to find it. Finally the worker gave up, saying, "Someone must have taken it." Danny became furious. "Who could do something like that to you! I will look for it; and if I find the guy who took the watch, I will beat him up, but good." So they went around the house asking boys whether they had seen the watch. Danny finally became restless. Suddenly he burst out, "You knew all the time that I had the watch. Why didn't you take it away from me?" And he returned the watch.

The worker had acted correctly. What bothered him was his inability to understand Dan's behavior. Why had he tried this stunt? Apparently Danny could hardly believe that the worker had a real interest in him and was a true friend; he had always been rejected and disliked by everybody. He apparently wanted to see if this particular act would provoke the same treatment which he had experienced all of his life. If the worker had succumbed to the provocation, he would have demanded the return of his watch, perhaps in a sharp way; the boy would have denied taking it, a struggle might have ensued, first with an argument, then perhaps leading to physical violence if the worker had tried to search the boy and to retrieve his watch. Thus the boy would have found his disbelief in friendship justified and reverted to the type of human relationship to which he was accustomed. This act of stealing was apparently a supreme test to which Danny subjected the worker, who passed it with flying colors. One decisive battle was won in the rehabilitation of Danny.

Violence and Brutality

The stubborn resistance to order often assumes terrifying forms. Sometimes it is limited to fits of anger, in which case the child retains a certain good will and excuses his eruptions of brutality afterward. But when these outbursts occur frequently and without pretext of being involuntary, the last vestige of good will has vanished and the naked antagonism is revealed. This bold-faced brutality presupposes a mixture of weakness and violent oppression on the side of the mother or father. Intelligent children can develop the most efficient techniques for getting at their parents' vulnerable spots and thus may become a real menace.

Seventeen-year-old Michael lay ill with the flu. His mother did not respond quickly enough to his desires, and he threw three glasses and two plates at her in a single day. When she withdrew, he got up with a temperature of 102 degrees, dressed, and went out on the street. He knew the sure way of reaching his mother's weakness.

Twelve-year-old John was the terror of his family. No one could manage him. He did whatever he pleased: stole money, refused to go to school, lay in bed all one day and stayed out the next day until one in the morning, lashed out at his mother and cursed her like a trooper. But when a stranger was present, someone whom he feared, he was a model of deportment and had a fine talent for explaining everything in a harmless light.

It is obvious that in such cases the blame lies with the parents themselves who, through their indulgence, have allowed the child to get completely out of hand. It is apparent, too, that they did not oppose the rising tide of conflict by pacific and friendly means. Otherwise they would have won him over, and his revolt would never have advanced to this stage. Often enough, the cruelty shown the child is the source of his own brutality. He reflects what he has experienced. Sometimes he may not actually have been abused, but nevertheless felt mistreated. Occasionally, brutality is merely a tool to experience the gratification of complete power over other beings.

Excessive strictness, especially whipping, may stir up rebellion and arouse brutal instincts. These are more likely to arise if one of the parents tries to compensate with compliance for the severity of the other. Neglect may have the same effect. In both cases the child feels more justified in his desire to seek revenge. Before any improvement of the child's behavior can be achieved, the conflict must be ended, at least on the side of the parent. The child must again feel accepted and liked, not feared. If a *natural* consequence cannot be easily and consistently applied, it is as well to do nothing at all. It may make a strong impression on him if he suddenly recognizes that he no longer can intimidate and hurt. Some few experiences of kind firmness may check the child and make him realize the futility of his behavior. They may suffice to reinstate the authority of order. Such effect cannot be attained by blows or other violent measures. If the physical strength or brutality of the child is so great that it is impossible to introduce natural consequences, the child should be removed from his parents and sent to an adequate home, preferably where he would be with several other youngsters. The earlier the parents resign themselves to this fact, the easier it will be for the child to learn to adapt himself to an orderly scheme of existence.

Extreme cruelty and brutality are sometimes observed in young children. The psychological mechanism in these cases seems to be slightly different. Their brutality is directed not so much against parents and against order, as against smaller, "weak" objects, such as animals, younger children, and even inanimate objects. Two factors seem to contribute to such behavior. One is the sensual stimulation produced through acts of violence. Children may have experienced such excitation either personally or by witnessing other children who were beaten, forcibly restricted, or abused. Sometimes stimulation has come from seeing pictures or listening to talk about violent action. Sensual stimulations have a tendency to continue in the same pattern. An experience which once aroused sensual feelings remains associated with the same response. It is sought again as a pleasure device. Sensual desire for brutality may be active or passive (sadistic or masochistic). Children who are frequently exposed to violence are impressed with its excitement. They seek similar sensations by biting or asking to be bitten, by hitting or provoking a blow. They like to suffer or to make others suffer as part of a sensual game. The psychological factors and the proper approach to its readjustment are the same as discussed in the section on sexual play.

Another dynamic factor causing cruelty and brutality in young children is in line with their general style of life. They may try to impress others with their "shocking" behavior (active-destructive A.G.M.), or they may want to demonstrate their power and forcefulness. Brutality against other children is often an expression of "masculinity." "See how strong I am." A desire to punish is frequently just an imitation of parental practices. While playing house, children demonstrate their interpretation of their parents' conduct. Parents who are horrified to see how their child treats his dolls, his "children" or "pupils" in his play, do not realize how the child's behavior reflects their own and how the child's relationship to others is an image of their own relationship to the child.

Bed-wetting

Bed-wetting is seldom due to physical causes, as is often falsely assumed. It is true that organ inferiorities of the bladder, the kidneys, or the spinal cord may facilitate its appearance. There are, however, no diseases which have as their only symptom an inability to retain the urine.

Five-year-old Frank began to wet his bed when his father put him in an orphanage. It never occurred when he slept at home. Eleven-year-old Alan was in conflict with a very strict father. When the latter gave him a severe lecture on school affairs, deprived him of free time, and struck him, the boy started to wet his bed. The purpose of the bed-wetting was very clear in the case of seven-year-old Charles, who went on a long visit to his aunt and, contrary to his previous habits, soiled the bed linen the very first night. When his aunt asked him why he had done this, he said that he only wanted to see whether she would put up with it.

When the antagonism against his environment has reached a certain intensity, the child no longer makes any effort to avoid unpleasantness. His sense of revengefulness is occasionally covered by a masochistic trait of self-abasement. Such children are often ostentatiously dirty. Their whole pride is fixed on *not* washing. They show a "downward ambition" (Wexberg). They achieve a kind of negative glory through the humiliations that they have to suffer, for they are really a sore burden on the entire household. No one knows what to do with them, and the dismay they cause gives them a particular satisfaction. Since this conflict has assumed the form of a physical disorder, it is likely that a doctor has been called in. However, medication will not help. The child must be given back his sense of honor, his faith in himself, and, even more, his faith in people. Heretofore he has been made to feel rejection without knowing that often he himself has provoked it.

But even if it were desirable to treat the symptom for itself, it would be a mistake to awaken the child at night. Apart from the fact that this evidence of concern would increase the satisfaction he receives from his conduct, it must not be the purpose of training to regulate his bladder functions by *outside* help. The child must control his functions of his own accord.

Waking the child during the night and putting him on the toilet is not advisable in any event. When the child is awakened during the night, he generally is not fully awake, even if he seems to be. Letting him perform his function in a state of semi-somnolence disturbs rather than stimulates a proper control. Normal control requires full wakefulness; the child must be able to suppress and control his urge until he is fully awakened to take care of himself.

If the training has not been successful in the past, it must now be undertaken in a better way. All you can do is to provide him with a lamp, pajamas, and—if he is old enough—a supply of fresh bed linen so that during the night he can completely take care of himself. He needs encouragement, to be sure. Children who wet the bed are generally deeply discouraged; they are disgusted with themselves and see no hope for improvement. They have to be told that it is up to them whether they want to lie dry or wet, but that they will learn eventually to take care of themselves. Everybody learns it, some sooner, some later. It is of utmost importance that this attitude not only be expressed to the child but actually felt by the parents. As long as the parents themselves are ashamed, disgusted, and desperate, they will of necessity have a bad influence on the child. They will, perhaps, have a false sympathy for him when he is small and relieve him of his natural consequences, for example, by permitting him to sleep in their bed when his is soiled. The first step toward curing bed-wetting is complete calmness and indifference on the side of the parents, who can then successfully attempt to win the child and instill in him new hope and an earnest desire to take care of himself. It is just as harmful to punish him if he is wet, as it is to praise him if he is "nice." That puts too much emphasis on the parents' approval, while it should be strictly his own concern.

D. Displaying Inadequacy

Children who give up completely in every regard, because they are so discouraged that they do not even move voluntarily, are very rare. In most instances the discouragement is only partial and, as a consequence, the child avoids only certain activities. However, it must be determined whether the child refuses participation in order to gain attention, to defy authority, to punish and hurt, or just because there is nothing to be hoped for. Only in the latter case does a child seek excuses and hides himself behind an inadequacy which may actually exist, but more frequently has been suggested to him by his environment. Sometimes the child assumes an inadequacy out of a wrong interpretation of certain experiences and succeeds in impressing others with it.

Indolence

Indolence is a special form of disorderliness. The child refuses to do his chores, he refuses to cooperate. Everyone has an occasional inclination toward laziness. Children may at times be so immersed in their thoughts, activities, or fantasies that they show no interest in the proceedings of the outside world. Scolding and reproaching a child for his real or supposed indolence will merely increase his unwillingness. One method only is effective—stimulating his interest. Once an interest is aroused, laziness disappears. If a child is so discouraged in schoolwork, for instance, that he considers his efforts futile, he lacks all incentive to action. Children who are left-handed and similarly children who for other reasons are convinced that they are awkward often show an inclination to put off a task. In all these instances it is not enough to arouse interest. The child must be encouraged to develop confidence in his abilities.

Indolence, therefore, is always a sign that the child needs assistance. But this assistance should not be supplied in too literal a sense, as a kind of prop or crutch, in the form of urging and exhorting him to work or, what is worse, performing his tasks for him. This would never aid him in meeting his problems. The help that he really needs consists of discussions and practical experiences which can fortify his self-confidence and strengthen his inner preparedness to apply himself happily and interestedly to tasks and to surmount his difficulties.

Stupidity

The child's attempt to evade obligations and to surrender to discouragement may give the impression of stupidity. Many children almost deliberately create this impression. One must consider, of course, the possibility of mental deficiency; but feeble-minded and defective children are rarely called "stupid." The "stupid" child, however, is reproached with his failing, since he is looked upon as normal. His stupidity is not always natural. Often enough it conceals an acquired mental inertness.

Once in a park I witnessed the following scene. A nurse was playing with several girls of about six or seven years of age. One pretty little child came running to her and asked for an apple. She plaintively inquired why the others, who previously had been given two apples apiece, were now presented again with two, while she herself had received only one apple again. The nurse took her on her lap and asked, "How much are one and one?" The happy little face became suddenly distorted and took on a terrified expression; the lips moved without uttering a word.

I knew nothing about this child, but we can sense what lay behind her problem. Could she really count? If not, how did she know the other girls had received two apples at a time? Apparently, it was only the formal "academic" question that she was unable to answer. This would indicate that her stupidity was only a mask. She had probably met with difficulties ever since she started school. Very spoiled children, who have led an easy life at home, often find it hard to adjust themselves to school. They are not used to being on their own. They cannot keep pace with their classmates, and quickly lose courage. Also children who were given a great deal of attention at home because of their charm, their "cuteness," or any other advantage that required no effort, are quite likely to be convinced, when they enter school, that the prescribed work is "too hard" for them. And then they give up; they simply stop trying.

Parents are usually horrified at their child's failure, and thus discourage him still more. Then the process of learning becomes an out-and-out torture to an already unwilling child. He is robbed of his leisure, disturbed at play, and given no peace even at meals. Time after time his parents remind him of his lessons and nag him with queries as to his progress. Is it any wonder that he goes on strike and flatly refuses to apply himself to anything resembling schoolwork? I had a patient once, a woman with an average I.Q., who barely had the formal knowledge of the fourth grade of elementary school. She had been reared in the manner just described, and hence acquired the reputation of being stupid. Yet she was in no way mentally retarded. The only trouble was that she was strikingly beautiful, and had come to depend entirely on her physical attractions. Thus there is such a thing as stupidity induced solely by discouragement. The child fails to learn since he believes himself incapable of understanding anything.

Other children *hide* behind their stupidity. They use "stupidity as an excuse" (Ida Loewy). They "play stupid" when they want to evade some obligation. Children who fail to get along in a particular subject at school will become discouraged; but their discouragement may have various results. Overambitious children who always want to play first fiddle will not make any effort unless they are sure that they can be on top. When they do not have this certainty they lose interest, claiming that they have no aptitude for the subject, and therefore just cannot learn it.

Even before school age children sometimes play this trick. The little boy who tried to cut his soup with a knife is an example. His parents groaned over his stupidity. Yet he knew well enough what he *should* do—and unfailingly did the opposite. Such children play stupid in order to hoax their parents into waiting on them. Here, too, stupidity is a means of evasion and a device for securing attention.

An only child or a youngest child may employ such tactics when he enters school. In this way he can force his mother to help him with his homework. When she is not sitting by him he can neither write nor do his arithmetic. And the anxious, ambitious mother regularly falls into the trap. She never notices that her child's inability and helplessness increase proportionately as she, surprised and alarmed, makes every effort to encourage him, corrects his mistakes, and ends up by working the problems and writing the themes herself. Some children retain their helplessness throughout their lives and are never capable of writing a letter or paper by themselves. Their minds are a blank when they pick up a pen.

It is not easy to break a child's determination to get the mother's aid and support. When she makes an effort to free herself from her child's domination, he will argue and wheedle. If she remains steadfast and insists that he do his lessons by himself as best he can—then he may come to her with every word or every figure to ask whether it is right. The child may finally agree to work by himself, if his mother will sit by him and watch him.

Accordingly, there are numerous situations in which the child attempts to make use of his stupidity. Analogous to the "play-dead reflex" (often employed by animals to elude their enemies), there is a "play-stupid reflex" that can be observed in children—and sometimes in adults, too. The one "reflex" generally serves its purpose of evasion as well as the other. For, in effect, the family and the environment generally do nothing to combat the real or apparent stupidity, but rather acknowledge its efficacy as means of evasion. Parents scold, criticize, and humiliate the child but at the same time they unwittingly fall for his trick; for, in the end, they relieve him of the work that he wants to avoid, or they put themselves into his service. They encourage his stupidity by their criticism and ridicule, which strengthen one of the main factors that produce stupidity, that is, the child's dependence, his lack of faith in his own ability.

How then, should one deal with a "stupid" child? It certainly requires a change in the attitude of the parents. They will have to stop scolding, confronting him with his incapacity, teasing and comparing him with a brilliant brother or sister; but they will also have to stop their laxity in allowing him to shirk his duties. That cannot be accomplished by urging and threatening, which makes a distasteful task even more disagreeable to the child. He should be made to feel the consequences of his dereliction. As matters stand, the *parents* feel punished when he fails, not he. Therefore, they try to prevent the unpleasant consequences. As a result, the child feels that he has to meet his obligations for the parents' sake, not for his own. Their concern over his progress relieves him of his own responsibility. If he fails in school, he punishes the parents.

It is the duty of the teacher to stimulate his interests, and parents should interfere as little as possible with schoolwork. However, they can help a great deal by stimulating the general interest and alertness of the child through interesting books, excursions to museums and zoos, through nature stories, and other discussions suitable to his age and development. Then he may take a greater interest in the corresponding school subject and find pleasure in his work.

Eight-year-old Rose is too "stupid" to play with other children. She cannot dress or undress herself or even speak properly. She swallows half her words and syllables. It goes without saying that she is behind in school. She is considered retarded and is so treated, although she is not feeble-minded and has an I.Q. of 91. When it comes to getting her own way, she is shrewd and even ingenious in maintaining an advantage once gained. She is never at a loss for an answer. Rose has a very clever sister who is one and one half years younger than she. The sister outshines her in every way; but Rose compensates through all the attention she gets. She even has her own nurse and, when she started school, got a private teacher. Stupidity often pays big dividends! Less fortunate children are just thrown overboard and left completely to themselves.

There are a great number of children with a low I.Q. who are for all practical purposes retarded and still are only pseudo-feeble-minded. They have either a brother or sister, usually the next older or younger one, who is extremely bright and excels intellectually and academically. His or her superior abilities discourage the other to such a degree that he gives up completely. Sometimes this total surrender is due to an extremely efficient mother or older sister, who takes full charge of everything so that there is nothing left for the child to do.

Proper treatment can do a great deal for children whose intelligence is under question. They sometimes blossom overnight and reach achievements which nobody had believed were possible for them. Even the I.Q. increases, to the discomfort of those who consider it unchangeable. Unfortunately, the differential diagnosis between true feeble-mindedness and pseudo-retardation can often be made only afterward, by the success or failure of the treatment. For this reason, a low I.Q. should never deter parents and teachers from taking every step possible to help the child. On the contrary, it should be an incentive to employ better and more effective methods to make use of the remaining aptitudes so that the child can become a useful member of the human society.

"Inaptitude"

A "natural" inaptitude is often assumed if a child notably lacks some ability. This assumption becomes a conviction if every effort to improve the child's deficiencies fails, especially if he himself seems to try hard.

The acquisition of skills and abilities is a complicated process. It requires considerable practice and training. Unfortunately, scientific insight into all the factors which affect the course of training, favorably or adversely, is in the earliest stages of development. Many inaptitudes and deficiencies are the result of unrecognized errors and oversights in the training of the child.

How can we stimulate a child to develop his latent potentialities? It is impossible to list all the methods. The issue becomes further confused because the same stimulation may produce the opposite effect in different children. The example of father and mother may stimulate one child to emulate them, and discourage another one who feels incapable of ever reaching their level. High expectations stimulate one child and hamper another one. Objections and prohibitions act like natural obstacles and organ inferiorities, impelling one child to special efforts and preventing another one from doing anything. Opposition or conformity, defiance or submission, self-confidence or discouragement, determine whether any given stimulation has a constructive or detrimental effect.

This bewildering diversity is responsible for the lack of clarity in the methods of fostering abilities and for the inclination to assume hereditary predisposition for certain skills. For this reason, many parents and teachers, as well as some psychologists, regard inaptitudes and deficiencies as the result of a lack of endowment. Examination of children and adults reveals, however, that improper training coupled with discouragement must be considered the main factor. One can always find the point in the training at which the child gave up. Some children never learn spelling. They are those who got so discouraged when they started school that they abandoned all effort. Others give up because they cannot excel. Certain children who are used to having their own way are not willing to agree that a word *must* always be spelled in the same way. They spell it as they are inclined to, once in one way, the next moment in another way. They finally get so confused that they no longer attempt to find out how the word should be spelled. There are many well-educated and well-read adults who have never learned to spell because their first teacher was unable to overcome their growing inferiority in regard to spelling; and now as grown-ups they are still frightened if they have to write a letter.

The inability to master mathematics may be due to an incidental initial discouragement in the process of studying.

Some overprotected children never learn to make their own decisions; they find it difficult to solve any mathematical problem which demands decisions in regard to procedure. These children may be excellent students in subjects where they can rely on information. But any activity that requires self-reliance and determination is closed to them.

I should like to demonstrate this fact in a field that heretofore has been looked upon as the exclusive domain of natural endowment—musical talent. There are people who take no pleasure at all in music, for whom it is even a torment. They may be "monotones," unable to sing even simple tunes —this generally is taken to indicate a complete lack of musical ability. But it has been proved in a great many instances that the assumed "lack of a musical ear" is nothing but a protest against musical activity as a result of discouragement— sometimes because of competition with an older sister or some other member of the family who showed a pronounced musical talent. Frequently, the typical contrast between first and second child leads to such "deficiencies."

When Eric was ten years old he seemed to be wholly unmusical. He could not be induced to listen to concerts and was incapable of singing even the simplest nursery songs. In his infancy he had shown some interest in music, but later he completely reversed his attitude. His father often conducted musicales in the home. The boy, who as an only child, had been spoiled by his mother, would not sit still while the music was being played, and finally had to be sent out of the room. From this time on he could not bear music. When he entered school he refused to sing with the others and was reprimanded and ridiculed. When his grandmother tried to teach him songs, he became irate and ran away. After he was ten the reasons for his attitude were carefully explained to him, and through his new understanding he was helped to overcome his antagonism to music. With the aid of an understanding teacher, he developed a "fine ear" and learned to sing very well.

Children who have never been taught to sing at home may be stigmatized as unmusical when they attempt to join in the unison singing at school and fail. They are impressed and dejected by the superior ability of their classmates, and their discouragement may easily be increased by thoughtless teachers who ridicule them, until in the end their want of musical ability is taken as an established fact, persisting despite all pseudo-effort and pseudo-practice. In later years—but perhaps not until quite late in life—such persons may finally be brought to realize that their lack of musical ability was a fiction, that they, like anyone else, can acquire a taste and a feeling for music. And then their "natural" inaptitude will come to a sudden and miraculous end.

The natural inclination of children toward music is often stifled by the parents' attitude in regard to practicing. Ambitious parents may insist that their children practice more. Little do they realize the damage which they do thereby to the musical development of their children. They transform an art which should provide enjoyment and inspiration into a tortuous and tedious task. To be sure, nothing can be achieved without training; but training requires *interest* and *stimulation*. Going through the motions of practicing will not do. The usual method of coaxing, reminding, threatening, and punishing certainly does not provide either stimulation of interest nor inspiration. It is up to the teacher to interest the child; parents should add stimulation, but not pressure. They can play records or take the child to concerts; they can help the child to appreciate good music; they can admire his progress. Of course, they can force him to sit at the piano, but in most cases they thereby kill his musical enthusiasm. When he fails as a result, they—and sometimes even the teacher—blame it on the lack of musical ability. Actually the conflict between parents and child and the ensuing wrong working habits of the child prevent proper training. His inability is the result.

A rather detailed discussion of musical talent has seemed appropriate since it shows so clearly how loosely and thoughtlessly the concepts of heredity and predisposition are accepted. Such pessimistic assumptions induce parents to increase the difficulties for the child instead of helping him to overcome them. Musical talent is quite analogous to all the specialized endowments. If a child seems to lack ability in drawing or composition, mathematics, languages, or other school subjects, one should first try to determine whether he has been discouraged and, if so, how; or whether and why he resists the demands of training. Persuasion and urging will of course have no more effect on him than scolding, fault-finding or, what is worse, exaggerating his supposed inaptitudes—all of which would only drive him further along the road toward failure. Raising the child's confidence, winning him over and thus overcoming his resistance, letting him realize his progress, strengthening his self-reliance, stimulating his interest and enthusiasm, and, above all, exercising patience throughout the necessary process of training—these are the means that often can rectify deficiencies that once seemed hopeless.

On the other hand, it is not feasible deliberately to create special abilities in the child. A particular talent develops only in the soil of a highly concentrated and intensive training, and this can hardly be imposed from without. Ambition will sometimes spur a child to exceptional attainments; but quite often it may lead him to shun activity if his courage and self-confidence do not balance his aspirations. In any event, one should keep a close check on his attitude toward his work, and advance his progress by means of encouragement. Many overzealous parents induce their child at an early age to a strenuous activity that gives promise of really remarkable achievements. For a time he may seem a prodigy, the fulfillment of all their expectations; but in far too many cases the ultimate result is collapse and wretchedness. Later generations of parents will perhaps renounce the methods that arouse antagonism and lead to discouragement, and they may have better success in drawing out the dormant potentialities of their children.

"Violent" Passivity

Children who are completely passive are very rare. Even children who are very dull and develop no abilities, either physical or mental, may show some active participation. The strongest impression of passivity is given by children who use their passivity deliberately as a means of resistance. True enough, they are discouraged and have given up in despair; however, their passivity is so strong that one can speak of it as "violent" passivity. These children show some signs of a desire for power and especially of vengeance; but their goals are achieved solely by passive methods. They drive parents—and teachers even more—to utter despair. There seems just nothing one can do to move them. One literally hits rock if one tries to influence or direct them.

John, nine years old, was brought to the Center because he refused to cooperate either at home or in school. He did not actually get into mischief, although he occasionally transgressed by lying, stealing, truancy, and the like. He offended more through what he did not do. He was lazy, very untidy and dirty, went to school half dressed, and was usually tardy. He failed in almost all subjects, did not do any homework; nor did he make any effort to pass his tests. He did not even play, either with his siblings or with other children. He was shoved around at home, constantly coaxed, threatened, and severely punished—without any effect. His behavior had become worse in the last two years. The decisive factor in his development was his brother, one year younger, who had surpassed him at home as well as in school. His brother was by no means a good student, but he passed; and John's behavior grew worse when his brother entered into the same grade and later stepped one grade ahead of him.

The first day at the Center John refused to come to the counseling room. The next time he came in with his mother but remained at the door. No invitation, kindly suggestion, or coaxing made any impression upon him. We let him stay there, and could observe that during the session his face revealed an interest in the proceedings. At the next session he was willing to sit down near the doctor, but he did not say one word, although he understood and responded with occasional smiles and slight gestures. When it was time for him to leave the room so that we could talk with his mother, he refused. He just did not get up. He had to be carried out on the chair, and he accepted this without any resistance.

John's violent passivity was eventually overcome by methods similar to those employed with children who show their power. The mother, a tense, rigid, and highly perfectionistic person who had punished him a great deal and even spanked him severely when he was slow and late to school, learned to restrain herself and instead to apply the natural consequences. John's first active participation was in a rhythm band at the Center. It was his first experience of pleasant cooperation with others. Later he joined a dancing class. In the meantime, he became more and more cooperative and friendly at the Guidance Center, expressing himself with increasing frankness and ease, and finally began to apply himself in the classroom. It was only natural that at this point his brother began to get into difficulties.

Forcefulness in fighting with passivity is even more impressive if it is limited.

Seven-year-old Jack refuses to talk except with his mother, who pampers him a great deal and submits to his whims. But that is the only relationship which Jack apparently accepts. At school he just does not say a word. He has learned to write and is willing to answer the teacher's questions in writing; he may make himself understood by gestures and signs, but he will not utter a word. He is outwardly conforming when addressed—he will do what he is told, but will not answer a question. At the Center he stares into space as if he could not hear what is said. He completely ignores communication.

As was stated before, it is questionable whether children who resort to violent passivity really belong in the fourth group. Their passivity seems sometimes to be more than just giving up. One should recognize the power element in doing nothing. Any pressure, coaxing, or punishment makes the child only more determined in his non-participation. The best response to his behavior is to leave him alone in such a way that he experiences the unpleasant effect of his passivity. As long as he can force the parents' hand and stimulate them to more activity and effort the child will find his method only too successful and comfortable.

E. Pathological Reactions

The resistance of the child may develop to such a degree that he may seem to be "abnormal." However, one must be careful what one considers pathological or abnormal in a child. As a rule, the child's reactions are not abnormal, even if they are extreme and seem out of the ordinary, because they are generally sensible and adequate responses to the situation as the child sees it. However, what is "normal" for the child may become "pathological" when it is carried into adult life where the reaction is no longer in accordance with the actual situation. Even if a child is quite different from the ordinary, he should not be called pathological, because such designation generally is based on a lack of insight into his relationships to parents, teachers, or society as a whole.

The term "pathological reaction" is justified only in describing certain reaction patterns, which, if they should be maintained in later life, would become typical psychopathological conditions. We can observe in children the first characteristic signs of these conditions, and case histories of adult patients reveal that often the first symptoms had appeared in early childhood. Such symptoms in children do not justify apprehension, fear, and pessimism. However, while some symptoms justify special care and consideration to prevent a continuation leading to pathological conditions, the parents, motivated by these emotions, may become more detrimental to an already disturbed adjustment.

Nervous Disorders

We have already cited typical neurotic mechanisms frequently found in children, when we discussed fear, overconscientiousness, temper tantrums, and the lack of concentration. Characteristic of every neurotic disturbance, in children and adults alike, is the tendency to maintain good intentions and to hide antagonism behind "symptoms" which are used as alibis. The child may have used these symptoms originally to excuse himself to the parents; but as soon as he believes his own excuses, the neurotic mechanism is established.

Many nervous symptoms may appear in early childhood. They are always aimed against the parent and against order. The child tries in this way to throw off certain responsibilites and secure consideration and assistance, or sometimes merely increased attention. The symptoms, accordingly, vary with the circumstances. They often follow the example that the child sees, and may be stimulated by casual experiences. *The development of a symptom depends on the manner in which the family reacts to its first appearance.* The stronger the effect that a symptom produces, the greater the likelihood of its further development. Ignoring it hastens its disappearance—at least in the beginning, when it is not yet firmly established.

Characteristic of the nervous child is the *tension* under which he lives. This arises from the difficulties with which he has to contend: from conflicts with parents, siblings, and teachers, from the dangers that threaten, from inordinate ambition. His whole organism is under the pressure of this strain; and thus any thought and emotion, any function of bodily organs to which his attention is directed, can develop into a nervous symptom. After whooping cough, the irritation may persist much longer than is warranted by the normal course of the illness; a stomach disorder caused by unwholesome foods may be maintained or repeated; cardiac complaint in the mother may lead the child to watch his own pulse and acquire nervous heart trouble. It is especially noteworthy that the nervous disorders of others are readily imitated by the child. And here again the family's perturbation over a disturbance—which often is regarded at first as a mere "bad habit"—encourages the child to adopt it permanently.

It is impossible to give even an approximate list of the neurotic disorders that appear in children. We shall briefly indicate a few.

A direct expression of tension is the so-called spasm. Spasms may appear in any muscular group, either over the entire body (in which case they often are falsely described as epileptic or heart attacks) or restricted to the eyelids (blepharospasm), the musculature of the jaw (trism), the facial muscles (*tic convulsif*, which leads to grimaces), the muscles of the throat and neck, or the shoulder, arm, and leg musculature. They may appear as yawning, sneezing, laughing, and crying fits, or as coughing spasms. Since sometimes these accompany a real physical complaint, a general medical examination is advisable in every case.

Tension can easily lead to nervous derangements of the gastrointestinal tract. Nervous children cannot eat when they are overwrought—before a trip, before going to the theater, and when anything disagreeable is in the offing. Going to school also affords opportunity, and for this reason breakfast may be difficult. Perhaps the child is in opposition to school, or he is very ambitious and dreads failure. In either event he seems incapable of taking nourishment in the mornings, especially before an examination or an unusual assignment. Coaxing may cause stomach spasms or nervous vomiting. The cramping of the pyloric orifice (pylorospasm) is often connected with reluctance to take food. Tension of the gastro-intestinal tract may lead to diarrhea or constipation.

Extreme tension may disturb the child's sleep. He tosses restlessly and screams or sometimes talks in his sleep. His brain still works on the problems that fill his daily life and give rise to emotional upheaval. Or perhaps he cannot sleep at all, because he is too much occupied with his problems. The vascular system reacts readily to strain, since anxiety and cardiac activity are interrelated in a physiological fear-mechanism. The results are palpitation, accelerated pulse-beat, blushing, and pallor—also increased sweat secretion, together with fear-sensations. Children exposed to much moral pressure may develop compulsive-obsessive symptoms.

The therapy consists first of quieting the child, and, above all, the parents. In cases of extreme excitement, medication does some good, but only as a temporary relief of the specific symptom. What was said earlier of children's faults is equally true of their nervous disorders: it is futile to treat only the symptom. *The child's personality and his relationship to the parents must be altered.* His whole situation needs drastic revision. Even ignoring of the symptom checks the development of only one particular manifestation. The general strain is not affected. In difficult cases, especially with older children, psychotherapeutic treatment is indispensable. But it is not enough to help the child out of his present predicament; treatment must include the parents and induce them to adopt a more sensible attitude.

Psychosis

The number of children who are classified today as psychotic is increasing. This may be due to the fact that heretofore they were not recognized as being different from severely retarded children. Actually, there are indications that these children, acting very much as if they were mentally deficient, have normal and often superior intelligence. Since their behavior seems to be utterly irrational and cannot be controlled with reason, they are called psychotic, often schizophrenic. However, their mental condition is quite different from that of adult schizophrenics, although they too seem to live in a world of their own, apparently little affected by events in their environment. Their distance and lack of contact are often expressed, not only by their unwillingness to listen, but by their inability to talk. Many of them are completely mute, and many seem to be deaf, while actually having no hearing defect. Because the nature of their "psychosis" is so little understood and because of the stigma attached to this term, these children are often not called psychotic, but "emotionally retarded."

No generally accepted explanation of the origin of this condition has been established. Some experts attribute it to an organic brain deficiency, particularly to a defective development; others consider the personality of the parents, particularly of the mother, as the cause of this form of abnormality. Our own observation would indicate that the parents of so-called psychotic children are not much different from those of normal children and—as a matter of fact—very often have other completely normal children. On the other hand, the assumption of an organic deficiency becomes dubious when we see—so far only in few cases—a complete recovery and adjustment. It may be possible that these children have what may be called an organ inferiority of the brain that makes them more susceptible to certain patterns of behavior.

The outstanding feature of all these children is the determination to have their own way and to disregard any pressure and demand from the outside. This resistance to pressure prompted some experts to assume that treatment should avoid any pressure. Our observations lead to opposite conclusions. Permissiveness usually intensifies the condition, while persistent firmness reduces the violence often exhibited. It is this determination of the child to resist the power of an authority, be it exerted by an individual or by the demands of the social situation, that may provide the clue to an understanding of this condition.

It seems to be a counterpart of the other extreme form of youthful rebellion, namely juvenile delinquency. Both occur to an extended degree at a time when parental authority diminishes in a democratic setting and the heretofore submissive group of children dare to express their defiance openly. In other words, childhood psychosis seems to indicate the extreme rebellion of a child who no longer fears retaliation and punishment, or at least takes it in his stride as the price for his perverted form of independence. This open rebellion is only possible in an era of parental overpermissiveness, when parents are no longer able and willing to "control" children. But it probably requires some organic predisposition for a child to let his inclinations sway him without any inner control.

There is little to be said about the prevention of such a mental state, except for pointing to the need for order and regularity within the family. This no longer can be brought about by direct pressure, but requires the wide range of training methods described in this book. The vulnerable, sick, or physically defective or handicapped child does not need any special methods of training, only a more careful observance of the basic principles. On the other hand, all handicaps and deficiencies make the maintenance of proper attitudes and procedures more difficult, and therefore demand from the parents more determination and perseverance in using the proper approaches.

Once a psychotic condition has developed, psychiatric help is needed. New drugs have been developed that influence the child in such a way as to make training methods more effective. These drugs do not cure the child but make him manageable; and the proper retraining then, in turn, may take its effect and permit either complete or partial adjustment. It is our experience that music therapy can often reach a child where all other therapeutic efforts have failed. Psychotic children are usually immune to a verbal approach; but the nonverbal approach of music can induce participation and contact. The rhythm also contributes to the therapeutic effectiveness of music. It implies order in a form to which the child can easily and more readily respond.

As in all severe power contests, the parents of a psychotic child need to be able to extricate themselves from the child's undue demands. It requires considerable fortitude to resist firmly but calmly the often considerable, vicious aggressiveness of such children. For the sake of maintaining their own independence and self-dignity, parents must have the fortitude and courage to stand up for their own rights and not to submit to the force of a sick child. Justifying a false considerateness and permissiveness on the grounds that "the poor child is sick" induces a child to become even more sick and to use his sickness as a club over his victims.

Psychopathic Personality

A misbehaving and rebellious young child may behave like a psychopathic personality without actually being one.[6] He does not share the values and moral concepts of the rest of the group to which he belongs. He may be defiant or self-indulgent; he may demand his own way and be completely unwilling to conform. However, a great number of these children, one may say the vast majority of them, adjust themselves later on without displaying any psychopathic tendencies. While their adjustment to home and school may have been inadequate, they succeed in adjusting themselves to society at large during the period of adolescence, once they become independent of those family relationships which disturbed their adjustment. On the other hand, children who did not previously show any obvious sign of nonconformity may be inclined to defiance during puberty if home and school either interfere with or neglect the necessary assistance and supervision. The resulting juvenile delinquency is largely a product of the lack of preparation for adolescence and of the inability of educational institutions like home and school to understand, appreciate, and stimulate the adolescent youngsters in proper channels.

Any trend to nonconformity and non-participation must be recognized and watched in children. It cannot be suppressed by force, or mitigated by indulgence. These two

[6] A psychopathic personality, as we understand it, can be defined as a person who has not developed an adequate conscience and does not accept the morals and values of the society in which he lives. Consequently, his behavior is socially disturbing. He considers his own interests as the only motivation which matters, without inhibition and restraint. We can distinguish three groups of psychopathic personalities: (1) the Indulgent Personalities—the alcohol and drug addicts, the gamblers, the liars, the perverts, the swindlers, the eccentric, the malingerers; then there are (2) the Defiant Personalities—the criminals and delinquents, the morally insane, the active sex offenders and prostitutes, the impulsive and quarrelsome; in this group belong (3) some Mentally Deficient Personalities, who have not learned to recognize right and wrong and have a limited knowledge of good and bad. They may be indulgent, defiant, or merely nonconforming, uninhibited, and impulsive.

methods of indulgence and suppression, applied predominantly today to misbehaving children, are mainly responsible for the great number of self-indulgent and defiant personalities. As long as schools cannot make up for this deficiency by winning the children over, integrating them in a harmonious way into the group, and adjusting them to order, psychopathic personalities will develop in ever-increasing number, especially in periods of change. The changing values of our time favor the defiance of moral concepts presented by parents and authorities. The more justified the children feel in rejecting the values of their parents, the more defiant they may grow in rejecting any moral value. Again it must be stated that such turmoil during puberty, which may even lead to delinquency, does not necessarily mean continuation of these psychopathic traits. However, punitive action by the authorities and overindulgence or neglect by the parents may drive the youngster deeper into social antagonism until finally his return to social participation may be permanently blocked.

Some children develop serious psychopathic traits of extreme defiance or extreme indulgence during puberty, some much earlier. The sex impulse may stimulate defiance and indulgence simultaneously. Such children may get completely out of control, as no force of parents or authorities is strong enough to prevent the victories of defiance. Gambling and drinking, vandalism, and uncontrollable self-indulgence in any kind of fun and pleasure, culminating in arson and rape, mark the development of a child who seeks significance outside the social order and the adult society.

It is unfair to blame parents alone for the increase in juvenile delinquency. After all, who helps the parents today in their superhuman task of raising children? Teachers, juvenile authorities, police, and courts equally must learn to understand the individual delinquent and his problems. A better understanding of those who have already come into conflict with the law may aid greatly in the public planning for the prevention of juvenile delinquency. Most of the youngsters with psychopathic traits are very ambitious but do not find adequate outlets in useful accomplishments. They want to be big and smart, and gain this objective more easily through misbehavior than through conformity. It is easier for them to feel grown up and important by emulating the vices of the adults than by fulfilling their tasks which, generally, offer them little recognition in the world of adults.

Once a child has turned against adults, it is difficult to influence him in a direct way. He is generally backed up by his contemporaries who think and feel as he does, since he can pick just those mates whose attitudes jibe with his. Therefore, remedial work with individual parents and children is not too efficacious; group approaches through new activities and especially through group discussions are much more promising. In that way it may be possible to influence and improve the social values and concepts of the whole group. It is easier to influence the group than it is to influence one individual, as one can find assistance from members within the group which can serve as a foundation on which to build.

As the psychopathic personality is characterized by denial of the social values of others and by exclusive consideration of one's own interest, the problem of mental retardation becomes necessarily related to it. It is true that some children are prevented by actual lack of intellectual capacity from grasping fully the more complex concepts of morals and values. But while children with extensive mental deficiencies are generally prevented from mixing with others and from doing damage to others and to themselves, children with a lesser deficiency can be a real danger. Many mentally deficient children, if carefully trained, stimulated, and supervised, could very well learn to participate adequately and even successfully in life. However, under present educational conditions, unsatisfactory at best, the additional problem of mental deficiency is too much for parents and teachers. Instead of getting better care, these children get far less training and sometimes none at all. Long before they enter school their limited abilities are already stifled through spoiling, overprotection, or neglect. It is true that training such children is difficult and does not promise any return comparable to the training of average or above average children. However, society as a whole pays a high price for its neglect in handling and training retarded children, through the part which they play in delinquency.

Concluding the discussion of the most disturbed children, we must call attention to the prevailing conditions under which they grow up. One can say: the more help and assistance a child needs, the less he receives. Proper treatment and stimulation on the part of parents, teachers, and others is given only to those who need the least, because they are well adjusted and can take care of themselves. They are treated with all the affection, attention, and consideration to which every child has a right. On the other hand, the most disturbed child receives the worst treatment, little or no understanding, assistance, and encouragement. He is pushed around, abused, humiliated, and driven into deeper rebellion and discouragement. This prevalent paradox can be overcome only through a wider knowledge of efficient training techniques and through a better preparation for the understanding of the personality of each child.

Chapter 7

Guidance and Readjustment

Iт is hoped that the foregoing presentation has helped you to recognize several of your mistakes, to gain a better understanding of your child, and perhaps even to improve your relationship with him. But you may still feel a need for further direction, especially if your own emotional equilibrium has been too upset or the child's behavior too disturbing. You may want to know about specific techniques used in guiding parents and children to a mutually constructive relationship. A discussion of actual cases treated in a guidance center will demonstrate how remedial techniques are used and may give you a clearer understanding of the methods I have attempted to describe in this book. Some of these techniques may be applicable to your own situation or may stimulate you to further thought and solutions. Perhaps you may decide to consult a similar center in your own community if you feel a need for professional assistance of the kind described.

Most parents know so little about the management of their children that outside help is essential in a great many instances. Teachers, too, are as a rule little prepared to understand fully a child who disturbs and misbehaves. Consequently, a great number of children need help beyond that which the classroom can provide. The fact that a child requires special assistance does not in any way indicate the presence of a pathological condition. A child becomes a problem only if parents and teachers do not know how to handle the problems which he presents. Not only does the child need assistance, but parents, too, require the objectivity of professional counsel. Their inefficiency in dealing with the child's problems is not their fault and does not necessarily indicate their inadequacy. But so long as parents and teachers lack proper preparation and training we must recognize the necessity for establishing agencies which are qualified to give the required assistance. Such agencies, serving the needs of parents, children, and teachers are commonly called Child Guidance Clinics. Their staff usually consists of a psychiatrist, a psychologist, and a social worker.

The appellation "Child Guidance Clinic" should, perhaps, be reconsidered. The word clinic generally implies a medical institution for the treatment of disease. As the function of Child Guidance Clinics is increasingly directed toward helping the *normal* child in his adjustment and growth, the term "Guidance Center" is more appropriate. (In Austria such institutions were called *Erziehungsberatungsstellen*, which means, literally translated, "centers for advice in rearing children.") In the future, we may very well have to distinguish between two types of Guidance Center: one, a clinic which deals mainly with extreme cases, where the disturbance is so severe that it may be called pathological and requires special treatment and management; and a Guidance Center for parents and children which serves the needs of the average parent, child, and teacher. Such Centers should be established in each community under public or private sponsorship, within the school system, and/or in community and settlement houses, churches, and similar institutions.

Various techniques of clinical guidance are used at the present time. Alfred Adler and his associates developed a particular technique for use in Guidance Centers. Its main principles are:

1. The focus of attention is directed toward the parent, as the parent is generally the problem, not the child. The child responds only to the treatment to which he is exposed. Younger

children, especially, cannot be helped as long as the parents' attitude does not change.

2. All parents consulting the Center participate simultaneously in a procedure that may be called "group therapy." In these sessions each case is openly discussed in front of the other parents. Any initial objection to such group participation disappears quickly when, at the first interview, the parents realize the spirit of mutual help and understanding. Confidential or embarrassing material is never brought up in the group, but is discussed at private interviews with the social worker or the psychiatrist, as the case requires. The advantage of group discussions is soon evident to any newcomer. Most parents gain greater insight into their own situation by listening to the discussion of problems of other parents, for it is easier to be objective in evaluating and understanding other people's problems.

3. The same guidance worker, whether psychiatrist, social worker, or psychologist, deals with the parents and with the child. All problems of children are problems of a disturbed parent-child relationship. In any case, the worker is confronted with a particular relationship and must approach it from both ends simultaneously. We have never felt any particular resistance by parent or child because we dealt with both; it is as easy to gain the confidence of both parties as that of the one. Our experience has indicated that working with one party alone is almost a handicap. The speed and course of the treatment depend upon the condition and receptivity of parent and child at a given moment; and these can be evaluated only if the worker is in close contact with both.

4. The problems of the child are frankly discussed with the child himself, regardless of his age. If the child understands the words, he also understands their psychological content. Contrary to a widespread belief, young children show amazing keenness in grasping and accepting psychological explanations. In general, it takes much longer for a parent to understand the psychological mechanisms of the problem; the child recognizes

them immediately. It is not that the child is more suggestible and therefore more easily "taken in" by suggestive remarks; his "recognition reflex" appears only when an interpretation is correct.

The child is called to the counseling room without his parent, and by his actions, his behavior, and his responses reveals his attitudes and characteristic approaches to life. The discussion is brief and directly attacks the basic problems; if it strikes home it generally makes a deep and lasting impression. Children are rarely embarrassed by the presence of adults; but, even if they are, they reveal in these difficult test situations more of their basic attitudes and reaction patterns, more of the true nature of their problems, than they do in "normal" situations at home or in their classrooms, where their true motivations may be covered up by compensatory and deeply entrenched behavior patterns.[1] Psychological tests are given if the diagnosis is not clear or special information seems necessary, but only few cases require such tests.

5. If the child is not an only child, we never deal with him alone. Each child in the family plays an important part, as the problem of any one child in the family is closely related to that of every other member of the group. We have to understand the whole group and the existing interrelationships, the lines of alliance, competition, and antagonism, really to understand the concepts and behavior of any one member. For this reason, we ask the parents to bring all their children.

When the children enter the guidance room, they are asked to sit together on a bench. The way in which they enter the room, how they sit down, their distribution and position on the bench, the way in which each one participates in the discussion, their facial expressions and other reactions during the discussion—all are definite clues to the relationships existing among them. This effort to deal with all of them simultaneously is the more necessary as any change which may be accomplished in one child is bound to affect the whole group sit-

[1] See below, case history of "The 'Teeter-Totter' Brothers."

uation. Often enough, if the "problem child" improves, the "good one" who is his more successful competitor becomes difficult. In many cases one can clearly see that the child with whom the parents have the greatest difficulty is not really the maladjusted one. At any rate, we cannot help any one child unless we establish a better equilibrium among all the children. The change in their relationships must be closely watched and the necessary steps taken to improve the attitudes of each child toward the group.

6. The main objective of our work is the change in the relationships between child and parent, and between the siblings. Only then can we alter the child's behavior, his life style, his approaches to social living, his concepts of himself in relation to others. The psychological guidance in each case is based on the interpretation of his family constellation and on the recognition of his goals. His difficulties are caused by his trying to gain attention (goal 1), to demonstrate his power (goal 2), to punish or get even (goal 3), or to demonstrate his inadequacy (goal 4).

The first interview at the Center (after the social worker presents the case history) is generally devoted to an explanation of the psychological factors behind the problem. As a rule, parent and child are told at the first interview why the child behaves as he does and what the parents do to create or increase his difficulties.

In some cases the first interview is used also to make suggestions for a change in the management of the child. We try to tackle one problem at a time, beginning with the most significant or with one which lends itself to an easy solution. The suggestions are always made as plain and simple as possible, although their execution is never as easy because they involve a change in the existing relationships.

The first suggestion which we invariably make—and which you, the reader, should consider before you try anything else —is to call a truce with the child. This first step is so important that it warrants detailed elaboration and emphasis.

Formerly the child and parent were at war. There must now be a lull in the struggle. It is necessary to convince parents that they must, for the time being, simply let the child go on as he is, being "bad" and making his mistakes. No harm will come of this, as he probably has misbehaved for some time. Meanwhile the parents have to learn to observe the child and themselves—with a better insight into what has been going on. First they must learn to restrain themselves. They must become aware of their tendency to harp repeatedly and learn to stop it. They must start to work on themselves. Many parents claim that they have "tried everything" without success. They generally overlook one possibility: *self-reform*. This is the value of a truce. Without an armistice there can be no peace. And it is their duty, and should be their earnest desire, to make peace with the child. Otherwise, no improvement in the child is possible. By learning to restrain themselves they gradually establish a new relationship between them.

We admit that this first step is the most difficult one. Few parents are able to about-face at once and to arrest their overactivity. If they can, we see results almost at once. In such cases the difficulties may disappear completely after one or two interviews. On the other hand, a slow beginning does not prevent eventual adjustment.

During the ensuing interviews new angles of the problem appear and are discussed. Each time one particular aspect is emphasized. It is necessary to repeat the same explanation and suggestion many times. After all, this is a training process, and training requires systematic repetition. No child will learn to read and write, no person will acquire a skill, by just being informed how to do it. The guidance worker must have as much patience with the parent as the parent must have with himself. If parents are overeager to improve, their anxiety will prevent their adjustment.

According to our experience only a small percentage of parents who seek advice are so deeply disturbed that they require psychotherapy, that is, help in their own emotional adjustment. The great majority require only information and guidance; then they can work out their problems with their children satisfactorily. Their emotional distress, their excitement and irritability, are often the result of their feeling of frustration because they do not know what to do and are nonplussed by the behavior of the child. As they begin to understand and discover different means to meet their problem, they lose their tension, anxiety, and distress. The problems which the child presents cease to be an affliction and become an interesting task, inviting experiment and creativeness. Such an attitude toward a problem situation is imperative, as children will always present problems. Whenever people live together problems exist because all human relationships involve conflicts of interest, clashes of opinion, opposition of desires and temperaments.

The case histories which we shall present are taken from the files of our Chicago Guidance Centers, the psychiatric clinic of the Chicago Medical School, and private practice. While they are similar to some already cited they will better demonstrate the step-by-step procedure. Success or failure depends entirely on the response of the *parents*. We work mostly with the mother; she is the most important person in the child's life, because she influences him more than any other person. If she does not change, accepting and applying our suggestions, the all-important relationship between mother and child remains based on a faulty equilibrium. "Improvement" of the child is by no means limited to the disappearance of certain behavior patterns of which the parents complain. Faulty behavior can be stopped sometimes by direct talks with the child alone; but unless the fundamental equilibrium within the family is changed, no lasting improvement can be expected.

Case Illustrations

Crying

Mrs. K. came to the Guidance Center because she was troubled with one specific situation. Her *six-months-old* daughter cried incessantly whenever she was put into her play-pen. Mother tried to ignore the crying, but after some length of time—sometimes after an entire hour—she just couldn't endure it and picked up the baby. What else could she do?

It became evident during a short discussion that both parents were very apprehensive about the welfare, growth, and development of the child. The child cried easily, and the mother especially became upset on such occasions. The baby's eating or sleeping, her weight, her slightest cold or discomfort were important problems and caused considerable concern.

The mother was informed that the atmosphere in which the child grows up is more important than any one single act or event. The child senses the anxiety and apprehension of the mother and has probably already discovered that she can rely on them for getting special attention. She finds it more pleasant to be in mother's arms, to be hugged and cuddled, than to be left by herself in the play-pen. Although mother is careful about what she does, she fails to check her emotions. Her anxiety and sympathy are expressed without words—and the child responds with her own excitement and self-pity.

Consequently, Mrs. K. was advised to leave the child alone in the pen without being afraid that crying will do harm. If she stays in the room, she has to remain completely calm; otherwise, it is preferable that she leave the room.

After one week, Mrs. K. returned and told of her amazement at what happened. The day following her visit to the Center she put the baby back in the pen as usual without saying anything. But this time the baby did not even start to cry at all. For the first time, she quietly accepted being left by herself; and since then, she had not cried when put into her pen.

Mrs. K. realized that it was actually her own attitudes and emotions which had acutely upset the child. The discussion had relieved her anxiety, and the child had sensed it immediately. From that time on, she carefully watched her attitude toward the child, thus altering her whole relationship with her.

Fear

Gilbert was nine years old when mother came with him for help. He was a fine boy, obedient and kind. But for about a year he had suffered from terrific fears. He had seen his grandfather die, and could not overcome the shock. Since then he had lived in constant fear that something might happen to his parents. He woke up during the night screaming and running to the parents' room to see whether they were all right. He is especially worried about mother. When she leaves the house, he is terror-stricken: something might happen to her. She must call home every hour. If she is five or ten minutes late, he gets frantic. The parents are very sympathetic. They do not fight or scold him, but they don't know what to do with him. Medicines do not quiet him down. Once they sent him to his grandparents' farm. For a few days Gilbert was all right. Then he woke up one night terror-stricken, waking his grandparents. He was convinced that his mother was dying. They had to call home in the middle of the night to reassure him. After that he couldn't stand it there any longer and was sent home.

A short examination of his past development revealed that while he had always been very close to mother, prior to his grandfather's death he had been well-adjusted at home and in school. There were no significant difficulties. He was affectionate and conforming, almost a model child. He even made a good adjustment when a little sister was born three years ago, and was affectionate and friendly toward her. All that had changed when the grandfather died.

At this first interview, no definite conclusion was reached. However, it seemed that the grandfather's death had become important only because of the extreme sympathy and concern which the parents showed about the shock which Gilbert had experienced. The event had occurred at a period in Gilbert's life when he probably felt insecure in the competition with his little sister, who was very cute at that time and attracted considerable attention. Gilbert, not trained for open rebellion and antagonism, undoubtedly capitalized on this new opportunity to gain the limelight and to keep mother even closer to himself than she had been, certainly closer than his age and development would warrant. He was, of course, unaware of this mechanism, as were his parents and other relatives. Mother was advised to stop being impressed by Gilbert's fears; the sympathy which he received only aggravated his condition. But she was also warned that it might take some time to give Gilbert a feeling of independence so that he would not have to resort to his fears.

During his interview, the boy appeared very frank and intelligent, sincere and kind. We had a brief talk with him, asking him first whether he knew why he was so afraid that mother might die. He shook his head. "May we explain it to you?" we asked. He was eager. So we told him that apparently he used his fears to keep his mother concerned with and close to himself, because he might be afraid of losing out to his little sister. Could that be? He grinned with the characteristic "recognition reflex." He had never thought of that before, but he admitted that it might be so. We asked him whether we should, perhaps, help him to overcome this feeling of insecurity. After all, he was a good boy and did not need mother so much any more. He was quite agreeable.

An appointment was made with mother and son for two weeks ahead. A few days before the appointment the mother called to cancel it. Gilbert's fears had completely disappeared.

The "Teeter-Totter" Brothers

The following case illustration may be worth mentioning, although no satisfactory results were obtained.

Mrs. D. had difficulties with her son, Tom, aged four. She reported that she became pregnant shortly after Tom was born, and her husband attended to his care. He put Tom to bed, held his hand, and took his part whenever there was an argument. Tom's behavior has become obstreperous. If he does not get his own way, he starts to scream. When he screams mother threatens to shut him in the closet and then he stops. Once, when he started to tease Fred, who is one year younger, she said she would give him an enema if he didn't stop. Mrs. D. uses a stick on both children when they misbehave.

Fred, the younger boy, fights all of Tom's battles. He frequently does cute things and everybody in the family admires him. At nursery school, Fred assumes a protective attitude toward Tom, and tries to console him when he cries.

When the children entered the counsel room, we found to our surprise that Tom was smiling and forward, while Fred trailed behind rather shyly and timidly. Tom answered all the questions, for Fred as well as for himself. Tom had a typical big-brother attitude, was friendly and pleasant, while Fred sat holding to his chair, wriggling and looking very mischievous and taking no part in the conversation.

It was obvious that in the unusual atmosphere of the Guidance Center, the children behaved differently than in the "normal" home and school situations to which they were accustomed. In the trying and embarrassing situation at the counsel room, Tom revealed himself as courageous and friendly toward other people. Apparently Fred was the problem child, contrary to the impression of the mother and teachers. It developed that mother had sided with Fred against the alliance of Tom and his father, thereby placing Fred in a position superior to that of his brother. Left alone to his own resources, Tom might well take care of himself. Under the present circumstances he has no chance to do so, as Fred discourages him and represses him with the approval of mother and teachers.

Mrs. D. was advised not to play one child against the other, or to take sides, but to send both children out of the room if they quarreled or misbehaved. Then she would not be in the position of having to threaten or to spank one or the other. Two weeks later Mrs. D. reported she had sent both children away from the table when they quarreled, and that they had ceased quarreling at mealtime. She further reported that before the last interview Tom had difficulty in dressing himself in the morning and Fred, the younger one, had helped his older brother to get dressed. However since the interview the circumstances have changed; now Tom dresses himself and Fred seems quite helpless and asks for help. The roles of the two children have reversed completely. Fred, no longer supported against his brother, has lost his temper many times and has also become quite negativistic in nursery school, where he has started to act in a helpless way in regard to dressing.

The children showed the same characteristic behavior as they had previously displayed when brought to the counsel room for their next interview. Fred walked hesitantly into the room, buttoning and unbuttoning his coat as he walked. When Tom entered, he said, "Hello, Fred," walked right over to the chair, and sat down. Then Fred followed and sat down, too. Fred did not answer any questions, completely ignoring them and just playing with his shoes. Fred's interest could be awakened only when he was told to show how well he could unbutton his coat; then his eyes gleamed, and he unbuttoned his coat and took off his coat and hat. Tom, who had been quite responsive up to then, slumped in his chair while Fred was performing and put his fingers in his mouth. When they were ready to leave, Tom again took the lead, stood up and invited Fred to come with him. Fred hesitated, followed slowly, and was coaxed by Tom.

It was explained to Mrs. D. how the children alternately play the baby role, according to which one of them is superior at the moment. Any partiality she shows increases the existing competition. If she wants her children to develop normally, she must establish a different relationship between them, and between herself and them. She was advised to leave the children alone to enjoy each other.

Although Mrs. D. came twice more to the Center, very little

progress was made. It was hard for her to change her attitude and methods, and she did not return to the Center again.

Several points are important in this case. First, the apparent problem child is not always the real problem; second, the peculiar and strained situation in the counseling room often permits a much better evaluation of the existing relationships than does the "normal" home or school situation; third, progress of one child often leads to regression of his competitor.

Although the mother did not cooperate enough to permit an adjustment of the children, our brief treatment produced at least some dynamic changes in the behavior of both children so that it can be hoped that a new equilibrium will finally result which will be sounder than the previous one, especially since the children's teachers realize the nature of the problem and will manage them accordingly.

The Bully

Mrs. P. is a very anxious mother. She describes her difficulties with Robert in great detail; she seems helpless, yet she is rigid in her own ideas of handling the child.

Robert, age six, has a sister three and a half years old. In her first interview, mother complains that Robert finds it difficult to make friends, is always alone, does not know what to do with his time; occasionally he draws, or listens to records. He bosses other children; sometimes he bribes them and then suddenly becomes belligerent. He is stubborn. Mother states, "It is hard to break his will." He cannot get along with anybody, wants his own way, and gets it by devious means. Mother "has to lick him occasionally." As a small child he was well behaved. Now he has to be called two or three times in the morning and he needs assistance in dressing. He eats well, but swings on his chair, sits on one foot, jumps up and down, and has to be reminded to sit quietly. He goes to bed only after much talking and coaxing. He does not put his clothes away.

The interview with Robert shows him as a frank, outspoken

little boy. He thinks mother likes baby more than she likes him. He becomes angry with his sister because she takes his books. He agrees that he wants to be the "big boss." He wants to become a doctor. He likes school and gets along in his classwork, but during recess periods the other children fight and kick him, and he does not know why.

Robert's behavior was interpreted first to him and then to his mother. We explained that Robert believes nobody really loves him, and therefore tries to find his place by demonstrating his power, mainly with his mother. She accepts this provocation and tries to enforce her own rule—without success, of course. Robert becomes convinced that what he needs is power; being liked is the sole privilege of the baby.

The boy understood and accepted our interpretation, which was verified by his "recognition reflex." Mother seemed to be dubious.

Mrs. P. was advised to stop fighting, reminding, coaxing, and punishing. She must win him, give him recognition and responsibility. She must not help him in the morning; that is *his* job and he must take care of himself. At the table, if he does not behave he must be sent away, without sharp words and criticism. Her main task is to improve her relationship with Robert. He does not trust human relationships. The pronounced masculinity of his father probably has some effect on Robert's desire to be "boss," but mother is still the most important factor in his development. Her feeling of helplessness induces her to use violence; although she fails to secure compliance, she stimulates Robert to force her hand.

At the next interview Mrs. P. reported on Robert's progress. He accepts more responsibility; he watches the clock in the morning in order to be in school on time. His table manners have improved considerably after he was sent away once. However, he still cannot play with others, nor by himself.

The boy was as outgoing and frank as he had been during the first interview. He admitted now that he had wanted to bully and boss everybody, including his mother and his school friends. He reported that he had stopped bossing the children, and that they were more friendly toward him.

Mrs. P. was advised to devote some time to playing with Robert—something she had never done before. It was also recommended that she invite other children to the home once a week and provide games for them to play with.

At the third interview, mother reported that Robert had improved considerably. He behaves better, does not resent her requests, is only occasionally disturbing, but sometimes still wants to prove that he can do as he wishes. Once she asked him to put on his galoshes, and he answered, "They are my feet, and I don't mind if they get wet." Mother's efforts to impress him with the consequences of getting sick were naturally unsuccessful. It was explained to her that the point at issue was not the galoshes, but the test of strength. It was less important whether he takes galoshes or not, than to have another contest of power. The mother was defeated because she still tried to impress him with her power of reasoning. The boy had frankly told her, "I am my own boss." He used his power of resistance when she tried to break his rebellion, proving to her *her* helplessness. If the struggle continued, he might even resort to an attitude of revenge. Her playing with him counteracts these tendencies. She herself observed that during their playtime he becomes more cooperative with her.

Mrs. P. reported that Robert is now able to play with children, even with his sister, without attempting to dominate them. The mother is inviting friends to the home. She feels much more relaxed. She stated that she can now keep her domestic help who previously had refused to stay because of Robert.

At the next interview, the question of Robert's going to bed came up. It takes considerable coaxing to get him to bed on time. He gets out of bed several times before he finally goes to sleep; sometimes he disturbs his parents during the night. Mrs. P. has contemplated possible natural consequences and reasoned that if Robert is so thoughtless about the parents' rest, they, too, should wake him up from his sleep!—an indication of how she still believes in retaliation, in the principle of "an eye for an eye." It was suggested to her that she find better and more logical consequences. She could make an agreement with Robert about the number of hours' sleep he needs; he would know at what time he should be in bed. Then she should watch *without saying one word.* If he is not in bed on time, he has to make up the sleep next evening by going to bed as many hours earlier as it took him to get to bed the night before. (It is advisable to let older children make up the lost time on *Saturday,* which may mean no dinner, no movies—depending on the amount of sleep lost during the week.)

The last interview showed marked improvement, not only in Robert's behavior, but in his relationship with his mother. Both are much happier. His going to bed is no longer a problem. He takes care of himself. He stopped indulging in temper displays after mother walked out of the house during one of his tantrums. He no longer tries to dominate her as she neither bosses nor pushes him around. He and mother play together and enjoy each other. His relationship with other children is much better. He likes to play with them. He is convinced now that he is liked by children and loved by his parents.

Robert's drive for power was inspired by his mother's attitude. First, she was overprotective and anxious, and when the situation became complicated, especially after the birth of the second child, when Robert felt left out, then she became rigid and punitive. Each recommendation made to her was directed toward changing their relationship. The changes in Robert's attitude toward mother—and hers toward him—were then reflected in the changed behavior of Robert outside of the house. Robert responded immediately to the interpretation, and mother was able to realize her errors and to adopt new methods. For this reason the adjustment of both was exceptionally fast.

The Baby Tyrant

Joe W., nine years old, was referred to the psychiatric clinic after passing through several other departments, because his overweight resisted all dietary and glandular treatment. Apparently, Mrs. W. was unable to control the food intake of the boy.

The mother reported that Joe does not maintain his diet. When he comes home from school he is hungry and asks for food. She reminds him that he should not eat between meals, but he goes to the pantry and takes what he wants. If she tries to stop him, he becomes furious, so she gives in. "After all, he is really hungry." Every day she has long talks with him about the need to control himself, but he is so hungry that he cannot refrain from eating more.

However, the difficulties which he causes are not only in regard to eating. He wets the bed. He is constantly around his mother. If she goes out, he is afraid she will not come home on time. When she leaves the house she has to tell him where she goes and when she expects to return. She plans her shopping trips so that she will be home before he returns from school. If she should be a few minutes late, he stands in front of the house and publicly makes a scene.

Another area of conflict is the radio. He listens to it as long as he likes to. He refuses to go to bed on time, goes only when the parents retire. He occasionally requires help in undressing and washing. He dresses himself in the morning, but does not lace his shoes. He cannot tie them. "Perhaps he is too fat for it," is mother's comment.

He is doing all right in school, but cannot get along with the children in the neighborhood. They are rough and gang up on him because he is Italian and they are Irish. They do damage to the neighborhood. Therefore, mother tells him that they are not the right company for him. He has one boy friend who is a little older but very dull and does everything Joe wants. When children visit him, he does not let them touch his toys because "they might spoil them." He takes a circuitous route on his way to school to avoid the other children of his neighborhood.

Joe has a brother who is twelve years older than he. He fights with him and feels that the brother tries to boss him. The brother becomes angry if Joe misbehaves or does not obey. Joe is jealous whenever his brother gets more than he or does what he is unable to do.

Summary: Joe is an overprotected child who dominates his mother and wants his way as compensation for being the youngest and smallest in the family. His excessive craving for food is his weapon to defeat his mother, as are his bed-wetting, his refusal to dress himself completely, his ascendancy in regard to radio and going to bed, and his control of mother's activities. His difficulties with children are the consequence of his desire to dominate and his refusal to participate on equal terms. Mother keeps him too close to herself and does not know how to manage him, fighting and giving in at the same time. The efforts of mother and brother to overpower him meet with the child's increased determination to overpower them.

The situation was explained to both mother and boy, who seemed to understand the interpretation. The boy acknowledged with the "recognition reflex" the suggestion that he might want to be the boss. Mother was advised to act rather than to argue. She should stop her talk about food but see to it that Joe ate nothing between meals; she should stop tying his shoelaces, and should turn off the radio at 9 P.M. If she would relinquish her fear and concern about him, he would learn to take care of himself. If she refused to succumb to his domination, he could not continue it. It is unnecessary to report to him where she is going and when she will return, or be on hand invariably when he gets home; he can assume responsibility for himself. Mother said she would carry out our recommendations.

Two weeks later Mrs. W. reported that the brother had

shown Joe how to tie his shoelaces, and Joe has tied them ever since. Mrs. W. has given him a key to the apartment, and he goes in when mother is absent and tends to his own needs. He now goes to bed at 9 P.M. except on one night a week when he is permitted to listen to one radio show. There is no argument about eating; he is given a little food after school occasionally; then he goes out to play. He has made friends with another boy. The principal remaining problem is his bed-wetting. He sleeps with his older brother, and they quarrel because of Joe's bed-wetting.

During the interview, Joe spoke little, looking away when addressed, but his facial expression and "reflex" reaction showed that he understood and agreed. We had a long discussion with him without his saying a word: his facial expressions indicated his responses. Asked whether he wanted, perhaps, to punish his brother by bed-wetting, because he felt bossed and pushed around by him, he answered positively with the "reflex."

This time Mrs. W. was advised merely to continue the diet and not to mention the bed-wetting. We wanted to see whether our discussion with the boy about this subject would have any effect.

Two weeks later: Joe gets along well. He ties his shoes. He no longer quarrels with mother if she is not home on time or refuses to tell him where she goes. In his relationships with other children, he still prefers his old friend whom he can boss. He is wetting his bed only two or three times a week, rather than nightly as he had been doing.

It was explained to Mrs. W. that Joe's improvement in regard to bed-wetting indicated that our explanation was probably correct and that she should stay out of this conflict between the brothers. However, she should try not to baby Joe and should so instruct his brother. Joe was more vocal during this interview.

Two weeks later: Joe dresses himself and goes to school

punctually without coaxing; he enters the home with his own key. There have been no arguments with mother about either homecoming, radio, or food. He wet the bed only twice in two weeks.

Two weeks later: Bed-wetting has stopped altogether. Joe behaves well, is in bed generally at 8:30, dresses and undresses himself alone, goes in and out of the house, makes less fuss about the food.

A new problem has arisen—Joe refuses to do his homework. Mother was advised to explain to him, without pleading or constant reminding, that he could not listen to the radio before he has finished his homework. Joe has dropped his old boy friend and turned to a new one who is much more his equal.

Two weeks later: Joe has wet the bed once. However, his homework is done every day. He has lost three pounds during the past two weeks. He gets along much better, not only with mother but also with children. He now plays with the Irish boys on the playground without complaining.

Two weeks later: No bed-wetting at all. Joe passed his school work with improved marks. He gets along well with children, has new friends. At home there is peace and order, no radio problem any more. Mother and Joe are happy over the improvement in their relationship. Case closed.

Joe's case is similar to the previous case of Robert. Here again the child and the mother caught on rather quickly to the interpretations of their mutual mistakes and began their reorientation immediately after the first interview. In this case, one has the feeling that the achieved adjustment had solved the immediate problems of the boy and certainly changed the mother-child relationship; but the peculiar position of the boy in the family set-up and a certain rigidity in both mother and child may lead to new complications whenever a new task finds them unprepared. In such a case each may revert to his old schemes.

The "Holy Terror"

Mrs. L. brought eight-year-old Mike to the Guidance Center without an appointment. She wanted immediate help and was unable to accept our request that she first make an appointment with the social worker who would take the history and background of the case. She remained in the counsel room, constantly causing disturbance either by running to the social worker for more information about the appointment or interrupting the discussion of another case by loudly asking the psychiatrist when he thought he could see her. Mike had been sent home from school the day before because he had jerks and convulsions. The teacher thought he had St. Vitus's dance.

At the appointed interview with mother and grandmother, we were informed that Mike had had tics for about two months, jerking his head, sniffling, clearing his throat, and, more recently, shaking his whole body rather violently.

Mother and father are seldom home and Mike is under the care of his maternal grandparents. There is a baby sister who is six and a half months old. All members of the family criticize each other in front of him. He can dress himself but refuses, so mother, rather than argue with him, dresses him. At the table he uses his fingers instead of his knife and fork, and messes up the floor. He refuses to eat anything but meat, and so he is constantly nagged at the table. He does not help around the house and is destructive. Children do not want to play with him because he hits them. He takes things away from others. He calls mother as if he were in great trouble; she runs to him in panic, and then he laughs and asks if he has worried her. The worst trouble is getting him to bed. Until last year mother had to wipe him after each bowel movement. She "cured" him by smearing the excreta on his face. Mother hits him frequently and nags him constantly. Mr. L. is stern and just sends him out. He scares Mike. Father holds mother responsible for the boy's behavior, and the parents are considering breaking up their marriage on these grounds. Both grandparents are extremely apprehensive; they overindulge Mike and always side with him.

Mike loves school and has good grades, but is rated poorly on self-control and courtesy. He talks out of turn, is destructive, and does not pay attention. One day he was sent home from school as a "punishment" for his tic.

Mother and grandparents are extremely alarmed about his present "nervous condition" and want immediate help. He has been given bromides and barbiturates for two months, but the condition has become worse. During the interview they repeatedly asked, "What can we do, what shall we do?" without waiting for any suggestions; when a suggestion was offered they immediately argued against it and refused to accept any advice, sometimes taking a stand against each other. The whole interview showed the family atmosphere—apprehension, excitement, conflict, and disorder.

The boy was very frank and outspoken during his interview. His body shook violently but his movements were not choreatic (typical for St. Vitus's dance). Asked why he trembled, he answered, "Shall I tell you why I do this? [jerking his head] Really something in my head tells me, 'Do it, do it.'" To another question he replied, "If you think I am jealous of sister— I ain't. They [the family] tell me this. I don't mind if they are busy with sister. I just go to my room and read comics." It was explained to him that his pride probably prevents him from admitting his jealousy, but that because of it he tries new and more potent tricks to make his family become more concerned with him. He wants to be the "boss" and the "baby" at the same time. While watching his jerking, we were impressed with the suddenness and vigor (drama?) of the movements. So we ventured a guess. Could it be that he used these mannerisms to frighten and impress mother and grandparents even more than he does with his other acts? He responded with the "recognition reflex." Then we demonstrated while talking to him, how terrifying such a sudden jerking movement is. He too, was startled—and smiled. Our discussion then ended.

We explained to mother and grandmother that Mike could not be helped until the whole home situation is changed. Before we could give advice, the fighting and bickering, arguing and attentiveness to Mike must stop. We assured them that Mike was not suffering from St. Vitus's dance; his symptoms were only his way of impressing them and getting more attention. Mother and grandmother declared their extreme eagerness to work out their problems with us and to come again next week.

We have not seen them again. When mother telephoned to break the next appointment, she overflowed with expressions of gratitude. Mike had stopped jerking the day after the interview, and had not twitched since. But he had started to swear, using terrible words. Mother broke the two following appointments with one excuse or another—and is still grateful that Mike does not jerk any more. Apparently that was all she was interested in.

Compulsive Neurosis

The development of a severe neurosis in young children is a rare occurrence. The case cited herein demonstrates that the severity of the symptoms in children does not have the same significance as similar symptoms have in adults whose treatment is generally very difficult and long.

During the first interview the following history was taken. Eight-year-old Sharon had been a "normal," healthy child until one month ago. She had been a charming, obedient, and kind little girl who performed equally well in school and at home. Suddenly she developed fears of blindness, of infantile paralysis, and of diphtheria. She could not breathe and was terrified of death. She repeatedly asked mother whether she would die or become sick, demanding reassurance and sympathy. For the last four days she had been afraid her food was poisoned, and mother had to taste all foods before she would eat. She drooled because she could not swallow her saliva, fearing the germs in it. She lived in constant expectation of disaster. She had many compulsive symptoms, counted the steps or other objects when she walked on the streets, and developed new symptoms each day. When she was not concerned about her symptoms she was impertinent, mocked her mother if scolded, and demanded continual reassurance that she was loved. One day she pointed a knife at her mother and on another occasion threw a ball violently at her parents when they were together. The parents always carefully avoided any demonstration of affection between them in the child's presence. At school, however, Sharon behaved well, was exceptionally advanced for her age, was liked by the children and played with them.

Past history: Three years ago Sharon had an episode of disturbance when she enrolled in school. She did not want to leave mother, was afraid mother would not be home when she came back from school. Mother had to go through a ritual of promising that she would be home, crossing her heart and repeating the same assurance many times. The child was taken to a psychiatrist who arranged play therapy for her once a week. She went for nine months and was completely well when discharged.

Her parents had been divorced when the child was two and a half years old. Since then, until recently, patient had lived alone with her mother. They were constantly together although the mother had remarried three years ago. But her second husband had been in the service and returned only two and a half months before mother and daughter came to us.

During the interview with the child, she maintained that she was happy, not at all sick, and she denied any fears. She said she did not need or want help. She denied ever having seen another doctor but spoke of a playroom in a hospital, of drawing pictures and eating candy. Upon further insistence she stated she did not want to talk, that she did not like the doctor, and stalked from the room.

The following impression was related to the mother at the first interview. It seemed that Sharon had been completely dependent on mother and wanted to possess her exclusively. Her first disturbance, three years ago, was directed against her mother's remarriage, but mainly against entering school. Apparently the play therapy induced her to accept temporary separation from mother and prepared her for school. The present episode seemed to be caused by the return of her stepfather, and by her fear of losing her monopoly on mother. Her symptoms were the expression of her rebellion and were her tools to occupy mother constantly, not only forcing uninterrupted attention, but also concern and worry. Normally, she never was openly rebellious and seemingly wanted to please mother and be a good girl. Now she could neither admit to herself her rebellion and opposition nor express them without the excuse of being sick. Furthermore, we suspected from her symptoms that the girl had been subjected to much subtle pressure. Behind the mutual closeness and affection existed a contest of power between two determined females.

Mother was perplexed about this explanation. She stated that her husband had expressed similar ideas about Sharon's using her symptoms coercively, but she had not accepted his explanation. However, now she could see that our impression might be correct.

She was advised to ignore the girl's behavior, though this treatment would probably increase Sharon's violence and symptoms. However, mother should not permit herself to be intimidated or dominated by the child's behavior. On the other hand, she should not become angry or impatient, should not show annoyance, but should be affectionate and play with the child. As a first step she would have to overcome her own apprehension and distress and would have to establish a new relationship with the child.

Three days later mother reported the following development. She was capable of maintaining an attitude of neutrality. The girl first pleaded, then raved, then attacked her with scissors and with a knife. She wrote on the walls, "Mother is a stinker." She was destructive, cut mother's nylons, and threw objects around. She begged mother to kiss her when she was in bed, to keep her, Sharon, from falling asleep as she was afraid of her dreams. Mother told her she was willing to kiss her because she loved her, but not after she had been bidden good night. Last night she wanted to get into mother's bed because she had been alarmed by a fire siren, but mother refused and the girl went to sleep on the floor. When mother paid no attention she got up in half an hour, asked for a phenobarbital, and retired to her own bed without any coaxing or other persuasion.

Sharon had expressed her anger at us to her mother and had protested that we had changed mother's personality. She asked mother why she did not get angry when she was destructive. She said, "I don't know what makes me so bad. God didn't make me like this. How can I be good?" Her mother advised her to talk it over with us. Sharon did not want to go to school.

We commended the mother for her attitude and for her ability to retain her composure in the face of the child's provocative behavior. She was advised to continue in the same way.

Mother came one week later to report that Sharon was recovering from a mild case of measles. Prior to her illness, her aggressiveness had subsided; now, in her convalescence, she again had become openly hostile, kicking mother and others. Her compulsions also had increased; she counted steps and spat her retained saliva on the floor. She placed an ashtray on mother's head when mother was seated; went into the parents' room after they had retired, turning on the lights; followed her mother everywhere about the house, wanting to hold her hand. Sharon was now afraid of contracting polio and, if mother was not with her all the time, was fearful lest she die in mother's absence. She did not want to listen to the radio because she might acquire new fears. Her eating habits also changed. After our first consultation Sharon had determined not to eat the same food as the parents but to have something special. Now she decided to take nothing but milk. On the other hand, she had asked mother to have me telephone her at home because she wanted help to overcome her worries.

At the next interview Sharon was willing to talk about her problems. She was quiet, friendly, cooperative, and attentive. An attempt was made to give her some understanding of the unconscious reasons behind her behavior—that she was accustomed to having mother to herself and had rebelled against her father's return because she did not want to share mother with father; that she used her fears to make mother become concerned about her; that she was angry with mother and annoyed both parents to punish them and to gain attention. Sharon listened attentively and responded several times with the "recognition reflex."

The next week the stepfather accompanied Sharon to our office because mother was sick. He reported much improvement. Sharon lost her temper only once a day. She continued, however, to swear at mother and father and to expectorate all over the house. She went for a ride with her girl friend, leaving the house without her parents for the first time. It was still difficult to get her out of the house to play with children; she generally followed mother from room to room. She ate better and did not demand that her food be tasted. For the first time she went to bed by herself without fussing.

The next interview with the mother, a few days later, indicated additional progress. Mother had learned to let Sharon experience the consequences of her actions. If Sharon became angry, mother simply left the room; when she returned, the girl generally was quiet and conformed to the necessary rules of order. Previously the selection of the daily wardrobe had been a major problem. Now, after a short discussion between mother and Sharon in which mother expressed her opinion but left the decision to Sharon, Sharon accepted mother's choice without remonstrance. When mother succumbed to a temptation to coax her, Sharon stopped her, saying, "That is none of your affair." Mother did not feel hurt, but smiled inwardly;

she recognized now how much pressure she had exerted before. It was still difficult for her at times to restrain herself; but she accepted increasingly her new role and relationship and no longer became upset by the child's coercive activity which she now recognized as a reflection of the forcefulness she had previously exerted. When Sharon started to demand reassurance about her symptoms and fears, mother referred her to the doctor and encouraged Sharon to seek advice there. (The previous evening Sharon had actually telephoned us and asked what she could do about her fears. Our answer was a reference to their purpose, that she wanted to absorb her mother's attention by demanding sympathy, consolation, and reassurance. She was praised for her cleverness in achieving her end, and told to continue her methods.[2] The girl seemed to be satisfied with the answer—sic!—and ended the call with friendly thanks.)

The principal remaining difficulty at the next interview was the girl's "inability" to swallow her saliva. The problem was discussed with Sharon. She volunteered the information during the discussion that she was bad and did not deserve to be happy. It was pointed out to her that one of the reasons for not swallowing the saliva was that she considered everything in herself to be bad, including her saliva, which she fancied was full of germs. She also was angry with her present situation, and expectorating was an emotional expression of her dissatisfaction and contempt for order and regulation, particularly since she no longer manifested her anger overtly through her temper tantrums.

During the discussion with mother a policy was established in regard to Sharon's expectorating. Mother was to tell her that she should go up to her own room if she wanted to expectorate on the floor instead of using the appropriate receptacle.

Two weeks later, the mother reported that the expectorating had stopped. Mother and daughter spent much time play-

[2] Such "anti-suggestion" is often very effective. Children seldom take such remarks as sarcastic, because they recognize what is meant.

ing together and there was little disturbance in the home. Only once during this period had a relapse occurred, shortly after Sharon had visited her own father. After this visit she berated her mother and struck at her several times. (Apparently the girl was unable to forgive her mother for having remarried instead of devoting the rest of her life exclusively to her!) Sharon did not like to have her hair combed and sometimes became angry on such occasions. (The rebellion against being overpowered or handled.)

During the next few weeks the child occasionally became moody as an appeal to mother for special consideration. Occasionally she struck mother who managed to ignore the abuse composedly.

After three months of treatment the case was closed as "recovered." She became "her old self" but on a different equilibrium with mother. Several months later, during a casual encounter, mother reported that Sharon had continued well and happy without a recurrence of any difficulties.

Mental Retardation

Geraldine at the age of seven behaves like a baby. She can neither dress nor undress herself; occasionally she rips her clothing when she tries to undress and gets angry at her inability to do so. She does not make any attempt to dress herself. She frequently loses her temper and kicks her parents if they do not give in. She does not go to bed by herself; mother has to lie down with her, or she will not fall asleep. During the night, she calls her parents frequently, and they always respond and quiet her. She started to talk at the age of five; her speech is unintelligible and guttural. She will not talk at all to strangers. The parents make her repeat each word to improve her enunciation. At the table she has to be fed, and mother must tell her stories or else she will not eat. She was entered in a parochial school at the age of five, but has recently been transferred to a public school, where she has been placed in an ungraded room. There she refuses to talk to the teacher and does not play with the children.

The school authorities informed the mother shortly before she came to the Center that they could not keep the girl, whom they considered mentally retarded, and advised the parents to send the child to a state institution for the feeble-minded. The parents were horrified at the prospect. They asked for postponement of the decision in order to seek psychiatric help. Although the teacher expressed doubt as to the possibility of any improvement, the parents pleaded and gained respite.

Geraldine is an only child and has had many serious illnesses during her childhood. The parents admit they have spoiled and overprotected her. At the interview Geraldine was completely passive and unresponsive.

The parents were told that it was impossible to make a diagnosis at the first interview. The child might be feeble-minded —but we felt unable to determine the extent of her mental deficiency so long as the parents did not give her a chance to develop her abilities. They would first have to change their approach to her. Geraldine must no longer be permitted to put them completely into her service. They must encourage her to act for herself. Since everything was done for her, there was no need for Geraldine to make any effort; she received too much by not functioning. Both parents were kind and sincere, although they admitted that they occasionally spanked the child when they did not know how to handle her, particularly when she threw a temper tantrum.

The parents understood our explanations fully. For the first time the child's behavior began to make sense to them. They expressed their willingness to cooperate in any way. During the first interview we offered more recommendations than we generally dare to give at this early stage, because the parents seemed to be ready for specific help. They were advised (1) to let the child go to bed alone in a separate room, to pay no attention to whatever she might do, and not to respond to any call during the night; (2) to leave the child alone when she had a fit of temper; (3) to disregard her bad speech, to stop making her repeat words, but, on the other hand, to ignore her when she speaks unintelligibly; (4) to play with her and to show her much affection, substituting this affection and play for the previous services to the child; (5) to stop scolding, nagging, coaxing, and spanking, but to remain calm whatever the child might do.

Two weeks later parents and child came again, reporting definite progress. The parents seemed to be much encouraged. Geraldine speaks more plainly; she goes to bed earlier and by herself; there is no longer any fussing; she undresses herself, although she still has difficulties in dressing; she and her parents play together, and whatever has to be done is discussed and agreed upon in advance. Geraldine asked them once why they no longer scolded or punished her; she expressed openly her surprise at this change.

This time the parents were counseled to let the child eat by herself and to send her away from the table if she threw her food around.

Two weeks later, the mother said that Geraldine is doing much more for herself; she now feeds herself and eats well. Her sleeping habits are very good. She goes to bed early and stays in bed. In the morning she arises upon being awakened, without having to be called or reminded. She talks much more, no longer mumbles, and her enunciation is much better and clearer. She can almost dress herself completely. She plays with blocks, with a ball, and with a xylophone, and wants to play with daddy. She expresses a desire to see her cousin. She does not mind if mother leaves her alone in the room. There are no more tantrums, no kickings, since parents ignore them completely. They, on their side, never scold or spank any more, are very careful never to raise their voices. Child and parents are happier than ever before. The one remaining difficulty is Geraldine's objection to having her hair combed, but mother

The situation in school has already changed. Geraldine is more friendly with the children and likes to play with them. She also talks freely with them. A few weeks ago the teacher had urged the removal of the child as a hopeless case, considering her moronic and "deaf." During the last week, the teacher has recognized and admitted the progress Geraldine has made, and is now cooperative in helping with the child's development. There is no longer any talk of removal and commitment.

The case was dismissed after three interviews. A final judgment of the child's mental ability has been postponed until the child has been given more time to develop.

Pseudo-Feeble-mindedness

Rick was four years old when his parents brought him to the Guidance Center to find out whether anything could be done for his development. He sat quietly between father and mother, leaning toward and holding onto his father with a sweet expression on his face. He did not respond to any questions, keeping his face blank and eventually turning himself away. He muttered something which was interpreted by his parents as "Go home."

The parents told of several severe operations which the child had undergone. They were in constant fear for the life of their only child and watched over him carefully. He started to walk at eighteen months, having been sick before. He has never learned to talk, nor does he listen. He cannot do anything, not even control his bladder. He is completely dependent on his parents. The parents had taken him previously for psychiatric and psychological examination. According to the mental test the boy *was diagnosed as feeble-minded and deafmute.* However, the parents had observed some reactions which may indicate that he is able to hear, at least some sounds.

It was evident that at the present time no decision could be made about Rick's mental condition and possible development because he was so overprotected. Therefore, the parents were advised to stop their overanxiety and apprehension, to let him alone and not be so much occupied with him. Whether he could hear and talk could be ascertained only after he had experienced that not talking or listening no longer produced the desired results. No other problem of Rick was discussed at this time.

At the next interview mother reported that, to their surprise, Rick had stopped bed-wetting during the night. She wanted to know now how to make him eat properly. He grabs the food at the table by the handful and stuffs it into his mouth. Mother was advised to give him a spoon to eat with, and if he refuses to use it, to take his plate away. We were informed that Rick becomes angry and agitated if he does not get what he wants, and the parents have tried up to now to upset him as little as possible. We pointed out that Rick has to learn that his anger will not produce results. The only way to teach him this is to leave the room whenever he gets angry; her mood, however, must not be unhappy or oversolicitous.

At this session Rick refused to go into the playroom with the other children, but stayed with his mother. He was somewhat restless, although he behaved rather well. This time he did not indicate a desire to go home.

The third week Rick showed further improvement. He had wet his bed but once, *after* he had awakened (as if to show that he still needs more care and attention). But he had learned to speak some words. Mother had refused to do things for him when he just pointed; so he started to name what he wanted. Mother had to be cautioned against urging him to speak plainly, which she had started to do. That is undue attention. She also had hesitated to take the food away when Rick did not use the spoon. Instead of applying the logical consequences, the parents had tried unsuccessfully to "teach him to eat with a spoon." Obviously, it was difficult for them to lose their concern and sympathy. It was pointed out to them that Rick needs to be encouraged and not to be served.

At the next session we heard of Rick's new trick to keep

mother's attention. Instead of wetting his bed, he asked several times during the night to be taken to the bathroom. His vocabulary increased, but he developed a new way of demonstrating that he was not listening: he turned his head away. He showed greater obedience to his father who is not home as much and does not give in so easily as mother. Rick now gets attention by stalling at bedtime and refusing to fall asleep until late. These new attention-getting mechanisms were explained to mother; she was told not to be deceived by such efforts. It is better to let him be awake until he is tired enough to fall asleep than to make a fuss or comment. He should be put on the toilet before he goes to bed, but under no circumstances should he be taken to the bathroom during the night; he must learn to control his bladder. So far Rick had not learned to exert himself in any direction.

The next week, according to the mother, was peaceful and happy. Rick did not wet his bed or ask for the toilet. He talked more and started to play with other children. His tantrums ceased. He was put to bed on time and fell asleep shortly after. Mother felt quite encouraged.

Rick still gave the impression of a very retarded child. At four he behaved liked a two-year-old. But for the first time he went to the playroom in the Center, starting to play by putting blocks one after the other to "build a train." He came into the counsel room, climbed clumsily on the bench, looking around for help. When he was not helped, he managed to get up by himself. However, he soon put himself in a precarious position, giving the impression that he would fall off at any moment, apparently to induce help and attention. He almost did fall—but, as nobody helped, he immediately regained control of himself and landed on his feet. He seemed to have discovered "poor muscle coordination" as a means of getting attention and service, but, if neither were given, he could take care of himself very well. He was very orderly in his play, showed a remarkable interest in minute details, such as examining tiny things like a hair, a blade of grass, a spider's web, or by drawing tiny figures in orderly arrangement. This seemed to indicate a rather well-developed intelligence.

At this point mother was advised to play with him a great deal.

After two weeks Rick's speech has improved further. He now uses not only nouns but also pronouns. Once he came to his mother and said, "I lost my mittens." When he was given salad, he said, "This is good." There is no longer the slightest question about his ability to hear. He sings some songs which he hears on the radio. He is beginning to dress himself.

This time he cried when brought to the counsel room. He refused to sit down or to pay any attention to what was said to him. Apparently he realized that his devices for extracting assistance were not effective here. One of his new tricks was to let his mother wait on the street while he followed her very slowly. Mother had to be reminded not to coax and urge him. She could ask him whether he wanted to come along or whether she should proceed by herself. Perhaps he could show her the way home? There was evidence that Rick still tried to run the show by making subtle demands on his mother to which she submitted, as usual.

This time Rick did not play with the children in the playroom but watched them from a distance.

Next week mother told us that Rick has begun to pick up his toys at night and to wash his hands and face. He also tries to put on his shoes and stockings. Nevertheless, he does occasionally become infantile and makes funny noises. He leans on his mother whenever he can. He dawdles, and mother finds it hard to refrain from reminding him; most of the time she merely watches him and he notices and seems to enjoy it. His table manners are much better since his food is taken away when he does not eat properly. On the street mother did try hiding around the corner when Rick refused to leave another boy to go home with her, and Rick has come promptly ever since.

At this session, Rick played contentedly in the playroom.

Mother has to be reminded again neither to help nor to direct Rick; instead of calling his attention to the consequences by reminding him of them, she must apply them without any further comment.

A month elapsed before the next visit to the Center. Rick has been getting along fine physically, his mother reported. He wets his bed rarely. He has started to go to nursery school and likes it very much. His teacher is satisfied, although he does not play much with other children.[3] He does not cry; he plays alone with blocks or builds long straight lines of trains. He does not always hear—or better, heed—what people say. During the nap period, he is restless and talks to himself. At lunch he first refused to ask for his dessert, but finally said, "Cake."

Rick came happily into the counsel room for his interview and talked to several people although his speech was not very clear. He was cheerful and pleasant and unafraid. He climbed on the bench and sat quietly. However, he did not respond when talked to and pretended not to hear. When we snapped a finger before his face, he assumed a blank expression, staring beyond us as if he could neither hear nor see; but after a while he tried to make a similar motion with his own fingers. His manner throughout the interview was haughty and oblivious of what was going on around him.

This session was also attended by Rick's nursery-school teacher. She was advised to let other children work with Rick when he built trains and to encourage him to participate in simple organized games. If he disturbed the other children during the rest period, his bed should be put in a separate room without scolding or fuss, and he should be permitted to come back when he was willing to be quiet.

Mother came again next week. She reported that Rick has discovered and enjoys colors. He goes around the house picking out all the blue objects, saying, "Blue," and does the same

---

[3] We did not attempt to give another psychological test because of the possible discouraging effect of another low I.Q.

with other colors. His speech is improving steadily. He can repeat the whole story of the "Three Little Pigs." He likes to set up his toy soldiers in marching formation.

During the interview Rick named all the colors and obviously enjoyed doing so. He counted his fingers, but refused to tell the story of the "Three Little Pigs."

Two weeks later, mother reported briefly that things were going well and she had no special problems. She is working now, and the family seems to be adjusting satisfactorily.

A week later: Rick has just recovered from a cold. During his illness he was inclined to whine and cry and to revert to his baby ways. He plays with blocks and does a lot of careful building, picking up his blocks when he is through playing with them. He likes to listen to stories. His speech is improving. A year ago he did not utter a word, a few months ago he said a number of single words, and now he is able to talk in sentences. He puts on his own shoes. At the interview he was very friendly, played with a pencil, and told what he was doing.

During the next few weeks, he had several colds, which threw him back somewhat in his behavior. However, he now learns very quickly, enjoys colors, numbers, and the alphabet, and knows all the letters. He is improving rapidly socially. He takes special delight in colors and he uses them as a social game to amuse guests. He designates all the people he knows by a color. His mother is "Red Mama," father is "Yellow Daddy," he himself is "Blue Rick." Relatives are "Pink Grace," "Purple Gertrude," and "Green Bessie." Young children are usually "white," older ones "orange." His grandparents are "Orange." This designation as colors is not done haphazardly. He always connects the same person with the same color. Apparently Rick associates emotions with color. At this interview he was very proud to mention the "colors" of the various persons present. He seems to use this particular stratagem to impress people and to gain special attention thereby.

In the nursery school he is not as cooperative as the other

children, but nevertheless is participating. Once he clumsily disturbed a game, and the other children refused to play with him. He became angry and knocked all the toys down. For the first time he was active and aggressive, and, in his case, this can be considered as progress. He plays nicely with a younger cousin. He is becoming a little more cooperative and sociable. However, since he quarreled with the children at school, he has shown a little reluctance to return to kindergarten. He sings the songs he learns at nursery school, but sometimes his words are still indistinct.

When he is ready to leave school he puts on his wraps alone, unless his mother is present; then he insists on help. Rick is generally amiable and occasionally a little boisterous. He has a one-track mind, and when he becomes interested in any one thing, he refuses to be diverted. He assumes a blank, stolid expression as if he could not see or hear what has been suggested, and willfully concentrates only on what he has in mind. Taken to the zoo, his interest seemed to be in the people rather than in the animals, at which he hardly looked. However, when he reached home, he pointed out the animals in his picture book, naming them and the parts of their bodies. "This is a lion, and this is his tail."

During the interview Rick refused to sit on the bench, but walked around the table and leaned against the social worker, lifting his arms as if he wanted to be picked up. He did not answer questions until asked about colors. He counted to twelve, counted his own fingers, and named the printed letters of the alphabet. But no response could be drawn from him on any other subject; he merely looked blank when anything else was mentioned.

Mother was advised that if Rick does not want to dress for school, she should assume that he is ill and put him to bed, giving him no toys and feeding him only liquids. Her manner should be kind and gentle, but firm. She was told, however, not to attempt it if she were doubtful of this procedure and of her ability to execute it without being tense and nervous.

The next report of the schoolteacher indicated that Rick is beginning to reach out to the group and to recede from his isolation. He got into a fight again. He is still somewhat backward in putting on his jacket and heavy pants. He makes friends with other children outside of school. He has not wet his bed for a long time. The mother was advised to be more careful not to help him dress, and it was suggested that she invite children to the home to play with Rick. Apparently the mother still gets angry with him sometimes, but she tries to do or say nothing on these occasions. Rick, too, loses his temper from time to time.

Whenever he is sick, it takes Rick a little time to readjust to school. On the street he greets acquaintances in a smiling manner. At times he still refuses to talk and assumes a remote look, but usually he smiles gaily when spoken to. Occasionally he will pretend not to hear. He is much happier than he has ever been, but is inclined not to trust everybody. Sometimes he antagonizes children and withdraws from the group, but most of the time he participates and cooperates.

At this session, Rick drew figures with neat, quick strokes and printed letters with both hands, shifting the pencil or crayon frequently from one hand to the other.

A few months later he became somewhat contrary after a period of respiratory disorders. He gets along beautifully with children younger than himself. He likes to teach, but cries when other children reject him. He sometimes acts tough, "I am going to beat you up—I am going to hit you." Mother still wavers between a growing anger and oversympathy if he misbehaves. Although she has learned much, she is not always as firm and objective with Rick as she should be.

During one interview he first sat down among the parents, pretending not to hear what was said to him. But then he came up to the bench, showed a drawing, and described what he did. He still has his own way, doing what he wants and rejecting what he dislikes, refusing to stop what he is doing. But he smiles all the time. When he was told that the interview was over, he pretended not to hear and went on writing. The teacher said that on some days he is more sociable than on others. Generally he is very cooperative when asked to do things.

In the playroom Rick colored rather rapidly and in a short time asked for several sheets of paper. He drew a picture of a train with flag, bell, smokestack, and many wheels on the engine.

After one and a half years' attendance at the Guidance Center, Rick had made real progress. Our prognosis was that an adequate adjustment could be expected eventually, although certain defects on the intellectual plane might remain. Both parents were cooperative and intelligent in the handling of the child and showed considerable insight, although their own emotional reaction was sometimes inadequate.

One year later, at the age of seven, Rick entered public school. His grades were all "Excellent," without any check for any particular difficulty. He is a charming, cooperative boy, but sometimes still displays a peculiar attitude of remoteness and aloofness. Then he looks like a prince who surveys the world around him. His overall adjustment, however, has been satisfactory. The latest information we have indicates that the boy is now far ahead of his class and the school is considering a double promotion.

This case is important for many reasons. It demonstrates first how wrong it is to be influenced by a first impression if the situation appears hopeless. Pessimism is never justifiable, as one can never really know how the situation will develop if the parents learn to deal with the problem more adequately. For this reason an early repetition of the first I.Q. test was omitted, as it would only have had discouraging effects on the parents and the child. At that time we could not know what became apparent later on—that the child was not retarded but actually had superior intelligence. We can further see in this case the ups and downs in the boy's development owing to the mother's inability to maintain a consistent approach.

Conclusion

Now that you are at the end of this book, you may examine what you have absorbed from it. While you were reading, many thoughts might have passed through your mind, stimulating or upsetting you, as the case may be. This is the time to integrate these thoughts. The process of thinking and rethinking after you are through will determine what value or use this book has for you.

I hope that one fact was brought home clearly and unmistakably—that it is within your power to bring about happiness and success for your children. I wish you would, then, stop for a moment and consider the larger implications of this fact. While it is only natural that you are concerned primarily with your own family, with your own children, you should not lose sight of the fact that you also hold in the palm of your hand the destiny of mankind. Each generation of parents is the foundation of the future. We cannot establish the extent to which external social conditions and our inner preparation decide the fate of humanity—whether we need first better individuals to form a better society, or a better society to produce better individuals. The two factors work hand in hand: the training of children influences the future social order, just as existing living conditions determine the forms of upbringing. The progressive evolution of mankind is inseparably linked with the improved spirit and technique of child-rearing. Man's imperfection today is in part conditioned by the training that he has heretofore received.

We have today a dim vision of the road that may lead from

this imperfection to heights previously unknown. The hypothesis of the evolution of new social forms, the idea of a great and unlimited expansion of the powers of the human intellect by a control of nature—these find a peculiar confirmation in our pedagogical experiences. A more adequate treatment of man beginning at infancy could completely unfold his creative faculties, and develop capabilities and qualities that now are all but inconceivable. We see only the first glimmerings of the light. But what we already know of the prevalent frustration and repression of the human powers gives us some idea of the myriad potentialities, ethical, intellectual, and emotional, that are obscured by training as hitherto practiced.

The previous belief in the omnipotence of heredity is now shaken. This credence was based on an understandable pessimism arising from the limited knowledge of the possibilities of proper training. Is it conceivable that, for millennia, really false principles of pedagogy were consistently applied? The previous tenets of education were not false; they were but the logical reflection of a culture-era that extends from the beginnings of civilization into our own day and age—an era marked by the conflict of man with man. Outside of our European-American culture there were, and still are, communities of a homogeneous type, tribes and clans which, within their own limits, have scarcely any notion of a hostile, competitive order (other than that involved in the relation of the sexes). Their education often proceeds from a wholly different premise, shuns personal punishment and abasement of children, and corroborates in many respects the experience of modern psychiatry.

It is certain that the shortcomings of the present methods of training have been emphasized by the special obstacles that our own times have laid in the way of parent and child. Yet it is beyond question that good parents, now as always, can discover and apply effectual training procedures. Our new understanding is built on the experience of untold predecessors. Many exceptional men and women, who towered above the general level of their contemporaries, were to a great extent the product of superior upbringing. (If their success were due solely to heredity, we would expect the children of geniuses to take after their parents more often than they do.) Nor is it mere coincidence when a certain graduating class of a high school produces a number of outstanding individuals that far surpasses the average. Here we see evidence of a blessed confluence of effort that is anything but chance, and of a pedagogical skill that has developed potentialities which under other circumstances might have lain fallow.

The extent to which a human being is capable of development can be shown by a simple illustration. If the child of a bushman were early transplanted and accepted into American culture he would develop powers and capacities that he could never possibly have attained in his original environment. Neither hereditary defects nor his assumed or actual inferior brain-development would prevent him from rising far above the norm of his own community. Hence we can conceive that, through better methods of training and improved living conditions, the men and women of the future will exceed our present cultural level as we ourselves exceed the level of primitive peoples. . . . We may well be stepping, right now, on the threshold of a new era of humanity.

Index